Promoting Behaviour for Learning in the Classroom

Promoting Behaviour for Learning in the Classroom offers essential support to help teachers develop capacity and confidence in managing behaviour in the group setting of the classroom.

It provides a concise analysis of established behaviour management strategies, recognising that no single approach will work for *all* pupils and that central to effective practice is an understanding of the different personal attributes and experiences teachers and pupils bring to the classroom.

Illustrated by examples from the classroom, *Promoting Behaviour for Learning in the Classroom* uses the tried and tested 'Behaviour for Learning' framework to show how teachers' expertise in promoting learning can be used to improve behaviour. Key issues considered include:

- developing positive relationships in the classroom
- understanding personal style and self-management
- effective use of positive feedback and rewards
- using positive correction and sanctions
- working with school systems and frameworks for managing behaviour
- individual differences and special educational needs
- dealing with challenging behaviour.

Written by experts in the field, *Promoting Behaviour for Learning in the Classroom* offers much-needed in-depth, realistic support and guidance to show teachers how to improve learning and behaviour in the group setting of the classroom.

Simon Ellis is a Senior Lecturer at Canterbury Christ Church University, UK. He has previously worked as a Key Stage 3 national strategy behaviour and attendance consultant and local authority behaviour support service manager.

Janet Tod is Emeritus Professor of Education at Canterbury Christ Church University, UK. She is a British Psychological Society (BPS) chartered educational and clinical psychologist.

Promoting Behaviour for Learning in the Classroom

Effective strategies, personal style and professionalism

Simon Ellis and Janet Tod

Routledge
Taylor & Francis Group

LONDON AND NEW YORK

First published 2015
by Routledge
2 Park Square, Milton Park, Abingdon, Oxon OX14 4RN

and by Routledge
711 Third Avenue, New York, NY 10017

Routledge is an imprint of the Taylor & Francis Group, an informa business

© 2015 Simon Ellis and Janet Tod

British Library Cataloguing in Publication Data
A catalogue record for this book is available from the British Library

Library of Congress Cataloging in Publication Data
A catalog record for this book has been requested

ISBN: 978-0-415-70448-9 (hbk)
ISBN: 978-0-415-70449-6 (pbk)
ISBN: 978-1-315-75398-0 (ebk)

Typeset in Bembo
by Swales & Willis Ltd, Exeter, Devon, UK

Printed and bound in the United States of America by Publishers Graphics, LLC on sustainably sourced paper.

Contents

Illustrations

Introduction

In 2012 the Government introduced additional guidance (TA 2012) intended to improve initial teacher training in relation to pupil behaviour. It provided a description of the knowledge, skills and understanding that trainees need in order to be able to manage their pupils' behaviour (TA 2012). The document reflected an established discourse (e.g. DfE 2010, 2012) based on teachers reportedly feeling underprepared in relation to behaviour management and pupil behaviour representing a significant concern. Although we would argue that this is an overly simplistic discourse in relation to the complexities of individual teachers' feelings of preparedness, it is evident from research (e.g. NASUWT 2012; NFER 2012) and our own experiences of working with teachers in the early stages of their careers that pupil behaviour can represent a source of some considerable anxiety.

The Professional Standards for teachers produced by the Labour Government (1997–2010) said relatively little specifically about pupil behaviour. Although these standards were revised during this period, the requirements relating to behaviour remained reasonably consistent. The 2007 standards stated that in order to achieve qualified teacher status (QTS) the trainee needed to:

- demonstrate the positive values, attitudes and behaviour they expect from children and young people (TDA 2007: 7)
- have a knowledge and understanding of a range of teaching, learning and behaviour management strategies and know how to use and adapt them, including how to personalise learning and provide opportunities for all learners to achieve their potential (TDA 2007: 8)
- establish a clear framework for classroom discipline to manage learners' behaviour constructively and promote their self-control and independence (TDA 2007: 12).

Reflecting a key theme in this book that behaviour cannot be viewed in isolation from other aspects of teaching and learning, there were, of course, other standards that potentially influenced behaviour in the classroom. The behaviour-specific standards set out above could be summarised as reflecting the need to act as a role model, know a range of behaviour management strategies, and establish and operate within a framework for classroom discipline. The Coalition Government moved away from this familiar set of standards and was a little more explicit in its expectations. Under the broad requirement to 'Manage behaviour effectively to ensure a good and safe learning environment' (DfE 2011a: 8) the document specified that teachers should:

- have clear rules and routines for behaviour in classrooms, and take responsibility for promoting good and courteous behaviour both in classrooms and around the school, in accordance with the school's behaviour policy
- have high expectations of behaviour, and establish a framework for discipline with a range of strategies, using praise, sanctions and rewards consistently and fairly
- manage classes effectively, using approaches which are appropriate to pupils' needs in order to involve and motivate them
- maintain good relationships with pupils, exercise appropriate authority, and act decisively when necessary.

(DfE 2011a: 8–9)

The additional guidance (TA 2012) produced in 2012 to supplement the new Teachers' Standards was developed by the Government's expert adviser on behaviour, Charlie Taylor. He was subsequently appointed as Chief Executive of the Teaching Agency (now the National College for Teaching and Leadership). The guidance covered eight broad areas:

- personal style
- self-management
- reflection
- school systems
- relationships
- classroom management
- more challenging behaviour
- theoretical knowledge.

(TA 2012)

The strength of this document is its explicit recognition that managing behaviour involves a broad range of interacting factors. Although, appropriately and necessarily, there is reference to knowledge of generic behaviour management systems and techniques, this is set within a broader context of teacher behaviours and attributes. There is a clear underlying message that the successful management of behaviour relies on far more than a set of strategies to draw upon when pupils misbehave. This book is, in part, a response to Charlie Taylor's guidance. We did not view anything in the guidance as particularly new or original. Many of the points represent enduring good practice principles that will continue to have relevance despite future changes of Government and revisions to the professional standards. The significance, however, is that the current Government was prepared to set down these ideas in a single document and promote them as the means to strengthen teacher training in relation to behaviour. In this book we use the Behaviour for Learning conceptual framework (Ellis and Tod 2009) to support the reader in developing the knowledge, skills and understanding contained in this guidance.

About the Behaviour for Learning conceptual framework

An inevitable feature of both past and current professional standards is that they largely reflect what the teacher will be doing rather than the pupils' response to this. Typically, understandably and necessarily, policy makers, teachers, training providers, authors and others have devoted considerable effort to honing the teacher's side of the relationship based on the premise that this will positively influence the pupils' response. And, of course, it does. There are good practice principles that if adhered to will lead to more positive outcomes more often with more pupils. Because the teacher is the more controllable variable in the relationship, it makes sense to be aware of these good practice principles and to know, rehearse and implement established and emerging strategies and approaches that reflect these. This book contains a number of chapters that consider a range of known effective strategies and set them within a behaviour for learning perspective. Where this book differs from many others is in the explicit acceptance of the principle that the pupil experiences and interprets classroom events, including the teacher's strategies for managing behaviour, as an individual. Acceptance of this principle encourages recognition of the need not just to focus on the teacher's side of the relationship but on the pupils' side as well.

The behaviour for learning approach makes use of the conceptual framework presented in Chapter 1. This framework links learning and behaviour, via the term 'learning behaviour', in order to reduce perceptions that 'promoting learning' and 'managing behaviour' are separate issues for teachers (McNally et al. 2005). Emphasis is explicitly placed on the social, emotional and cognitive factors that underpin learning and behaviour in school contexts. The influence of such factors is likely to be well known to many readers, even if not expressed in these terms. For example, you may have heard a teacher say, or said yourself, that a pupil's misbehaviour is due to their low self-esteem. This attributes the behaviour to an emotional factor. Disputes during group work may be explained in terms of a lack of social skills. The attribution here is to social factors. Failure to engage with or complete a task might be due to the lack of skills necessary to tackle it. This represents a cognitive or curricular factor. Of course, as a teacher you can exert an influence. If the suspected cause is low self-esteem, you might break the task down into more achievable sections so that the pupil experiences success and you can provide positive feedback on this. It is because of this interaction between factors related to the pupil (their low self-esteem) and factors related to the teacher (their capacity to change the task) that within the behaviour for learning approach we refer to a set of relationships. These are:

- relationship with others (predominantly social)
- relationship with self (predominantly emotional)
- relationship with the curriculum (predominantly cognitive).

The self-esteem example earlier is a simple illustration. In reality, of course, the relationships need to be understood as changing, interdependent and reciprocal. They do not lend themselves to any one quick-fix set of strategies but allow teachers and others to plan for such relationships and for pupils to contribute positively to their development.

Importantly the behaviour for learning approach does not seek to pathologise individual pupil behaviour. The development of learning behaviour and the maintenance and enhancement of the three relationships that underpin this are considered important in relation to all learners, not just those who present with problematic behaviour.

The relationship with our previous book

Our previous book, *Behaviour for Learning: Proactive Approaches to Behaviour Management* (Ellis and Tod 2009), sought to take the conceptual framework that emerged from a systematic literature review (Powell and Tod 2004) and, drawing on our experience of working with groups of teachers and trainees, develop its application to practice. In a number of its chapters, the book allowed the reader to share in the development of our thinking in relation to the key components of the conceptual framework. This was important in justifying through an evidence base of literature how we had arrived at this point. Readers who feel they require this level of understanding may wish to seek out that publication. However, in writing this second book, which we regard as a sister publication, we were very conscious that there are many teachers, particularly at the early stages of their careers, who do not currently want or need such an in-depth understanding of the behaviour for learning approach but may find the principles and practices helpful.

Ways of using this book

As with many educational texts, it is more likely that many readers will home in on particular chapters based on time and need. There may be a temptation to move straight to those chapters whose titles imply a more practical focus. We do not underestimate some readers' need to find something that they can try out tomorrow. Providing you have read the surrounding text and assured yourself that you are not inadvertently adopting an approach that we have actually included as an example of questionable practice, such cherry picking may address the immediate need. When presenting the more practical guidance we have only included material that, if applied in the spirit and manner intended, is broadly compatible with the behaviour for learning approach. We would hope, however, that readers find time to read a broader range of chapters. Chapter 1 is pivotal and even for those readers who are adopting a selective approach to reading this book we would suggest that this should be read first. This will provide a working understanding of the Behaviour for Learning conceptual framework and its relationship to the more conventional behaviour management approach. The summary below provides a guide to the focus of each chapter.

Chapter 1 The Behaviour for Learning framework

This chapter presents the behaviour for learning approach as a way of improving practice in relation to pupil behaviour in the classroom by enhancing the links between behaviour and learning. The Behaviour for Learning conceptual framework that underpins this book is introduced and the key terms 'learning behaviour', 'relationship with the curriculum', 'relationship with others' and 'relationship with self' are defined and discussed. An overview of day-to-day, core and extended use of the behaviour for learning approach is provided.

Chapter 2 Developing relationships for learning

This chapter roots classroom practice within the building and maintenance of positive relationships. It explores the rationale behind the language of relationships within the Behaviour for Learning conceptual framework. Each of the three relationships – with self, with others and with the curriculum – are considered in detail. The learning behaviours that characterise effective learning relationships are defined and strategies for their development are discussed.

Chapter 3 Motivation for learning and behaviour: applying the behaviour for learning approach

This chapter takes motivation as an example of a cluster of learning behaviours that teachers typically want to promote in groups and individuals. It explores how the behaviour for learning approach can be applied to the challenge of fostering increased motivation for learning as a strategy for improving learning and addressing behavioural issues in the classroom.

Chapter 4 Personal style and self-management

This chapter recognises that a teacher's personal style is influenced by their professional knowledge and skills in relation to pupil behaviour, their abilities in forming effective relationships for learning and a set of 'within teacher' factors that influence how they experience, interpret and respond to classroom events. The Behaviour for Learning conceptual framework is used as a means of exploring and understanding these three interdependent elements. Self-management is conceptualised as the awareness and management of the 'within teacher' factors that contribute to a teacher's personal and professional resilience.

Chapter 5 School systems and frameworks for managing behaviour

This chapter looks specifically at whole school behaviour policies. Typically the classroom teacher will be expected to operate within the context of a combination of rules, rewards and sanctions specified in their school's policy. However, schools vary in the amount of responsibility individual teachers are expected to take in determining a framework for managing behaviour within their own classrooms that reflects the policy. The chapter examines some of the key elements that feature in most schools' behaviour policies and evaluates their potential compatibility with the principles of the behaviour for learning approach.

Chapter 6 Effective use of positive feedback and rewards

This chapter focuses on the role of positive feedback and rewards within a framework for promoting positive behaviour within the classroom. The reader is encouraged to reflect on the use of positive feedback and rewards with regard to the Behaviour for Learning conceptual framework – in particular, considering how any positive comment or reward may be experienced and interpreted by the pupil.

Chapter 7 Effective use of positive corrections and sanctions

This chapter focuses on the role of positive correction and sanctions within a framework for promoting positive behaviour within the classroom. It is recognised that there will be occasions when pupils do not adhere to the school rules and general expectations of behaviour, and the teacher will need to intervene to address this. The reader is encouraged to reflect on the use of positive correction and sanctions with regard to the Behaviour for Learning conceptual framework – in particular, considering how any verbal correction or sanction may be experienced and interpreted by the pupil.

Chapter 8 Individual differences and special educational needs

In referring to individual differences and special educational needs (SEN), this chapter encompasses those pupils whose behaviour gives considerable cause for concern, not just those who are classified as having a special educational need. Changing perspectives (DfE 2014a) on the identification of behaviour as a special educational need are discussed. Through the Behaviour for Learning conceptual framework the reader is encouraged to reframe SEN in terms of the individual's differences in their social, emotional and cognitive behaviour.

The framework is used as a means of understanding the reasons behind the behaviour, informing intervention planning and supporting evaluation.

Chapter 9 Dealing with more challenging behaviour

This chapter focuses on behaviour that is rarer and more extreme than the more predictable behaviours that teachers routinely encounter. Such behaviour is typically underpinned by strong emotions. A recurring message within this book is the importance of understanding how the pupil is experiencing and interpreting events. Nowhere is this more important than in relation to such emotionally driven behaviour. The assault cycle (Breakwell 1997) is presented as a means of understanding a pupil's behaviour in terms of what they are experiencing and, based on this, identifying the teacher's priorities at each stage. Consideration is also given to the issue of physical intervention.

Chapter 10 Professional development, reflection and theory

The final chapter recognises that, as professionals, teachers should seek to extend the depth and breadth of their knowledge, skills and understanding. This principle is considered in the context of professional growth in relation to pupil behaviour. The reader is encouraged to use the Behaviour for Learning conceptual framework as a means of setting priorities for their development. Consideration is given to the role of theory and evidence bases in informing practice.

A note on terminology: the B4L approach

Throughout the book, when it is beneficial in terms of brevity and a more precise distinction is not required, we have used the term 'B4L approach'. This should be understood as referring to the Behaviour for Learning conceptual framework (see Chapter 1, Figure 1.1), the perspective on behaviour it engenders and the enactment of practices that reflect its principles.

Chapter 1

The Behaviour for Learning framework

Introduction

The term 'behaviour management' is an established part of the discourse on behaviour in schools, appearing no less than nineteen times in the Steer Report (DfES 2005a) and five times in the DCSF (2009a) guidance on *School Discipline and Pupil-Behaviour Policies*. Current professional standards (DfE 2011a: 8) do not use the term, but they do require teachers to 'manage behaviour effectively'. Additional guidance intended to improve teacher training in relation to behaviour set out to describe 'the knowledge, skills and understanding that trainees will need in order to be able to manage their pupils' behaviour' (TA 2012: 1). A search of a popular online bookseller's website using the term 'behaviour management' will produce a plethora of texts on the subject. It is also likely that many readers will have read books about behaviour management and attended courses to learn about it. The phrase has a respectable, quasi-professional tone and its provenance is rarely explored. This chapter invites the reader to critically consider the limitations of a focus on behaviour management when narrowly construed to mean a set of methods used to establish and maintain control over pupil behaviour. The Behaviour for Learning conceptual framework is then introduced as a means of reframing behaviour management in terms of promoting *learning behaviour*.

Behaviour management: truisms and part truths

A popular text on behaviour management begins: 'Behaviour management: if you get it right, your life is easy, you're free to do what you're meant to do, which is of course to teach!' (Cowley 2003: xiii).

In some respects Cowley is right; there are undoubtedly some ways of responding to pupil behaviour that are less effective than others and either escalate the situation or lead to the teacher becoming embroiled in an extended disciplinary interaction at the expense of the pace and flow of the lesson. Both outcomes get in the way of the teacher's core focus, which is the promotion of learning. Yet, as we argued in our previous book (Ellis and Tod 2009), Cowley's comment typifies a separation between learning and behaviour that may ultimately be unhelpful. The implication of an emphasis on behaviour management is that there is a discrete set of skills that can be learned by the teacher. In itself, this notion is not a problem and may even have some value in challenging any assumption that skills in behaviour management are a natural gift (DES 1989). The problematic element is when these skills are seen as a distinct aspect of the teacher's role without due recognition of the influence of factors such as the curriculum, teaching approaches and the teacher–pupil relationship. Ofsted have highlighted the link between behaviour and the quality of teaching, suggesting:

> Where teaching does not meet pupils' needs or does not engage pupils sufficiently they can lose attention, demonstrate poor attitudes to learning and eventually interrupt the learning of others. In these cases teaching can then focus too much on continually managing low-level disruption at the expense of providing interesting and relevant opportunities for pupils to learn.
>
> (Ofsted 2011: 59)

Assuming Ofsted's attribution of cause to be correct, the priority in such situations would seem not to be working on becoming better at behaviour management in order 'to do what you're meant to do, which is of course to teach!' (Cowley 2003: xiii) but to strengthen the quality of teaching. Yet in making this point there is the risk that we, and Ofsted, are guilty of ' . . . the pious platitude that provided you have spent enough time preparing your lessons properly, you will never have discipline problems' (Wheldall and Glynn 1989: 2).

The challenge is to live with the complexity rather than dealing in truisms and part truths. The influential Elton Report was clear that 'Reducing misbehaviour is a realistic aim. Eliminating it completely is not' (DES 1989: 65). The implication is that inevitably, however well planned and executed the lesson, there will be times when a teacher will need to respond to unwanted behaviour. There are some principles and practices that, if learned and rehearsed, can allow teachers to deal swiftly and effectively with behaviour more often and with more pupils. It would be professionally foolhardy not to develop capacity in this area. However, in acknowledging this, it should not lead us to neglect the potentially powerful influence of the curriculum and teaching and learning approaches in securing more positive behaviour within the classroom.

The problem of an undue emphasis on behaviour management

McNally *et al.* (2005) argue that *behaviour management* might have some value as a temporary conceptualisation for trainees, but if too much emphasis is placed on the management of behaviour there is a risk that 'it occludes a superior focus on learning, trivialises the life problems of pupils and demeans the place of teacher–pupil interactions in relation to these problems' (McNally *et al.* 2005: 183). Essentially McNally *et al.*'s (2005) argument is that the term 'behaviour management' influences trainees' priorities and limits understanding of a range of interacting variables that may lie behind the behaviour.

Typically behaviour management strategies are conceptualised as a set of techniques used by a teacher to both encourage and maintain positive behaviour and to address behaviour that is problematic in a classroom context. Attention is usually focused on rules, teacher language, rewards and sanctions. This positions the teacher as the manager and the pupil as the managed. The pupil is constructed as a relatively passive recipient of the teacher's management techniques rather than an active participant in a relationship. In reality of course, the pupil brings a range of life experiences to this relationship and also experiences and interprets any classroom events, including the teacher's behaviour management strategies, as an individual (Ellis and Tod 2009). This offers the potential for the pupil to react in an entirely different way from what might be expected, whatever the good practice credentials of the strategy employed. This represents a problem depending on the teacher's interpretation of such an event. One interpretation may be to discard the strategy employed because it has seemingly failed operationally and to embark on a quest for the definitive set of strategies that will provide the solution. The sheer volume of materials produced on behaviour management should be evidence enough that such a set does not exist – if it did, then it would surely have been discovered by now and the definitive text produced. The other interpretation may be that, because the pupil's behaviour is not ameliorated by the typical approaches to behaviour management, they are in need of something different and possibly more specialised than the classroom teacher can provide. The teacher might even begin to question whether the pupil's behaviour represents a form of special educational need.

Ultimately, realism is needed. It is not realistic for a teacher to anticipate and prepare for the entire range of pupil responses they will experience in the classroom (Powell and Tod 2004). There are numerous interacting variables that influence classroom behaviour and mean that classroom events will be unpredictable to a degree. As Watkins (2011) points out, in addition to their unpredictable nature, classroom events are multidimensional, with those present having a variety of purposes, experiences, interests and goals, and they often occur simultaneously. Classrooms are also very public places with both the teacher's and the pupil's behaviour visible to everybody else in the class. When set in this context, the notion that it is possible to *manage* every individual's behaviour through a set of learned behaviour management techniques seems unrealistic. It is therefore important that behaviour management strategies are afforded an appropriate rather than an elevated status. They form a necessary part of a teacher's repertoire of professional skills. They can be thought of as improving the odds; the types of strategies we talk about in Chapters 5, 6 and 7 are intended to lead to more positive outcomes, with more pupils on more occasions. In themselves, however, they are unlikely to be sufficient to address the range of behaviours that might be encountered in the classroom. Unless teachers can accept this, the risk is that they 'continue to seek more and more strategies in the hope that they will be better able to cope with anticipated classroom disruption' (Powell and Tod 2004: 2).

Origins of the behaviour for learning approach

The term 'behaviour for learning' has found considerable popularity, probably because it captures the idea that schools should have a focus on learning and that in order for pupils to learn together in relatively large groups there needs to be a reasonable standard of behaviour. However, there is no shared understanding of the term 'behaviour for learning' and it is used to describe a variety of approaches. The use of the term in this book refers specifically to a conceptual framework that developed from a piece of research (Powell and Tod 2004) commissioned by the Teacher Training Agency (TTA). This framework is presented and explained later in this chapter. Powell and Tod (2004), together with a team of colleagues from Canterbury Christ Church University, conducted a systematic literature review with the overall aim of informing initial teacher training tutors about the theoretical underpinnings of learning behaviours in school contexts in order to enhance initial teacher training in relation to behaviour management. The central concern was that the review should contribute to training that allowed trainees to reflect upon the *purpose* of behaviour management. The team held the view that the fostering of learning behaviour or 'behaviour for learning' was the foundation for effective behaviour management, and argued that this represented a contrast with the more common perception that behaviour management is solely concerned with establishing control over disruptive pupils. The use of the terms 'learning behaviour' and 'behaviour for learning' was intended to reduce perceptions that 'promoting learning' and 'managing behaviour' were separate issues for teachers (McNally *et al.* 2005).

What is the behaviour for learning approach?

The behaviour for learning (B4L) approach offers an alternative way of thinking about pupil behaviour that addresses some of the previously outlined problems associated with a focus on behaviour management. It is underpinned by a conceptual framework depicted in Figure 1.1. The rationale behind this model is likely to be familiar to most, if not all, readers through their own experiences as learners.

When thinking about your own learning at school, the factors that influenced your behaviour in class probably included:

- how interested and capable you were in the subject
- how well you got on with your teacher and peers in the class
- how you were feeling emotionally.

These factors reflect the three B4L relationships. These are:

- relationship with the curriculum (predominantly cognitive)
- relationship with others (predominantly social)
- relationship with self (predominantly emotional).

We use the term 'relationship' to reflect the dynamic reciprocity that is inherent in curricular, social and personal experiences. To illustrate what we mean by this, if we return to your recollections from your own schooldays, you can probably recall that your interest in the subject, how well you got on with your teacher and peers in the class and how you felt emotionally were influenced by factors such as:

- the way the particular teacher presented the lesson
- the type of tasks they set
- your perception of how the teacher viewed you as a learner and as a person
- how the teacher related to you and your classmates
- who you were with when you were learning.

Therefore, although you are likely to have brought to your school-based learning various influencing skills, dispositions and previous experiences, your interest in the subject, how well you got on with your teacher and peers in the class and how you felt emotionally were also influenced for better or worse by a range of contextual variables. The B4L approach does not leave the interaction between these elements to chance. The class teacher aims to be aware of the effect on behaviour of these variables, and to work positively with them to foster the development of learning behaviour.

Reflecting upon your own experiences as a learner in a group setting is helpful in developing a working knowledge of the key components of the B4L conceptual framework. We will now look in more detail at the components represented in Figure 1.1:

- *Learning behaviour* is placed at the centre of the triangle in recognition that the promotion of learning behaviour provides a shared aim for teachers and others with responsibility for providing appropriate learning experiences for children and young people. The identified learning behaviour provides the focus for assessment, intervention and positive change.
- The triangle surrounding the term 'learning behaviour' is used to indicate that the development of learning behaviour is influenced by *social*, *emotional* and *cognitive* factors. We sometimes refer to this triangle as the 'triangle of influence'.

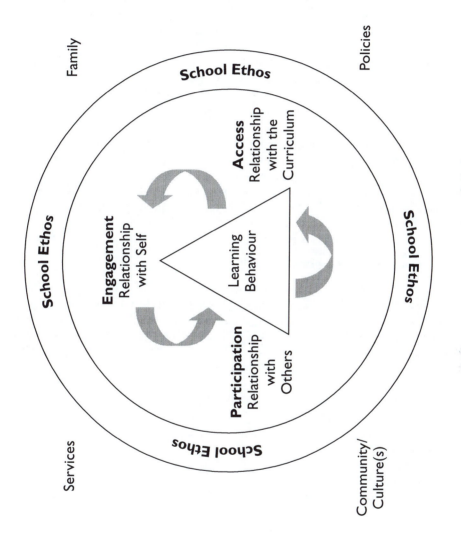

Figure 1.1 The Behaviour for Learning conceptual framework

Adapted from Powell and Tod 2004

- Explicitly recognising the influence of social, emotional and cognitive factors allows learning behaviour to be explored and addressed through the three *relationships* (with self, others and the curriculum) experienced by the individual within the classroom.
- The arrows that surround the triangle represent the *dynamic* nature of learning and reflect the *reciprocal* influence that these social, emotional and cognitive factors have on the development of learning behaviour.
- The terms 'engagement', 'access' and 'participation' in the diagram are used to reflect the essential components of effective inclusion in group settings. In practical terms, the learner is not viewed as a passive recipient of the disciplinary frameworks and learning opportunities available within the classroom and school. This places the *experience* of the pupil at the heart of effective practice.
- The circle surrounding the triangle of influence, entitled *School Ethos*, and the terms that lie outside this circle acknowledge that the development of learning behaviours takes place in a *context* that itself exerts an *influence*.

The overall purpose of the Behaviour for Learning conceptual framework is to encourage teachers to focus on what learning behaviour they need to develop in order to replace or reduce the problematic behaviour a pupil currently exhibits. The framework's acknowledgement that behaviours have a cognitive, social and emotional component provides a means by which teachers can select the most appropriate strategies and evaluate their efficacy.

What is a learning behaviour?

A learning behaviour can be thought of as a behaviour that is necessary for a person to learn effectively in the group setting of the classroom. In their systematic literature review, Powell and Tod (2004) identified a set of learning behaviours drawn from the TTA standards for QTS (TTA/DfES 2002) that could usefully be used in school practice. These behaviours were:

- engagement
- collaboration
- participation
- communication
- motivation
- independent activity
- responsiveness
- self-regard and self-esteem
- responsibility.

The list was not intended to be definitive or exhaustive but simply to encourage consideration of the possible learning behaviours a teacher might seek to promote. As illustrated in the example of *Collaboration* (see Figure 1.2), for operational purposes each of these broad learning behaviours would need to be broken down into observable indicators of their development.

The suggestions in Figure 1.2 vary in their level of sophistication. For example, sharing equipment might be a learning behaviour we would aim to develop in a young child whereas self-monitoring one's own contribution is a more advanced skill. We can

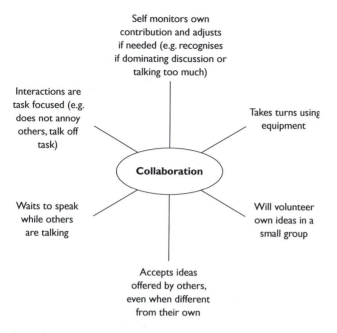

Figure 1.2 Identifying learning behaviours

probably all bring to mind some adults who seem to struggle with this one sometimes. In practice. when conducting such a mind-mapping exercise, the learning behaviours should be relevant to the pupil's stage of development.

The Appendix contains further examples of learning behaviours because, from our experiences in training sessions, we have found that teachers often find it difficult initially to identify the learning behaviours they wish to promote. Again, the intention is that these examples act as a stimulus rather than being viewed as a definitive or exhaustive list.

Learning behaviours may take the form of skills and dispositions. Claxton (2006) summarises the distinction stating:

> Put crudely, when you have learned a skill, you are able to do something you couldn't do before. But you may not spontaneously make use of that ability when it is relevant in the future, if you do not realise its relevance; or if you still need a degree of support or encouragement that is not available. In common parlance, it is not much use being *able* if you are not also *ready* and *willing*.
>
> (Claxton 2006: 6)

Claxton's observation highlights the distinction between what we might term 'skill' and 'will'. Some of the problematic behaviour encountered in classrooms may be because the pupil does not have the cognitive, physical or social and emotional competences necessary to understand and follow a school rule. This could be due to the fact that they are either not developmentally ready or they have never been taught the skills they need to regulate their emotions or behave appropriately in social situations. Other pupils may have the necessary understanding and competences to follow the school rules but for a variety of reasons demonstrate non-compliance.

Although not mutually exclusive, recognising the distinction between behaviour that represents a 'skill' issue and behaviour that represents a 'will' issue is important in influencing strategy choice.

The three relationships that underpin the promotion of learning behaviour

It has become something of an accepted belief with considerable face validity that good teaching is rooted in relationships. The B4L approach moves beyond unquestioning acceptance of the importance of relationships towards a critical understanding of their nature and influence. The use of three core relationships within the model does not deny the complexity of classroom interactions. The choice of these three relationships is based on the finding from the original Evidence for Policy and Practice Information and Co-ordinating Centre (EPPI-Centre) review that the original literature sources used theories that combined cognitive, affective and/or social perspectives (Powell and Tod 2004).

If we apply a relationship model to our approach to pupil behaviour, then we would still do many of the things in classrooms that are currently in operation, but we would be *thinking* differently. Rather than approaching behaviour from the perspective of 'if the pupil does *x* then the teacher does *y*', attention is instead focused on the *interaction* between the teacher, the pupil and their peers. This places the teacher in the role of continually monitoring and being responsive to the pupil's response. Consequently, the choice of strategies, approaches and interventions is based on its likely impact on sustaining and improving the pupil's contribution to the relationship. The overall emphasis is on building positive relationships for learning within the classroom.

The teacher is also able to capitalise on the interdependence between the three relationships in their selection of strategies and approaches. For example, a teacher might find that a pupil's limited liking for or interest in a particular curriculum area can be strengthened by planning the lesson so that some activities can be undertaken in a group with friends. Similarly, many teachers find that showing an interest in what interests the pupil (e.g. sport, music, films, television), and exchanging some brief conversation about this from time to time, is sufficient to foster at least tolerance for the curriculum area they are teaching. From this tolerance increased interest and motivation may develop. In both examples, a social dimension (i.e. relationship with others) is having an impact on a relationship with the curriculum issue.

Establishing a behaviour for learning classroom

In day-to-day practice the priority is to protect and enhance the three B4L relationships. This requires the teacher to keep a watchful eye on these and look for opportunities through the curriculum, the behaviour they model and their routine interactions with pupils to develop learning behaviours. It is possible to identify some example characteristics of a behaviour for learning classroom:

- Strategies and approaches to learning and behaviour are selected and evaluated against their likely impact on the three relationships. Those that risk damaging or undermining the relationships, promoting unhelpful behaviours or hindering the development of positive learning behaviours are avoided.

- Curriculum planning includes consideration of the opportunities for practising and developing learning behaviours within activities set.
- In planning tasks, the teacher considers the demand on the *existing* learning behaviours of the individual, group and class, and recognises the implications for support and the scaffolding of learning.
- The teacher provides positive feedback (see Chapter 6) on the learning behaviours demonstrated by the individual, group and class.
- Pupils are encouraged to feed back in the plenary on learning behaviours used during the task by themselves and others.
- When the opportunity presents itself or can be created, the teacher draws attention to learning behaviours (e.g. resourcefulness, resilience, perseverance) demonstrated (or not) by fictional characters, and historical and contemporary figures.
- When supporting pupils, teaching assistants keep a focus not just on the task but on the learning behaviours fostered by the mode of support. The aim should be to promote independence and resourcefulness rather than dependency.
- In the case of certain pupils, a teacher will intuitively vary their approach and responses based on awareness of the three relationships. For example, if a pupil displays some vulnerability with regard to their relationship with self, the teacher might think more carefully about the phrasing of any developmental comments on a completed task and combine these with attention to its positive qualities. Similarly, if a pupil finds it difficult to collaborate with others (relationship with others), the teacher might include them in a more supportive group in which there are positive role models.

Although we hope readers will reflect on these broader characteristics, the primary focus of this book is the B4L approach as it relates to the management of behaviour within the classroom. Chapters 6 and 7 outline some known effective strategies but places them within the behaviour for learning perspective. It is likely that most readers will encounter other strategies too through classroom observations and the formal and informal advice of colleagues. There is also a wide range of texts available on behaviour management. We do not seek to prescribe a specific set of strategies and approaches. The B4L approach encourages teachers to harness the plethora of strategies currently available, while always keeping a critical eye on these two consistent questions:

- Does the strategy have the potential to promote, or at least not undermine, learning behaviour?
- Does the strategy have the potential to promote, or at least not undermine, the three relationships that underpin the development of learning behaviour?

Even in an immediate management situation, a teacher should aspire through their verbal and non-verbal communication to ensure that they do not do anything that undermines the three relationships or promote what we might term a 'negative' learning behaviour. Strategies, for example, that are intended to cause fear or embarrassment, although superficially effective in that the class becomes quiet, may promote alienation, resentment, reticence, an unwillingness to take risks in learning and a preoccupation with remaining unnoticed by the teacher. If a strategy or approach risks compromising any of the three relationships or models, or otherwise encourages the development of undesirable behaviours, then it is to be avoided.

For most pupils the day-to-day use of the B4L approach described here will be sufficient.

Moving beyond day-to-day use of the behaviour for learning approach

What we have just described as *the behaviour for learning classroom* can be seen as a *quality first teaching* approach to behaviour for learning. Although no longer used in current Government guidance, quality first teaching was a regularly used term in a range of National Strategy documents (e.g. DfES 2002, 2005b, 2006) produced during the Labour Government's administration (1997–2010). In summary, quality first teaching refers to the incorporation into standard classroom practice of teaching and learning strategies, support and resources that encompass the learning and behavioural needs of the widest range of pupils possible. However, this should not be viewed as a fixed or externally defined offer; rather, it is responsive to the profile of the class and school. Quality first teaching was presented as wave 1 of a three-wave model of provision. Wave 2 involved targeted intervention, typically for small groups, and wave 3 involved more individualised interventions. Importantly, the waves model was not intended to represent a progression through a sequence of stages; the pupil would continue to be exposed to quality first teaching in addition to receiving interventions at waves 2 or 3.

Within the B4L approach, it is explicitly recognised that for some individual pupils it may be necessary to adopt a more explicit focus on the learning behaviour to be developed or a more in-depth focus on particular issues associated with their relationship with the curriculum, self or others. We do not talk of 'waves' but we do advocate a tiered approach as set out in Figure 1.3.

Core use: focusing on a specific learning behaviour

In the case of some pupils, it may be that the development of one or two learning behaviours appears to be the priority. Through careful observation the teacher will have recognised that if these specific behaviours were developed then there would be a significant positive effect on the pupils' behaviour in school. Activity 1.1 may be helpful in identifying these learning behaviours.

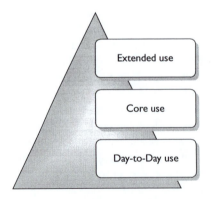

Figure 1.3 Different levels of use of the behaviour for learning approach

Activity 1.1

Fold a piece of paper in half vertically to create two columns. Label the left-hand column 'Problematic Behaviours' and the right-hand column 'Learning Behaviours' (see Figure 1.4). In the left-hand column, write down any behaviours that currently cause concern. In the right-hand column, write down any positive behaviours that you would like to see emerging.

Problematic Behaviours	Learning Behaviours

Figure 1.4 Example recording format

In some cases the problematic behaviours will lend themselves to a directly opposite positive learning behaviour. For example, if a pupil rarely takes turns in group activities, then the desired learning behaviour may be that the pupil does this more often.

Sometimes, however, there is no direct correspondence. For example, you may be concerned that a pupil is regularly out of their seat. You might decide that a learning behaviour of 'sustains attention on task' is appropriate because this is incompatible with the pupil being out of their seat but also with other forms of behaviour such as talking to or otherwise distracting others.

Once you have your two columns, tear your piece of paper in half. Put the unwanted behaviours away somewhere safe – these behaviours have a purpose for the child and so they contain important intelligence for the teacher – you may want to refer back to them. Your focus, however, are the learning behaviours you have identified.

It may be necessary to refine the learning behaviours identified in Activity 1.1. There are a number of points to consider:

- The behaviour should be positively expressed. For example, 'puts hand up to seek teacher attention or to ask or answer a question', rather than 'does not call out'.
- The learning behaviour should be checked against the dead man test. In 1965, Lindsley put forward what he referred to as the 'dead man test' in response to 'a rash of very poor alleged "measures" of classroom behavior' (Lindsley 1991: 457). His particular concern was studies that referred to 'time on task' when what was described 'were actually only records of minutes spent sitting at a desk in arithmetic position'. He also questioned the value of 'time spent without a tantrum' (Lindsley 1991: 457) as a measure. The basic premise of the dead man test is that if a dead man can perform the behaviour it is not a suitable target. The behaviour for learning approach is based on developing learning behaviours that represent alternative ways of responding that are incompatible with the problematic behaviours. The hope is that these will reduce as the new behaviours develop. Consequently, the learning behaviours need to have an active component.
- The learning behaviour should be observable and measurable in itself, or lend itself to the identification of other behaviours that provide evidence of its development. This point needs to be qualified, lest it encourage a focus on valuing what is measurable rather than measuring what is valuable. Some learning behaviours may be quite broad. For example, we might want a pupil who regularly says, 'This is boring' when set a task, and/or engages in more appealing distractions that may be available during the lesson, 'to show an interest in tasks set'. This is an important learning behaviour but thought is required in order to identify the specific things a pupil might do to indicate that they are developing an interest in tasks set. One example might be that the pupil volunteers information about the task in the plenary. Another might be that the pupil asks a question for clarification related to the task. The pupil does not need to demonstrate all the indicators but it is important that in setting a broad learning behaviour the teacher has in mind what some of the indicators might be.

Once the target learning behaviours have been established, the next decision is whether to target these via relationship with the curriculum, relationship with others or relationship with self. In making the decision, the teacher should take into account not only what is likely to be best for the pupil but also their own confidence or competence in relation to particular areas.

The case study below illustrates how a teacher is able to make effective use of the interdependence of the three relationships. Although the presenting lack of confidence may suggest relationship with self as the focus for intervention, the teacher can choose to adopt strategies and approaches related to one (or more) of the other relationships in order to develop the required learning behaviour.

Case study

Through observation the science teacher has decided that Katie, Year 7, needs to develop more confidence when tackling practical tasks because she currently appears very reticent and allows others to dominate.

The teacher might seek to address these issues via one or more of the three B4L relationships:

- Working via relationship with the curriculum, the teacher might decide to plan the lesson differently so that some activities are undertaken in pairs on the premise that this will necessitate more active involvement from Katie and her confidence will develop.
- Working via relationship with others, the teacher might change the group so that Katie is with less dominant or more supportive peers. Alternatively, the teacher might assign roles to group members on the assumption that once Katie does take an active part she will find that she can do it and it is not so daunting.
- Working via relationship with self, the teacher might increase their vigilance in order to notice those occasions when Katie is less reticent and provide positive feedback on her performance.

This Case study represents a fairly straightforward example but sometimes a teacher may need to access additional advice and guidance from others in the school, such as the Special Educational Needs Coordinator (SENCO), before deciding on a course of action. In some cases a pupil may need a specific, targeted intervention led by somebody other than the teacher. For example, a pupil might be included within a social skills group led by a teaching assistant.

Monitoring and evaluation

Monitoring and evaluation are based on the emergence of the target learning behaviour(s) or other indicators that demonstrate progress towards the development of the learning behaviour. It is for this reason that it is necessary to spend time thinking carefully about the learning behaviour to develop and, when this is quite broad, to consider carefully the indicators that will show the learning behaviour is developing.

A summary of the key questions involved in core use of the B4L approach is shown in Table 1.1.

Extended use: focusing on a specific relationship area

In the case of some pupils it may be that the development of a particular relationship area is the priority. Although schools may not be accustomed to using this terminology, it is not uncommon for a teacher to say that a pupil's difficulties relate to low self-esteem.

Table 1.1 Summary of the decision-making process for core use

- What is the learning behaviour that I need to promote?
- Where should I concentrate my effort? In order to promote this, will it be most effective to work in the area of relationship with self, relationship with others or relationship with the curriculum, or a combination?
- What strategies, interventions and approaches can I use to work in the selected area(s)?
- Can I do this on my own or do I need help? What help or support do I need?
- Is there a relationship area that I feel more confident or competent to work in initially?
- What are my evaluation criteria? How will I know if I'm being successful in promoting this learning behaviour?

If the reference were to global low self-esteem, then in behaviour for learning terms this would represent an issue related to relationship with self. Identifying the particular relationship does not commit the teacher to directly focusing on that area. A distinctive aspect of the teacher's expertise, compared with that of a therapist or social worker, is their knowledge, skills and understanding in relation to curriculum, pedagogy and classroom management, and so there may be variables associated with the curriculum, teaching methods and pupil groupings that can be manipulated to have a positive impact on relationship with self. In such a scenario, the teacher would be working via the pupil's relationship with the curriculum or relationship with others to have an impact on the target relationship. The decision should be strongly influenced by what is likely to be better for the pupil. For example, some pupils who exhibit problematic behaviour may be resistant to the continued focus on their difficulties through direct attempts to improve their self-esteem by talking to them about their feelings or engaging them in 'special' activities that they do not see any of their peers undertaking. The other factor in the decision-making process is the teacher's confidence and competence in relation to a particular relationship area. As the teacher's primary area of expertise, it is useful to consider first what can be done via relationship with the curriculum through curricular and pedagogic variables.

Having identified the target relationship area, the teacher needs to identify specific learning behaviours that would represent indicators of progress in this area – even if it is being tackled indirectly by one of the other relationships. The list of learning behaviours in the Appendix is organised to reflect those that relate to each of the three relationships. One practical approach to identifying these learning behaviours is to plan a mindmapping exercise (see Figure 1.5), either to be completed individually by the teacher or in dialogue with others who work with or encounter the pupil. In this example, it is assumed that the relationship that is in need of development is the pupil's relationship with self and the presenting difficulties in this area are associated with low esteem.

In generating the learning behaviours that reflect the selected relationship area, it is important to continually question whether these are specific enough to allow monitoring of progress. We have illustrated this in Figure 1.5 through the example of confidence. In this case, indicators of confidence have been selected that relate to interactions with others. Just as we would know, for example, the steps involved in mastering a mathematical concept, it is important we think about the steps involved in developing a particular learning behaviour.

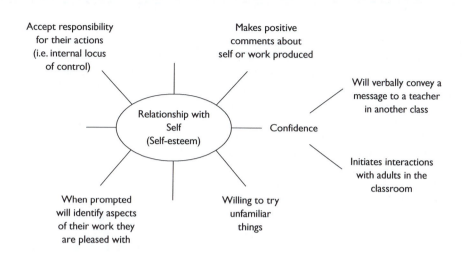

Figure 1.5 Identifying indicators of progress in a relationship area

So far we have identified the target relationship area, the learning behaviours that might indicate progress in this area and, if applicable, the other relationship area(s) that might be used indirectly. The next step is to consider the strategies, interventions and approaches that could be used to promote the targeted relationship area. These will, of course, vary from case to case. An individual teacher is likely to have knowledge of the pupil as well as a body of knowledge, skills and understanding that they can bring to bear in determining strategies. The expertise housed within the school among the staff team should not be neglected either. However, it is possible that additional strategies and approaches will need to be sought. It should be recognised that the original literature review (Powell and Tod 2004) that gave rise to the Behaviour for Learning conceptual framework identified the three relationship areas because the literature related to the development of learning behaviour in school contexts broadly fell into three different categories – social, cognitive and affective. Hypothesising that a pupil's difficulties lie in a particular relationship area signposts the way to a body of knowledge if it is necessary to research additional information to formulate strategies.

For some pupils external agency involvement may be necessary. This may take the form of direct working with the pupil, more detailed or specialised assessment of need, or advice and guidance to extend the capacity of school staff. In such situations the Behaviour for Learning framework can help to provide a common focus for intervention.

Pupils themselves will have their own strengths and weaknesses across the three relationship areas as well as their own understanding of the difficulties they are currently experiencing. The B4L approach is based on relationships and so it is important to understand a pupil's perspective rather than imposing interventions on an 'adult knows best' basis. This understanding is likely to be achieved by talking to the pupil, listening to their views and relating these to the intelligence already gathered. The latter is important for corroboration purposes. It should be recognised that pupils, like adults, may give what they believe to be expected answers, answers that portray them in a more positive light, answers that deflect blame and answers that avoid opening up potentially uncomfortable areas. Having listened to the pupil, consider whether what they have said seems plausible in light of intelligence previously gathered through observation and from those who encounter the pupil. For example, the pupil might identify that support from a teaching assistant would be helpful, but previous observation may have shown that they were uncooperative when this was provided. Further discussion with the pupil would therefore need to take place to ascertain the form the support should take for it to be successful. The following questions need to be considered:

- What purpose does the current behaviour appear to serve for the pupil?
- To what extent does the pupil view the behaviour as a problem or consider there to be a need for change?
- What learning behaviours does the pupil want to develop and is there a reasonable degree of match with those defined by the teacher?
- What benefits does the pupil associate with the development of these learning behaviours?
- What costs does the pupil associate with the development of these learning behaviours?
- What strengths does the pupil have that could help in the development of these learning behaviours?
- What type of support or intervention does the pupil feel would be most helpful in developing these learning behaviours?
- What type of support or intervention does the pupil feel would be least helpful in developing these learning behaviours?

Monitoring and evaluation

When employing the B4L approach at the level of extended use, monitoring and evaluation are based on the emergence of learning behaviours associated with the targeted relationship. It is for this reason that it is necessary to spend time thinking carefully about the learning behaviours associated with this relationship early in the planning process. However, it is important to retain an open mind, balancing an awareness of a range of indicative behaviours with the flexibility to recognise other behaviours that may also signify improvements in the focus relationship area. For this reason, we consider the look, listen and note approach to continuous assessment encouraged within the previous Government's Foundation Stage guidance (DCSF 2008) to be helpful for pupils of all ages when employing the B4L approach at the level of extended use. The look, listen and note approach, which typically involves the teacher noting on a sticky note or similar their observations as part of daily practice, seems preferable to working to a rigid checklist of learning behaviours associated with a specific relationship area. It allows the teacher to note observations that may be of interest and collate and interpret these later in order to make judgements about improvements in the selected relationship area.

A summary of the key questions involved in extended use of the B4L approach are shown in Table 1.2.

Table 1.2 Summary of the decision-making process for extended use

- What is the relationship that I need to promote for learning in a group setting?
- Is it better for the individual pupil if I focus directly on the target relationship or seek to develop it via one of the other two?
- Is there a relationship area that I feel more confident or competent to work in initially?
- Which cluster of learning behaviours (or a specific significant learning behaviour) do I need to promote in order to have a pervasive, positive effect on the relationship?
- What strategies, interventions and approaches can I use to promote the targeted relationship?
- What knowledge, skills and understanding does the pupil bring to this relationship?
- What knowledge, skills and understanding can I contribute to this relationship?
- Do I need any additional advice, guidance and support from within my school or from multi-agency partners?
- How will I know if I'm being successful in promoting the target relationship?

Conclusion

This chapter has provided a rationale for the B4L approach, a summary of its key components and an introduction to its practical application. At the level of day-to-day, whole-class use, the B4L approach provides a way of selecting and evaluating strategies based on the principle that no approach adopted should compromise the three relationships or the development of learning behaviour. It is hoped that this principle will guide teachers in selecting from the plethora of material available related to pupil behaviour the strategies and approaches it is appropriate to incorporate within their own professional repertoires.

For some pupils it will be necessary to move beyond day-to-day use and to adopt a more systematic approach to the promotion of learning behaviour. Core use and extended use of the B4L approach represent a graduated response, moving from a more explicit focus on the desirable learning behaviours through to the targeting of one or more behaviour for learning relationships. The representation of the different levels of use in Figure 1.3 is intended to convey the clear message that we do not expect teachers to employ such systematic approaches for all pupils. Extended use in particular is likely to be reserved for those pupils where there is either a feeling of 'stuckness' on the part of school staff or the complexity of the case means there is a need to better understand the interacting factors in order to determine the areas for intervention.

Chapter 2

Developing relationships for learning

Introduction

This chapter focuses on the development and maintenance of particular types of relationships – namely, *relationships for learning* – that are considered relevant to learning and behaviour in the group setting of the classroom.

The importance of relationships has been stressed in Government guidance on the knowledge, skills and understanding needed by trainees in order to be able to manage pupils' behaviour. This stated that: 'Trainees should understand that good relationships are at the heart of good behaviour management. They should be able to form positive, appropriate, professional relationships with their pupils' (TA 2012: 2).

Most schools and their teachers would also probably agree with the view that good teacher–pupil relationships are crucial to the development of an effective learning environment. This has been endorsed by research (Hattie 2009). The quality of peer relationships experienced by pupils in school affects their academic performance, well-being and engagement, absenteeism, vulnerability to bullying, behavioural difficulties, drug usage, social difficulties, and mental health (McGrath and Noble 2010). Good teacher–pupil relationships at age 14 are positively associated with progress between Key Stage 3 and Key Stage 4 and consistently negatively associated with engagement in risky behaviours at the ages of 14 and 16 (Chowdry *et al.* 2009). Peer-assisted learning strategies, including peer tutoring, have been cited as a 'high impact low cost strategy', with benefits for both tutee and tutor that typically equate to a GCSE grade (Higgins *et al.* 2011).

Our everyday experiences also tell us that relationships are important but can be complex and demanding. For this reason, this chapter applies the Behaviour for Learning conceptual framework (see Chapter 1, Figure 1.1) to the challenge of promoting positive relationships for learning in the classroom. It is hoped that it will be of use to teachers in developing a critical understanding of the nature and influence of relationships on behaviour.

The role of schools and their teachers in developing positive relationships

Teacher involvement in the building of positive relationships with pupils is of paramount importance given that the behavioural difficulties exhibited by some pupils can be attributed to factors outside the school context. Some pupils may bring to school a view that much of school learning is boring and irrelevant to their lives. They may also have developed a perception of themselves that leads us to attribute their behavioural problems to low self-esteem or a lack of self-efficacy. Some have developed relationship styles with others that are characterised by being very loud, aggressive, demanding of attention or withdrawn. Such behaviours can become habitual if they have developed over time and are reinforced by others influential in a pupil's life.

The school offers a very different environment from that experienced by some pupils outside it. For example:

- The school offers structure, stability, purpose, behavioural expectations, rewards and sanctions that apply to *all* pupils.
- Teachers are expected to model communications that convey respect, fairness, interest and concern for their pupils.
- Teachers are trained to promote learning, achievement and appropriate social behaviour in their pupils.

There are two main strands to the development of a focus on relationships in schools (Roffey 2010). One concerns the influence of a school culture and climate that values, models and fosters positive relationships. The other is the use of curricular opportunities (e.g. DfES 2005c, 2007) to directly or indirectly teach social, emotional and behavioural skills. Teachers have a professional responsibility to build relationships with pupils that support progress and learning. The school has a role in providing the contexts, the curriculum and the conditions that allow pupils to learn how to develop and improve their relationship skills with others. The importance of relationships in school is frequently acknowledged and few teachers, or others working with children and young people, would argue with the view that: 'positive relationships with significant others are cornerstones of young people's capacity to function effectively in the social, affective and academic domains' (Martin and Dowson 2009: 351).

However, there are inherent difficulties in securing an evidence base that can be used to guide and develop practice. Personal qualities identified as desirable for relationship building are often referred to as 'soft skills' that include competences in areas such as communication, empathy, conflict resolution, active listening and creative problem solving. The effectiveness of any relationship cannot be unilaterally judged but is dependent on the *subjective* experiences and interpretations of the individual participants. A relationship style that is effective for most of a class might still be perceived and experienced as negative by an individual member of that class.

'Relationships in action' in your classroom

The moment you walk into your classroom or greet the pupils waiting outside, you are actively involved in building '*relationships for learning*'. You will always need to be mindful of how what you are saying and doing is being received and interpreted by your pupils.

Your lesson 'starter' seeks to get your pupils involved in their 'relationship' with the subject area. Within the B4L approach we refer to this as 'relationship with the curriculum'. Pupils' behaviour will communicate to you the level of their engagement. Those who are actively engaged will ask and answer questions or demonstrate interest in what you are saying just as they would if they were actively relating to another person. Other pupils may not engage and will communicate this to you by their behaviour. For example, they may start fiddling with their pens or chatting. Some 'disengaged' and/or 'disaffected' pupils may be less easy to identify because they do not overtly demonstrate behaviour problems. These may be the pupils who display 'on task' behaviours, such as looking at the teacher or responding to requests, but who in fact are not actively engaged and are probably taking a line of least resistance and adopting a low profile.

Your response to noting pupils who are not actively involved in their relationship with the curriculum will be crucial. You will be aiming to effect a behaviour change in them that will get them back 'on task'. You may do this by telling them to stop what they are doing or, if following the advice on positive correction in Chapter 7, by telling them directly what behaviour you want (see Chapter 7). Alternatively, you might ask a question that will reorient them back into the relationship, such as:

'David, can you tell me what I have just asked the class to do?'

This may suffice to hook David back into engaging with his work. However, it should be recognised that you are in the public arena of the classroom and David may prefer to opt for relating to his peers by starting an argument or saying:

'It's boring, Miss, and I don't know what we are supposed to do . . . '

You might then be tempted in this instance to react emotionally and defend your position by saying:

'If you had been listening, David, you would know what it is you had to do – others in the class are interested in getting on with this work.'

Reacting emotionally directs attention away from your key purpose of building classroom relationships, which is to 'promote learning'. David now has the controlling role in the relationship and may have secured peer attention and support.

Your response to his behaviour should demonstrate to him that he has not distracted you from your focus on learning. You need to remain calm, comment on David's *behaviour* (avoiding any personal comments such as 'Why is it always you that is causing trouble?') and redirect his attention to the learning behaviour you want from him. You may choose to address issues relating to his self-efficacy or his need for peer approval by comments such as:

'David, tell me why you think what I have asked you to do is important?'

Or:

'You are good with ideas and it will be useful for others in the class.'

From this scenario we can get a feeling for the link between building positive relationships for learning and pupil behaviour. Of course, by 'unpicking' an incident that may be only a few minutes in duration you may well be thinking that, while looking closely at relationships in this way is interesting, it would not be feasible to apply this level of analysis within day-to-day teaching. Such thinking is entirely justified and it is worth noting that for the most part pupils and their teachers adapt to the learning relationships that are conducted in the public arena of the classroom. As they progress through stages of their education, most pupils learn to accept the behavioural expectations of this environment.

Within this chapter the purpose of placing a focus on relationships for learning is so that, as a class teacher, you keep a focus on ensuring classroom relationships remain positive. You will also be aiming, when appropriate, to strengthen these relationships.

The general principles for this endeavour, emerging from the scenario described earlier, are:

- As with all other relationships interactions are *reciprocal* and *dynamic* – you do something, the pupil responds, you react to that response and so on.
- Each person in the relationship experiences/*interprets* what the other is saying/doing. As the professional in the relationship, you have to try to understand how pupils are experiencing and interpreting your behaviour.
- Relationships, like all communication, have *cognitive, emotional* and *social* components. What another person says to us influences how we feel and what we do next. This interdependence of social, emotional and cognitive factors allows us to build and repair relationships in a variety of ways. This might be through reasoning, showing empathy and understanding, and sharing interests and activities.
- Your professional role in developing relationships in the classroom differs from your personal relationships in that you have to keep the focus on relationships that support *learning* in the group setting of the classroom.
- You are looking, within the relationships, to develop *learning behaviours* and reduce/ eliminate behaviours that prevent the class or individuals from taking part in, and benefitting from, the learning opportunities of the school/class.
- Relationship building takes place in the *public arena* and as such you are expected to remain calm and model appropriate relationship behaviour.
- Individual pupils are conscious of the public nature of the classroom and their behaviour may communicate to you that they seek to *preserve their individuality* (e.g. through non-compliance) or to gain the attention and *approval of their peers* (e.g. by chatting, messing about).
- We cannot know what another individual is thinking and so we tend to use their *behaviour* as a guide to how the relationship is progressing.
- Within the classroom the speed and interdependence of cognitive, emotional and social interactions make for an ever-changing situation. Timely action is needed if situations are to be de-escalated.
- Teachers need to develop an awareness of how their *personal style* of communicating has an impact on their professional responsibility for 'building relationships for learning' (see Chapter 4).

As these points illustrate, classroom interactions happen at a fast pace and involve a complex interdependence of the many variables that make up the context and conditions of the classroom. For that reason, this chapter applies the Behaviour for Learning conceptual framework to the task of unpicking and understanding how relationships have an impact on learning and behaviour.

Using the behaviour for learning model to support relationship development

All teachers are aware of the importance of classroom relationships and make decisions about what kind of relationships they want to establish in their classrooms. These tend to change over time (Wubbels *et al.* 2006). There is no blueprint for building an effective relationship with pupils and most teachers experience times when they wish, on reflection, that they had responded differently. However, in practice, the aim is to become more aware of, and more consistent in applying, some core principles that underpin the development of effective relationships for learning. The two core features of relationships that can be used by teachers to improve pupil learning and behaviour are as follows:

1   Learning relationships are *reciprocal.*
2   They are influenced by context and can be *changed* and *improved.*

In essence, the first point means that teachers, individual pupils and their peers always need to be aware of how what they say and do affects others in the classroom. Teachers need to think about their own behaviour from a pupil's viewpoint. For example, a teacher might say, 'If you do not get on with your work you will not get your GCSE grades and you will not get a job' as an intended pupil motivator. While the comment may be valid from the teacher's perspective, the pupil may be functioning in the 'here and now'. The threat of a delayed negative outcome is unlikely to serve to quell the pupil's immediate need for some social chatting and attention.

The positive dimension of the second core feature of relationships noted above is that teachers do have considerable influence over the context and conditions of their classroom. This gives them opportunities to make adjustments that can serve to strengthen or repair relationships for learning in their classrooms.

The Behaviour for Learning conceptual framework has been fully described and explained in Chapter 1. In this chapter, the model is intended primarily to be useful when teachers are trying to 'problem solve' around a particular pupil and/or group exhibiting behavioural problems in class. Interestingly, there is a tendency to focus more on teacher, pupil and peer relationships when a problem arises. Less emphasis is placed on understanding how it is that, for most of the time, teachers and their diverse range of pupils adapt to the range of interpersonal interactions they experience during the school day.

How does the behaviour for learning approach help in building relationships?

In the classroom a pupil may feel confident about their relationship with the subject, competent relating to others and comfortable in their relationship with themselves. In this case the individual is likely to be responsive, responsible and resilient within these three relationships and their behaviour does not cause concern. However, consider how a pupil might behave if they were not very good at their subject, lacked self-belief, and kept falling out with their peers and teacher. As outlined in Chapter 1, in classroom contexts the Behaviour for Learning conceptual framework illustrates a focus on:

* Relationships with the Curriculum – mainly the *cognitive* component of learning
* Relationships with Others – mainly the *social* component of learning
* Relationships with Self – mainly the *emotional* component of learning.

In all three areas the relationship is reciprocal and interdependent. These three relationships allow us to unpick and understand how what the pupil is doing, how they are feeling and who they are with are influencing their learning behaviour. It also allows teachers to use one of the relationships to strengthen another. For example, the use of collaborative group work (relationship with others) may serve to improve a pupil's relationship with the curriculum if they experience learning as 'more fun' by doing it with others.

Using the Behaviour for Learning conceptual framework at whole class level: maintaining equilibrium

Although within the Behaviour for Learning conceptual framework (Chapter 1, Figure 1.1) relationships with self, curriculum and others are separated out, in reality of course the pupil does not experience these separately. The model is just a model. The aim for the teacher is to maintain a *balance* between these three relationships so that an understandable emphasis on subject teaching and academic attainment does not damage the pupil's belief about themselves or their relationships with their peers and teacher. Overly competitive cultures and a lack of consideration for how individual pupils are experiencing this in the classroom can lead to an imbalance between the three learning relationships.

At whole class level, it is useful for teachers to ask themselves:

1   Am I making sure that in my relationship building I have kept a clear focus on the learning behaviours I want to develop?
2   For example, if I am seeking to establish mutual 'respect' between myself and pupils, do we both know the learning behaviours that are expected from us, such as:

- will listen to and consider another's opinion
- will come to the lesson prepared and on time
- will keep agreements
- can and will show manners
- will be fair
- will not make assumptions.

3   Am I achieving a good *balance* between teaching for academic outcomes, being aware of pupils' feelings and self-esteem, and taking advantage of the learning resource and enjoyment factor offered by peers?
4   Am I taking full advantage of the *two supporting relationships* (i.e. relationship with self and relationship with others) to improve pupils' relationship with and progress within my subject area?

The next section discusses each of the relationships for learning in turn, along with suggestions that will inform strategy choice.

Relationship with the curriculum

The pupil's relationship with the curriculum can be defined as 'The dynamic interactions that make up the reciprocal activity between the learner and the school curriculum/subject. This involves being able to access, process and respond to the information available through the subject areas of the curriculum' (Ellis and Tod 2009: 94).

Building and maintaining a positive relationship with the curriculum involves fostering learning behaviours

In using the word 'relationship' alongside the word 'curriculum' there is a deliberate attempt within the Behaviour for Learning conceptual framework to move forward from notions of the teacher delivering the curriculum, setting specific targets and measuring predefined 'outputs'.

When approaching behaviour from the perspective that it is influenced by the pupil's relationship with the curriculum, it is important to identify when and why they have 'disengaged' from the curriculum and to direct them back into the relationship. We need to promote behaviours that allow the pupil to be involved in a positive, dynamic relationship with the subject. Although behaviours such as sitting still, following instructions and paying attention might be desirable, they do not *in themselves* equate with the pupil actively engaging with and/ or relating to the curriculum (Boyle *et al.* 2001). The kind of behaviours expected from, for example, a secondary school pupil in an English lesson might include that they:

- check if they understand, if necessary requesting further information or telling the teacher what aspects they do not understand
- sometimes seek reasons for aspects of the work they are undertaking
- plan a general strategy before starting
- anticipate and predict possible outcomes
- offer or seek links between different activities and ideas, different topics or subjects and schoolwork and personal life
- search for weaknesses in their own understandings and check the consistency of their explanations across different situations
- suggest new activities and alternative procedures
- challenge the text or an answer the teacher sanctions as correct
- offer ideas, new insights and alternative explanations
- justify opinions
- react and refer to comments of other students.

(based on PEEL 2009)

Teachers seek to develop these behaviours in their pupils through the instructions they give, the tasks they set and the feedback they provide. In a primary school setting, teachers aim to teach these behaviours in their simpler form – for example, by having visual reminders of self-help strategies or by making the required behaviours explicit through verbal instructions such as 'Check you have finished' or 'Decide what to do next'.

In pre-school and primary settings we can see how play encourages children to develop the learning behaviours that are related to those listed in the eleven bullet points earlier. The features of play include the following:

- the child initiates
- the child has chosen to direct their attention to the activity
- adult intervention is through shared and not directed attention
- the child monitors their own pace and direction
- the involvement of other children is unintentional but valued
- there is not necessarily a prescribed end point
- the reward is intrinsic to the activity and the child uses different and creative ways to explore the situation.

Examples of desirable learning behaviours needed for a positive relationship with the curriculum

There are many learning behaviours that it is important to develop in order to foster pupils' positive relationship with the curriculum (see the Appendix) It is often helpful to think in terms of the pupil having to access, engage with and respond to the curriculum – just as a person would have to do if they were taking part in a conversation. These learning behaviours reflect the need to have a *disposition,* or personal willingness, to take part in the lesson, and the organisational and planning *skills* to absorb the necessary information within a group setting.

Examples of positive learning behaviours include that the child:

- can focus attention primarily on the task
- actively listens to the teacher and monitors their own understanding of instructions
- actively seeks coherence, relevance and meaning – i.e. is an active not a passive learner
- can identify when they need help and can take appropriate action
- asks 'why' they went wrong
- is willing to offer an opinion and is able to justify it
- refers to previous work before asking the teacher for help
- can plan and produce a response that is understandable to the recipient within the time frame
- checks work against the teacher's and their own expectations
- takes appropriate responsibility for their own learning.

Strategies for enabling pupils to build a positive relationship with the curriculum

There are some basic principles that can be applied at whole class level in order to address any emergent behavioural problems in some pupils:

1   Place emphasis on differentiation. Check that pupils have opportunities for a variety of inputs and outputs through, for example, the use of visual, auditory and, if feasible, kinaesthetic presentation modes, and the use of a variety of tasks that demonstrate their learning.
2   Actively seek meaningfulness and interest from the *pupil's* perspective in order to engage them emotionally.
3   Keep instructions simple – do not assume *all* pupils will be able to listen, think and write simultaneously.
4   Explicitly encourage the development of metacognition so that individual learners remain active in their personal relationship with the curriculum. Open up debate with pupils about their learning by asking them to consider how they are approaching learning or to identify the learning strategies they are using that are successful.
5   Foster motivation (see Chapter 3). In order to be motivated within the class group, a pupil needs to feel they belong, are valued, can achieve and have some control (McLean 2009). Much of the established effective practice for behaviour management (see Chapters 5, 6 and 7) is based on this view and seeks to meet these pupil needs by, for example, affording and rewarding success, giving the pupil choice and

showing them respect. The following approaches may be helpful in fostering learning by meeting pupils' motivational needs:

- involving pupils in some of the decision making within the classroom
- making sure pupils fully understand the *purpose* of the work and the hoped-for outcomes
- involving pupils in the identification of criteria that demonstrate success, and in the evaluation of their learning
- providing choice as to how activities and tasks are completed and information presented
- allowing pupils to determine their own questions for enquiry and debate
- using behaviour management techniques that encourage children to make choices about their behaviour
- providing opportunities for children to determine class and playground rules and routines.

(based on DfES 2005c: 26)

Evaluation of the efficacy of strategies

A particular strength of using the Behaviour for Learning conceptual framework is that it provides teachers with a way of evaluating the efficacy of the strategies they have put in place to effect a behaviour change in their pupils. This applies to all three relationships that are intrinsic to the conceptual framework: namely, relationship with the curriculum, relationship with self and relationship with others. Typically pupils are constantly monitored against academic targets and/or a reduction in or cessation of behaviour problems. A low-achieving pupil who exhibits behaviour difficulties is thus at risk of receiving an imbalance of negative feedback. Focusing on the learning behaviours that are required from the pupil in order for them to improve their learning and behaviour provides an alternative, more positive focus for monitoring and evaluation.

This enables the teacher to model, encourage and reward this behaviour and use it as a measure of pupil progress.

Relationship with self

The pupil's relationship with self can be defined as the dynamic interaction between the individual's existing thoughts, perceptions and feelings about themselves.

The individual in the group

We have noted earlier that pupil behaviour has both a 'skill' and a 'will' element. We can attribute the reason for the pupil's behaviour either to the fact that they did not have the required skill to behave appropriately or that they knew how to behave but did not have the will and/or disposition to do so. Strategy choice for teachers depends on whether their aim is to:

- teach and/or develop the appropriate behaviour, or
- try to bring about a change in the pupil's 'attitude' to learning.

The classroom situation for individual pupils requires them to:

- adapt to sharing adult attention with others
- make effort with work that they are not necessarily interested in
- be compared with others, sometimes openly
- work alongside and sometimes collaboratively with peers they may not know or like
- conform to rules and other expectations they may not see the point of.

The individual has to keep a balance between 'fitting in with the group' and retaining their individuality. Those who seek to 'fit in' risk becoming passive recipients of the learning opportunities available in the classroom. Although not displaying behavioural problems, they are likely to underperform. Those who seek to impose their individuality within the group can become loud, argumentative, bossy, demanding of attention and so on.

Teachers have to use the school systems, routines and rewards to encourage some conformity but at the same time to keep a focus on ensuring that the individual pupil is recognised and valued. Some individual pupils exhibit behaviour problems that ensure they are 'noticed'. In such cases teachers might usefully pay explicit attention to the way they respond to that individual pupil in class. Suggestions for relationship building responses include the following:

- show interest in the pupil as a person – ask them about their interests, views, etc.
- give them some time and attention
- listen to their viewpoint and take it on board
- ask their opinion
- refer to them by name
- convey that the behaviour is the problem, not the person
- provide positive feedback – explicitly note good behaviours and positive characteristics
- protect them from failure, rejection and humiliation
- empathise, showing concern about their progress and well-being
- be fair
- when necessary, explain the reasons for your having given a reward or sanction
- be straight, honest and clear with them
- be trustworthy and reliable
- be positive – give them hope. Avoid phrases like 'You never know how to behave' or 'It's always you, isn't it?' that convey little faith in their ability to change
- do not patronise the pupil or use sarcasm.

While use of the phrase 'relationship with self' may be less familiar, teachers typically acknowledge that behaviour is influenced by how a pupil thinks and feels about themselves. Some teachers may, for example, explain a pupil's behaviour by saying:

'I think he is messing about because he thinks he is not as clever as he would like to be' (i.e. a self-esteem issue).

'He knows how to do the work but he doesn't think he can sustain the effort to succeed' (i.e. a self-efficacy issue).

'He isn't going to change because he thinks that it's someone else's fault that he is the way he is. He thinks it's up to the school or his teachers to make things better for him' (i.e. a locus of control issue).

These behaviours largely reflect the emotional component of learning. They involve the pupil developing the interest, commitment and belief that allows them to actively process the curriculum, respond to feedback, monitor their own progress and develop some responsibility for their own learning. As such, 'relationship with self' contributes to the development of both positive and negative learning behaviours.

Pupils bring to school with them a unique combination of characteristics and experiences. Once in the classroom they may change some of their perceptions of self or seek to select information that reinforces the view of self they have already constructed.

It is useful at this stage to take a brief look at three constructs, mentioned earlier, that we sometimes use to 'explain' emotional aspects of a pupil's behaviour.

Self-esteem

Self-esteem is an umbrella term we often use to describe any aspect of the pupil's relationship with self. Although a term frequently used to *explain* pupil behaviour, there remains a lack of consensus about the nature and impact of self-esteem (O'Brien and Guiney 2001; Butler and Gasson 2005). There is, however, some agreement that self-esteem involves the individual making comparisons between their 'ideal self' and their own 'self image' (e.g. Coopersmith 1967; Lawrence 2006).

Self image can be thought of as how a person perceives themselves. It is a perception that has been formed and continues to be influenced by a range of feedback and experiences. *Ideal self* relates to how a person believes they should be and would like to be seen. There are many sources of information that can contribute to the development of an individual's *ideal self* including feedback from parents, peers and the media. If a pupil perceives that there is a significant discrepancy between their self image and ideal self, then we presume that they will experience low self-esteem. On the other hand, if the pupil perceives that they are closely matched to their ideal self, then we might say that they have high self-esteem.

Working with this view, we can see that in the social and academic context of the classroom there are considerable opportunities to enable the individual to either confirm or reject the judgements they are making about themselves.

For the purpose of this chapter, we are looking to bring about changes to a pupil's expression of their relationship with self – namely, their behaviour and their self-reference statements. We would seek, for example, to reduce the number of '*I can't do this*' statements by asking the pupil to identify at the start of a task which parts of it they are able to do.

Working with self-esteem

Pupils present numerous behaviours that teachers and others may be inclined to attribute to self-esteem. Working with the construct of self-esteem allows teachers to:

- think about why the behaviour makes sense from the pupil's perspective – even if it does not seem sensible from the teacher's perspective
- consider strategies that address the distance between the pupil's own self image and their ideal self. This can be achieved in two compatible ways:

  1   The teacher can make the 'ideal self' more realistic for the pupil. They can do this by working with the pupil to reappraise the evidence that has led them to

construct their view of 'ideal self'. The overall aim is to adjust ideal self so that it is closer to that to which the pupil could realistically aspire.

2   The teacher can work with the pupil with a view to re-conceptualising their own view of themselves. This would normally involve supporting the pupil to move away from an over-emphasis on negative self-judgements towards a realistically positive self-appraisal.

What behaviours are associated with self-esteem issues?

In thinking about these, we are in effect trying to *guess* how any one individual feels about themselves by the behaviours they exhibit and the things they say. The behaviours associated by teachers with low self-esteem typically include:

- reluctance to try new things
- being easily frustrated by lack of immediate success or understanding
- attitudes that are hypercritical, negative, sarcastic or cynical
- withdrawal, depression and unwillingness to communicate
- blaming behaviour outside themselves
- dependency on others to tell them what to do, what is good, what is acceptable
- lying
- non-compliance to authority.

(Ellis and Tod 2009: 119)

Others include:

- being overconfident, often without justification
- showing off or boasting
- being disruptive
- having a negative outlook
- falling out with peers
- lacking in motivation
- seeking approval.

(informed from Miller and Moran 2005)

What learning behaviours is it desirable to develop?

In order to improve a pupil's relationship with self, it is desirable to foster certain behaviours and dispositions so that the child:

- makes some positive comments about self
- demonstrates some interest in subject/school work/other areas of the school curriculum
- is willing and able to control mood changes (e.g. anger and annoyance)
- has an appropriate sense of self-efficacy
- can tolerate some failure
- is willing to take appropriate responsibility for own learning
- is prepared to try new things and 'take risks'
- is willing to make mistakes and 'move on'

- knows how and is prepared to get help
- can manage distractions
- is willing to work independently as appropriate.

Notice that, when seeking to develop learning behaviours relating to self, any intervention needs to place emphasis on a pupil's *disposition* and *skill*. The teacher may tackle this initially by ensuring that the pupil *is able* to exhibit the desirable behaviour. Once they demonstrate the learning behaviour, are rewarded for it and find that it can be beneficial, they are more likely to gradually develop the *will* to continue with this learning behaviour. See the Appendix for more examples of learning behaviours.

Although working with the construct of self-esteem has benefits, it clearly does not suffice to address the range of behavioural problems linked to 'self'. There are other explanations that we can usefully consider. One relates to the pupil's self-belief about their own competence, the other to their perceptions about who is in control of their behaviour. These constructs are known respectively as 'self-efficacy' and 'locus of control'.

Self-efficacy

Self-efficacy can be defined as an individual's judgement of their ability to successfully execute a required behaviour (Bandura 2002; Gibson and Dembo 1984). If, for example, a pupil is told '*Come on, you can do it if you try*', they may agree with the teacher's statement but judge themselves to be incapable of making and sustaining the effort required. The importance of this construct in schools is endorsed through Poulou and Norwich's (2000) suggestion that an individual's conviction in their own effectiveness is likely to affect how much *effort* they will expend and how long they will *persist* in the face of obstacles and adverse circumstances.

Working with self-efficacy and behaviour

In school settings self-efficacy is a useful construct for teachers when dealing with behaviour that is linked to engagement and effort. Encouraging pupils to put more effort into their work is of crucial importance, particularly for pupils who need to work harder than others in order to achieve success (see Chapter 3).

Making effort explicit

Claxton (2002), in his book *Building Learning Power*, noted the need to develop perseverance in learners in schools and not just assume that it develops with chronological age. As they go through the education system, pupils need to learn to sustain effort that is uncomfortable, and which may clash with other competing social and personal agendas, if they are to achieve success.

The importance of understanding the construct of self-efficacy is that if a pupil *believes* that they cannot successfully complete a task they develop behaviours in support of that belief. This in effect results in their being rooted in a vicious circle of experiencing a lack of success that serves to fuel their beliefs surrounding self-efficacy. Based on this assumption, it follows that the most effective way to break a pupil's 'low self-efficacy—low successful task completion—low self-efficacy' cycle is to adopt teaching strategies that serve to enable the pupil to experience an increase in successful task completion.

Whole class strategy suggestions for self-efficacy

- Discuss with the class what they mean by 'making an effort with their work':
  - Do they think it is doing the same thing for longer?
  - Do they have a purpose behind their effort other than being praised for making it?
  - How do they judge their own effort?
  - How do they judge others' effort?
  - What strategies do they use to sustain effort?
  - Do they find it easier to sustain effort on some things (e.g. computer games) than others?
  - What have they experienced as the benefits of effort?
  - When have they experienced that effort has not been worth it?
  - What barriers have they experienced to their making an effort?
  - What makes effort effective?
  - What do they think is the difference between perseverance and shorter term channelling of focused mental effort towards a solution?
- Grade pupil effort and achievement
- Share with pupils how you judge 'effort'
- Draw on the media, films, books and history to highlight individuals who have persisted in spite of adversity
- Reward progress throughout the task as well as the final outcome.

Secondary level teachers may feel that pupils *should* be able to sustain effort. However, if this stance persists and the pupil maintains and preserves their stance on self-efficacy, then stalemate is reached. In a study focused specifically on low-attaining secondary aged pupils Dunne *et al.* (2007) identified that effective teaching involved manipulating interest, fun, ease and success in order to re-engage them. Clearly there is a balance to be achieved in meeting pupil preferences for lessons because they also need to experience that learning is sometimes difficult, requires repetitive practice and involves setbacks. However, the first priority has to be to secure pupil engagement. This may require that for some pupils teachers have to prioritise their interests and preferences for learning as part of the process of bringing about changes to their behaviour and learning.

The strategies listed earlier are designed to support pupils to think again about their own competence and confidence, and to break the cycle of their fulfilling the beliefs that they have brought with them to the school context. As pupils progress through school, there is of course an expectation that they will develop increasing *responsibility* for their own learning. The next section examines how an understanding of where pupils locate control for their behaviour can support teachers in promoting the behaviours that are associated with responsibility.

Locus of control

As mentioned earlier in relation to motivation, individuals need to believe that they have some control over what happens to them. An important construct relating to self is concerned with our beliefs about whom or what is responsible for what happens to us. If we believe that what happens to us is completely beyond our control we are said to have an *external* locus of control. On the other hand if we believe that we determine or are responsible for what happens to us then we have an *internal* locus of control. Most individuals balance their beliefs, with control placed between these extremes. For example, if we had an unsuccessful job interview we might say it was due to a combination of factors, some beyond our control (e.g. there was a favoured internal candidate) and some within our control (e.g. we didn't prepare well enough).

We can make judgements about a pupil's locus of control through the attributions they make (Weiner 2000). We can consider this through two examples:

- After a fight or argument, a pupil might say, 'It wasn't me, Miss, he started it.'
- When confronted with a task, a pupil might say, 'I can't do it, I'm dyslexic.'

The pupils concerned have generated explanations (or 'attributions') about the cause of their behaviour. In both cases they are unlikely to make changes to their behaviour because they perceive that the cause of their behaviour is outside their control. The teacher has a role in guiding the pupil towards taking at least *some* responsibility for their own behaviour. When discussing the 'fight' situation (when things have calmed down), the teacher can encourage the pupil to think about how they could have stopped themselves from getting involved. In the other example, although the pupil has a learning difficulty that is beyond their control, they still have control over how they react to that difficulty.

It can be useful for teachers to consider the attributional style of those pupils whose explanations for their own and others' behaviour lie at extreme ends of the locus of control continuum and have become entrenched and habitual. If pupils generally believe that their environment or other people control what happens to them, they are unlikely to make an effort to change. Such pupils could be at risk of adopting a position of 'learned helplessness' (Seligman 1975). A stance like this can render them vulnerable to becoming passive recipients of things that happen to them.

It is important that pupils are supported to develop responsibility for their behaviour by locating control of their behaviour within themselves. It is also the case that there will be factors that contribute to a pupil's behaviour over which they may have limited or no control, and they will need to develop resilience to these factors if they are to avoid accepting a role as victims of circumstance.

Strategies for working with locus of control include the following:

- Encourage pupils to look at their style of attributions and consider how that affects their behaviour and motivation to change.
- Seek to challenge with them their beliefs about the causes of their behaviour and aim to secure a more balanced style of attribution based on recognition that '*some* of what happens to me is not in my control but I can change my responses to that'.
- Aim to see things from their perspective and let them see that you want them to progress for *their* benefit and that they do have some control.
- Identify with them which aspects of their behaviour they do have control over. What steps could be taken by them to manage that behaviour?
- Encourage collaborative work so that success (and failure) can be experienced with others and locus of control 'shared' such that the pupil has a stake in that control.
- Use examples from literature, the media, others and role-play so that individuals can reflect upon issues associated with, and the effect of, locus of control judgements without being hampered by their personal involvement.
- Discuss ways of coping with 'failure' that may be resulting from factors over which the pupil has limited control. For example, the work may be too difficult, the pace may be too fast or they may be required to study subjects that are of no interest to

them. Although their perception may be largely valid, it is important that they do not locate themselves exclusively in an 'externally' controlled situation. Encourage them to talk about why they are experiencing difficulties, and what action they could take to bring about improvements.

As with all other constructs relating to self, we are dealing not with realities but with a pupil's *belief*. Teachers have a valuable role to play in enabling pupils to question the beliefs they have constructed and to use available evidence to support any reappraisal thought to be beneficial to the pupil.

The group setting of the classroom provides a rich source of information for individuals to compare and contrast their own behaviour with peers and reappraise the causal attributions and behavioural responses they have made, hopefully in a safe and responsive setting. An understanding of the theory that surrounds 'relationship with self' should be helpful in supporting teachers to effectively harness this resource.

Relationships with others

A pupil's relationship with others can be defined as being able and willing to take a positive and active part in learning that involves others.

Within school contexts pupils are required to take part in learning that involves others. Teachers can take advantage of the opportunities that are available within the group setting of the classroom to improve academic and social outcomes. The evidence for the efficacy of peer tutoring and peer-assisted learning in raising attainment and improving behaviour is strong (McGrath and Noble 2010; Higgins *et al.* 2011).

As pupils progress through school, they tend to show a preference for teaching that includes activity and engagement with peers (Smith *et al.* 2005). The low-level chatter that results from this pursuit of social interaction is very annoying to some teachers. This difference between the teacher and pupil in terms of social preferences for learning may be exacerbated by the increased levels of peer–peer interaction outside the classroom through social networking sites, mobile phones, emails and other forms of electronic communication. This electronic communication is distinct from that experienced in face-to-face situations because it allows individuals to practise making relationships in a context in which they have more perceived control. The electronic medium can allow individuals time to make (and edit) their written response. They do not have to deal with interruptions, or monitor recipients' non-verbal reactions, and they can control when to end the relationship by 'switching off'. They can gauge the approval/disapproval rates of responses of others and can make use of others' skills by copying or agreeing with the responses generated by those involved (Ellis and Tod 2009). On the more negative side, 'relationships' conducted through electronic media place individuals at risk of receiving information and feedback from a range of sources that can be upsetting and/or harmful.

In thinking about social behaviour in schools and classrooms, the Teachers' Standards state that teachers should: 'have clear rules and routines for behaviour in classrooms, and take responsibility for promoting good and courteous behaviour both in classrooms and around the school, in accordance with the school's behaviour policy' (DfE 2011a: 8).

When using the B4L approach, we are concerned with developing the learning behaviours that not only reflect the Government requirements for 'good and courteous behaviour' but also facilitate learning in the group setting of the classroom.

Children arrive at school having experienced a variety of relationships with others, and they consequently display a range of behaviours for relating to their teachers and peers. Teachers, particularly in Early Years settings, expect to have to place emphasis on developing behaviours that enable pupils to learn in the group setting of the classroom. These behaviours include listening, taking turns, sharing attention and resources, and accepting adult direction.

Although some behaviour problems can reliably be attributed to social influences outside the school, teachers are in an influential position to make changes to pupils' relationships with others.

In looking at how teachers can influence the development of pupils' relationships with others, it is important to revisit and consider the points made about relationships at the start of this chapter. These are that:

- learning relationships are *reciprocal*
- they are influenced by context and can be *changed* and *improved*.

Teachers have control over their part in their relationships with pupils and through this can seek to bring about change in pupils' responses. This will be noted throughout this book when effective behaviour management strategies are characterised by an emphasis being placed on the quality of teachers' interactions with their pupils. This includes being calm, respectful, allowing choice and keeping the emphasis on the behaviour not the pupil's personal characteristics.

Learning behaviours associated with 'relationship with others'

Teachers on our courses have noted the following breakdown points in their relationship with their classes:

- When pupils will not listen when asked. When they appear blasé and just don't seem to care.
- When they accuse you of having been unfair when you were not.
- When they are simply not interested in you and ignore you.
- When they repeatedly do something that you have asked them not to do.
- When they deny doing something when you have seen them do it.
- When they criticise your teaching or compare you unfavourably with another teacher.

Activity 2.1

1   Identify one or two learning behaviours from the earlier list (p.41) that you would want to develop to address these behavioural issues.
2   How might a view that 'teaching is all about relationships' help to analyse what has gone wrong in these instances?
3   Choose one learning behaviour you have identified and consider how you might bring about changes to your own behaviour and planning for teaching that would promote the development of this behaviour.

Most schools, through their behaviour policy, make the social behaviours expected from their pupils explicit. These form the basis for creating a social environment in which pupils can learn safely and cooperatively with others. However, the cessation of some of these behaviours (e.g. 'no swearing', 'no running in the corridors') do not necessarily lead to improved learning behaviour. In this chapter we are concerned with the development of the type of relationship with others that fosters improved learning in the classroom.

Your engagement in Activity 2.1 should have directed your attention towards the learning behaviours that you want to promote in your classroom. As mentioned earlier, these behaviours will include social, cognitive and emotional aspects of learning. Within the classroom there is a need to develop relationships with others that allow for both effective communication and collaborative working. There is a range of behaviours needed for this. The following lists provide some examples but, of course, are not exhaustive.

Behaviours that support effective communication for learning

- responds positively to instruction
- waits turn to speak. Interacts respectfully with the teacher
- seeks attention appropriately
- uses appropriate tone of voice for task (e.g. is not aggressive)
- shows concern and understanding for others' opinions and progress
- is able to respond to the teacher in a non-confrontational manner
- is able to put own point of view across calmly
- is able to show emotional engagement without resorting to physical aggression towards adults or other pupils
- is able to give positive feedback to others
- is able to regulate behaviour based on a prediction of how a cruel or spiteful comment will impact on others
- has some strategies to manage feelings of anger.

It is of course acknowledged that effective communication is needed for all learning activities in the classroom. While there is less consensus about the impact of group work on pupil progress, it offers potential for the following to occur:

- Through mutual feedback and debate, peers can motivate one another to abandon misconceptions and search for better solutions.
- Peer communication can help a child master social processes, such as participation and argumentation, and cognitive processes, such as verification and criticism.
- Collaboration between peers can provide a forum for discovery learning and encourage creative thinking.
- Peer interaction can introduce children to the process of generating ideas.

(Damon 1984: 335, cited in Slavin 2004: 284)

The use of the word 'can' in these bullet points is of course pertinent because, although there is the potential for collaborative learning to achieve these aims, it very much depends on the make-up of the group and how the activities are structured, designed and evaluated. Obviously just getting pupils to work in groups will not in itself suffice. The important point to note is that in order for collaborative group work to be more effective than pupils just working alongside one another, it is necessary to be explicit about the following:

- the nature and purpose of the social relationships within the group. These depend on roles given to participants (Maloney (2007)
- the learning behaviours required for those relationships to be effective.

Behaviours that support collaborative learning in the classroom

- respects other pupils and uses appropriate language to work with them
- treats other pupils as equals and does not dominate them by intimidation or abuse
- is able to sustain attention on the shared task
- is able to share attention with others
- is able to control behaviour that distracts or disrupts others
- is respectful of others' property
- is able to contribute to group work (e.g. takes part in discussions)
- listens well in groups
- is able to seek attention appropriately and does not interrupt or interfere with others
- listens to what others have to say and consequently adds positively to group discussions
- is able to identify what individual contribution can be made to the task that will benefit the group

Teachers, of course, would not be expected to explicitly teach all these behaviours before setting pupils a group task. However, it is important to think about the learning behaviours needed for your group task to be successful and to identify any pupils you think might need to be either taught the required behaviours or explicitly reminded of the behaviours you are looking for.

Classroom strategies for improving relationships with peers

Schools and their teachers have an important role to play in improving their pupils' relationships with others. One of the criteria Ofsted takes into account when inspecting schools is 'pupils' behaviour towards, and respect for, other young people and adults, and their freedom from bullying, harassment, and discrimination' (Ofsted 2014: 19).

Strategies available to teachers include:

- building and repairing appropriate professional relationships with all pupils, keeping an eye on the reciprocal nature of the relationship
- having high expectations for the behaviour of participants in the relationship, including themselves
- modelling appropriate professional relationship behaviour and knowing how to respond effectively to poor behaviour
- being aware of the school's behaviour policy in respect of interpersonal relationships between teachers, pupils and peers
- knowing the hierarchy of rewards and sanctions and applying the behaviour policy consistently and fairly to all pupils in all situations at all times (see Chapter 5)

- delivering rewards with due regard for the need to explicitly recognise appropriate social behaviour
- implementing any necessary sanctions with care, compassion and clarity, and aiming to use a favourable ratio of rewards to sanctions, such as the 5:1 frequently advocated (e.g. DfES 2005a; Dix 2007)
- brokering effective social relationships through the curriculum by:
  - o choosing tasks and grouping strategies that place emphasis on the social learning behaviours needed to achieve success
  - o illustrating successful and unsuccessful social relationships (e.g. through story time or text analysis)
  - o role-playing different social scenarios
  - o teaching social skills explicitly to the class and through targeted group work.

- regularly reminding pupils what social learning behaviours are required so that those who do not know how to behave have information to work on
- using the resource of the whole class group to model, reward and debate socially appropriate behaviour.

While it is clear that building relationships for learning must take advantage of the potential of the class peer group for improving behaviour, it is crucial that close attention is paid to how this potential can be maximised (Roseth *et al.* 2008). It is the grouping of pupils – in other words, the 'relationship mix' – that may require more thought than a simple instruction to 'get into groups' if the intended learning outcomes are to be met.

The strength of using the curriculum and, for example, group assemblies and tutor group meetings to foster awareness of effective social relationships is that the target pupil(s) can reflect upon the information without being overly emotionally involved. If a pupil's own behaviour is used as a basis for analysis (as might be the case following an altercation with a peer), they are often too emotionally involved in defending their position to listen to reason. 'Depersonalisation' through the curriculum as a means of modelling and developing appropriate relationship behaviour, along with fair use of the school's rewards and sanctions policy, is a resource that is unique to schools in their quest to foster appropriate learning relationships with others.

Conclusion

There is consensus from research that the quality and nature of relationships experienced by individual pupils have an impact on both their learning and behaviour. This chapter has sought to harness the power of relationships as a route to improving pupil behaviour in the classroom.

The Behaviour for Learning conceptual framework enables teachers to understand and unpick the complexity of classroom relationships. By tackling learning and behavioural issues from the perspectives of relationship building, teachers can focus on the importance of *reciprocity* in addressing pupil behaviour. This allows attention to be diverted away from the behaviour problem itself towards the social interactions, subjective interpretations and emotional experiences that characterise relationships.

It is acknowledged that pupil behaviour can often be attributed to relationships pupils have developed and experienced outside the school context. Schools and their teachers are in a unique position to influence the development of particular kinds of relationships – namely, relationships for learning.

In order to learn and achieve in school, pupils need to actively and positively relate to the curriculum. Individual pupils also need to develop a balanced relationship with themselves that will allow them to belong to the class, but also retain their individuality. School learning takes place largely in groups and it is important that pupils develop positive relationships with their peers and their teachers.

In the context of whole class teaching, it is not feasible to expect class teachers to monitor relationships at an individual pupil level unless a particular behavioural need arises. However, it is important that teachers are consciously aware of how their own behaviour influences the trajectory and quality of the relationships that their pupils are experiencing in the classroom. Teachers can influence the development of these relationships by explicitly thinking about how their pupils are *experiencing* them.

Within the classroom, teachers should seek to retain a balance between the social, emotional and cognitive aspects of pupil relationships. They need also to be vigilant that their behaviour does not do harm to the three learning relationships outlined in this chapter.

There is no blueprint for how to build relationships with, and between, pupils that can guarantee improvements in behaviour. All pupils are unique but share the common need to experience that they belong and are valued, can achieve and also have some control (McLean 2009). Pupils throughout their schooling need to be taught, or facilitated to develop, behaviours that allow these needs to be met. For some pupils, school offers a unique opportunity to experience conditions and contexts that facilitate the development of positive relationships that in turn influence their behaviour.

Chapter 3

Motivation for learning and behaviour

Applying the behaviour for learning approach

Introduction

This chapter seeks to explain how the behaviour for learning approach can be applied to the challenge of fostering motivation in the group setting of the classroom. The rationale for a focus on motivation is clear. Motivation is the 'golden' learning behaviour that all teachers seek to develop, and direct in their pupils. If pupils developed motivation towards their school learning, it is likely there would be both less problematic behaviour and higher levels of achievement.

The Teachers' Standards (DfE 2011a) include references to the teacher's role in developing pupil motivation. Teachers are expected to 'set high expectations which inspire, *motivate* and challenge' (our emphasis) (DfE 2011a: 7) and ' . . . manage classes effectively, using approaches which are appropriate to pupils' needs in order to involve and *motivate* them (our emphasis) (DfE 2011a: 9).

When tackling motivational issues, it is important to note that pupils who experience difficulty with their schoolwork may need *more* motivation than those whose general aptitude for school-based learning means they can succeed in most activities that they are set. The same is likely to be true of a pupil who has an established pattern of difficult behaviour. They may require more motivation to comply with classroom expectations than a pupil for whom positive behaviour is more or less second nature.

Changing behaviour

Pupils with behavioural difficulties do not necessarily lack motivation. They may just not have the motivation to do the things that are asked of them in the classroom. It can seem – and in some cases be the reality – that these pupils have plenty of motivation for developing strategies to avoid work, annoy their teachers and chatter to friends. It is also likely that outside a school context there are things that motivate them. Some of these may be positive, such as hobbies and pastimes; others may not be, such as vandalism and other forms of socially unacceptable activity. The challenge for teachers is to motivate their pupils to behave in such a way that they are able to benefit from the learning opportunities available in their school and classroom.

Most pupils, as they go through school, learn the rules and regulations for 'school behaviour' and it becomes a habit that does not require the ongoing regulation of the school's systems of rewards and sanctions. That is, they have learned not to be loud and disruptive in class but are not doing this because they are actively fearing sanctions or seeking rewards. They are motivated by their own need to fit in and achieve and as such are described as being *intrinsically* motivated. Teachers strive to develop and maintain intrinsic motivation for learning so that pupils will engage willingly with their work. With younger children rewards and sanctions are more often used to encourage the development of appropriate behaviour. Pupils are praised for being quiet or for not running around and this serves to get appropriate classroom behaviour established. Teachers expect this *extrinsically* motivated behaviour to develop into intrinsically rewarded behaviour so that pupils' behaviour becomes self-controlled and self-directed.

For some pupils, it is not this 'class appropriate' behaviour that becomes the dominant internally driven behaviour but that which meets the individual's own *immediate* needs and provides personal gratification. The refusal to comply that is exhibited by a 3 year old meets the same personal need for control that is exhibited by a defiant secondary aged pupil who refuses to get on with their work.

Teachers can manipulate the context and conditions of the classroom in order to influence the direction that pupil motivation takes as a means of improving learning or behaviour. However, ultimately a pupil owns their own motivation. Their motivational preferences have been influenced by outside school experiences such as home and other social and cultural factors. Changing an individual's motivational behaviour in a way that leads to improved learning and behaviour in the classroom is not something that can be done quickly or without collaboration with others – in particular, the individual themselves and their parents. If the pupil has been brought up in a culture that does not value effort, achievement and education, then teachers are in a position where they are constantly trying to persuade them to redirect their motivation away from their own personal pursuits towards those that are required in the classroom.

Teachers bring to this task knowledge about their own motivational struggles and also a knowledge of, and motivation for, their subject. Teacher training offers a plethora of information and strategies that seek to encourage pupils to develop motivation for subject learning. Deployment and ongoing evaluation of the efficacy of these strategies is one way in which teachers can continually improve their pupils' motivation for learning. The other is to develop an increased understanding as to why some pupils are motivated away from learning and towards disruptive behaviour. The B4L approach offers one way for teachers to unpick the complexity of classroom motivation for behaviour so that they can employ their skills in promoting learning to address behavioural concerns.

Motivation to learn and motivation to behave: two sides of the same coin?

The B4L approach differs from other approaches to improving motivation for learning in that it links the *behavioural* and *learning* aspects of motivation through use of the term 'learning behaviour'. In so doing, it is acknowledging that teachers want their pupils to be *both* motivated to behave well *and* motivated to learn.

The separation of learning and behaviour

In school contexts there tend to be different systems for 'behaviour and discipline' and 'teaching and learning'. So while systems for behaviour and discipline seek to promote motivation to comply and conform, teaching and learning policies aim to promote learning that is self-directed, imaginative, problem solving, creative and purposeful. The former tend to use *extrinsic* factors such as systems of rewards and sanctions that apply to *all* pupils in order to encourage motivation for behaving appropriately in the group setting of the school. In contrast, policies for teaching and learning acknowledge that individuals learn differently and that this prescribes the need to adopt a more personalised approach to encourage pupils to be *intrinsically* driven to learn and achieve. We can see this different policy stance for behaviour and learning in the following statements from national documents. In a guidance document on personalised learning it was stated that:

> Personalised learning, tailoring teaching and learning to individual need, is essential in helping children to achieve the best possible progress and outcomes. It is critical in raising standards and narrowing the attainment gaps that exist between different groups of pupils.
>
> (DCSF 2010a: 1)

In contrast, in evidence submitted to the House of Commons Education Committee's report *Behaviour and Discipline in Schools* behaviour consultant Paul Dix suggested:

> The best schools have absolute consistency. I don't care whether the system they use is behaviourist or whether the system they use is extremely old-fashioned, the critical difference is that people sign up to it and teachers act with one voice and one message: 'This is how we do it here.'
>
> (House of Commons Education Committee 2011: 25)

Current Government guidance on school behaviour policies conveys a similar message, stating:

> A clear school behaviour policy, consistently and fairly applied, underpins effective education. School staff, pupils and parents should all be clear of the high standards of behaviour expected of all pupils at all times.
>
> (DfE 2014b: 8)

Government guidance for discipline and behaviour (DfE 2014b) appears to support a view that 'one size fits all' albeit with caveats for some flexibility if disability rights are threatened. As with many policies and practices concerning behaviour and learning, there is a separation. The attitudes and beliefs reflected in these policy differences basically risk conveying the following messages to pupils (and their parents):

- If you have problems with learning we are prepared to tailor our teaching to suit your needs. In fact we will differentiate our lessons and assessments, and be innovative and creative in our teaching in order to keep you motivated and maximise the chances of you experiencing success.
- If you have problems with behaviour then you must conform to our rules and sanctions. If you continue to behave badly then we will not let you be part of our school.

For the most part this does not seem to be a problem for schools in terms of the impact on pupil behaviour because Ofsted reports that 'the great majority of children and young people enjoy learning, work hard and behave well' (Ofsted 2005: 3). Ofsted (2011) has also reported more recently that behaviour is good or outstanding in around 90% of schools.

The separation of learning and behaviour is potentially problematic from the viewpoint of both the teacher and the pupil because neither of them *experiences* learning and behaviour as separate (Ellis and Tod, 2009). Teachers are encouraged to adapt their teaching so that increased pupil interest and engagement is fostered, and disruptive behaviour reduced.

The B4L approach seeks to harness behaviour and learning for motivation in the following ways.

- Identifying and developing the learning behaviours that are judged by teachers to characterise 'being motivated' (i.e. behaviour that reflects initiation, self-direction and persistence).
- Giving particular attention to considering how you think the pupil is experiencing your teaching. This 'seeing things from the pupil's viewpoint' will help to focus attention on trying to secure their interest and, when feasible, including motivational activities such as competitive group work, team challenges, emphasis on anticipation of immediate tangible rewards and so on. The aim of such approaches is to engineer enhanced intrinsic motivation in those pupils who you feel need to be more actively engaged in their lessons.

If we approach motivation from the perspective of these two strands then, for example, if a pupil keeps talking to peers we would have to ask ourselves whether they need more motivation for learning or less motivation for talking.

What do we mean when we say, 'I want my pupils to be more motivated'?

In our everyday use of the term, we tend to think of motivation as an unobservable energy that resides within the individual. In the classroom it is a categorisation that we apply to a set of behaviours. This view reflects Miller's (1989) stance that 'Motivation can be understood not as something that the individual *has* but rather as something the individual *does*' (Miller 1989: 69, emphasis in original).

Motivation within this chapter is considered to be a descriptor given to a set of behaviours a person exhibits that we associate with being motivated. If a person demonstrates these behaviours, we say they have the quality or disposition of motivation.

Most definitions of motivation incorporate the components of direction, persistence and intensity (Capel and Gervis 2005). For example, Coles and Werquin (2005) defined learner motivation as covering 'a range of an individual's behaviours in terms of the way they personally initiate things, determine the way things are done, do something with intensity and show perseverance to see something through to an end' (Coles and Werquin 2005; cited in Lord and O'Donnell 2005: 4).

Such definitions can be viewed as generic descriptions of motivation. They are applicable in a range of settings and are arguably value-neutral in the sense that they could be demonstrated by an individual in relation to anti-social or self-injurious activities as well as in the context of more positive pursuits.

While we can be clear about what we describe as being motivated we are less clear about the components of such motivation. In their exploration of strategies to raise pupils' motivational effort in Key Stage 4 Mathematics, Kyriacou and Goulding (2006) suggest that when we say that a pupil is highly motivated towards mathematics this typically includes a mixture of:

- positive attitudes towards the subject
- positive beliefs about self-efficacy
- positive intention
- positive action.

Arguably these represent the key elements involved in motivation in relation to all school-based learning. Kyriacou and Goulding (2006) make the important point that the relationship between these elements is complex with, for example, the relationship between enjoyment in a subject and efforts made not always being positively linked. It follows that in setting the conditions for motivated school learning a focus just on securing pupil enjoyment would not necessarily suffice. The pupil would also need to believe that they could succeed (self-efficacy) and be able to take the actions necessary to actualise that belief.

A further area for consideration in relation to motivation and behaviour is the nature of motivation needed for an individual to *change* their behaviour. This is relevant in relation to children and young people who are locked into patterns of behaviour that, as adults, we recognise as harmful in some form. This might be direct harm in terms of the individual placing themselves at immediate risk or longer term consequences resulting from engaging in certain types of behaviour. The issue of what makes an individual *want* to change is complex. It involves developing the will and/or disposition to change as well as the skills and knowledge needed to enact a change in behaviour. Motivation belongs to one person, yet it can be understood to result from the interactions between the individual and other people or environmental factors (United States Department of Health and Human Services 1999).

Intrinsic to the B4L approach is a core focus on developing *learning behaviours*. A teacher who wants their pupils to be more motivated to learn in the classroom needs to be clear about what behaviours constitute 'being motivated'. Once these behaviours have been identified, there is a need to foster, develop and maintain them in the classroom.

Changing motivations and motivation to change

If we consider motivational behaviour from the pupil's perspective, we need to take on board that once in class they are required to learn and achieve in the context of a curriculum that is largely prescribed, and to conform to disciplinary frameworks of the school that have been designed to facilitate learning in group settings. They also have to spend most of their time in a group with peers whom they have not normally chosen. As we have noted previously in Chapter 2, if we think about being placed in such a context, we can see that individual pupils have to:

- make effort with work that they are not necessarily interested in
- be compared with others, sometimes openly

- work alongside and sometimes collaboratively with peers they may not know or like
- conform to rules they may not see the point of
- share attention with others.

Seen from this viewpoint, we can understand why some pupils respond to this particular situation by exhibiting behaviour that results in their being described by their teachers as 'poorly motivated'. It is important to stress the uniqueness of the classroom situation for the pupil when compared with other situations outside school. This can help us to identify which particular factors are influencing their behaviour and in so doing seek to modify the impact of these factors on pupil motivation for learning.

As discussed previously, the B4L approach places emphasis on the dynamic interaction of the *cognitive, emotional and social* aspects of learning and behaviour. When we apply the B4L approach, we use the term 'relationship' to emphasise that these cognitive, social and emotional factors are dynamic and changing. As stated in earlier chapters, we use these terms as follows:

- Cognitive: curriculum influences on learning – what the pupil is required to learn and the teacher is required to teach. We term this 'relationship with the curriculum'.
- Emotional: what the pupil is feeling and how they make sense of their world. We term this 'relationship with self'.
- Social: relationships with peers and teachers in the classroom. We term this 'relationship with others'.

Teachers are all too aware that pupils' motivation varies both between and within lessons. A pupil can arrive at a lesson feeling motivated, experience difficulty with the work, play up to the class, get told off and leave feeling negative about the subject and their teacher. Likewise, low motivation for a lesson on arrival can be changed if the content grips the pupil's interest, they are enabled to achieve and they enjoy being with their peers.

Clearly motivation is influenced by the way the individual thinks and feels and whom they are with. In schools, the Government largely prescribes what pupils should be taught and when and how they will be assessed. The social mix in the classroom and the teacher are also mainly a 'given' for the pupils. If this school context is compared with factors that influence motivation for a hobby or leisure pursuit where the individual chooses the activity, has optimism that they can achieve and/or enjoy it, and may have some choice over whom they interact with, then it can be appreciated that motivating pupils to learn and behave in classrooms provides an ongoing and significant challenge for teachers.

Teachers cannot *make* individuals learn and behave in a way that is deemed desirable. If behaviour is to be improved, then there is a need to harness both the *will* and *skill* of individual pupils. It is this balance of will and skill that is often conceptualised as 'motivation' and that reflects the interaction of social, emotional and cognitive factors in the classroom setting. It is important to identify whether pupil motivation is an issue in class because they have:

- the will but not the skill: the pupil wants to achieve and behave but the work is too difficult and/or they have not yet developed the skills needed to learn and behave with others in a class group

- the skill but not the will: the pupil does not want to learn and/or behave although they are able to do so if they choose
- limited will and limited skill: in this case the pupil has not fully automated the skills needed to learn in a group setting and has not fully developed strategies to overcome feelings of being bored or uninterested; such pupils may require constant reminders to keep them on task and behaving well.

By recognising the skill and will components of motivation (sometimes referred to as the 'can't' and 'won't' of behaviour), it is clear that teachers will need access to a range of strategies for tackling motivation and be able to select which ones are most likely to work. The use of a rewards and sanctions approach to motivating a pupil would not be effective if that pupil did not have the skills to produce the required work or behaviour. However, such a strategy might be effective with a pupil who was able to produce the required work or behaviour by providing the necessary stimulus for them to apply their existing skills.

Choice of strategies will depend on such factors as class mix, the experience of the teacher, the nature of the subject being taught and its associated learning objectives, the amount, if any, of additional support accessible by the teacher, the overall attitude and maturity of the class group, and the number of pupils with learning and/or behavioural difficulties.

Because of the dynamic nature of motivation and its dependence on the effect of a wide range of interacting classroom variables related to learning and behaviour, there is no one simple answer to the question: '*How do I get my pupils to be more motivated to learn and behave in my lessons?*' The application of the B4L approach will, however, support teachers in making sense of the complexity of classroom motivation and in pursuing the selection, development and evaluation of strategies designed to improve pupil learning and behaviour.

Increasing motivation in the classroom: starting points

Some teachers may not experience any particular difficulties in motivating their class to learn and it is not expected that the B4L approach will need to be applied routinely within classroom teaching. Rather, it is intended that the approach should be applied judiciously when the need to address behaviour problems linked to motivation arises.

Practical application of the behaviour for learning approach

Chapter 1 (see Table 1.1) provided a sequence of questions to use when making core use of the B4L approach. Table 3.1 sets out these questions and provides an example of possible responses to them in relation to the promotion or development of motivational learning behaviours. The use of such a table, completed individually or with colleagues, can be helpful when working through the B4L framework to problem solve in relation to individual pupils or groups of pupils whose motivation for classroom learning is currently limited.

Choosing a strategy

A range of strategies for motivating pupils is included in this chapter. You are also likely to have been exposed to a number of strategies during your training, some of which are

Table 3.1 Example of a planning framework for developing motivational learning behaviour

Behaviour for learning questions	Answer	Reason for answer
What is the desired learning behaviour to promote?	Can get started – knows how to get self-started on task	This is to replace the 'messing about' procrastinating behaviour that sets the tone for a non-productive lesson and moves the focus away from learning to controlling behaviour – 'getting started' is often one of the core difficulties with motivation for tasks that have not been chosen by the individual.
Where should I concentrate my effort?	Mainly on the pupils' relationship with the curriculum. May use 'relationship with others' to enhance class engagement and also relationship with self.	I feel more confident in working in my subject area – that is my area of expertise. I am not yet sure of the names and nature of the pupils in this class so I aim to keep a sharp focus on learning so that I do not get distracted into dealing with behavioural issues.
What strategies could I select?	I will aim to improve my planning for the 'starter' activity by placing an emphasis on 'motivational starters'. There are documented features of 'motivational' tasks (e.g. McLean 2009: 68–86) that I could increasingly include in some of my starters. These are tasks that stimulate and encourage engagement and have structure and feedback.	Most pupils do get on with their work but a few remain resistant and exhibit low level disruptive behaviours that distract themselves and peers from learning.
What help/support do I need?	I will ask other colleagues in my subject department about getting pupils engaged quickly at the start of a lesson.	Most teachers are concerned with 'motivation' and are likely to have developed a good resource bank of strategies. It makes good sense to make use of that knowledge and experience.
What strategy best matches my strengths?	Planning lessons to strengthen motivational aspects.	I feel comfortable teaching my subject and confident that I can make some changes to delivery and assessment that will enhance pupil motivation.
What are my evaluation criteria?	I will record the number of pupils who start and complete the brief lesson starter work before and after my strategy use.	Note to self: I may have to record 'starters' and 'finishers' under two categories to note those who persist to completion.

effective for *some* pupils but not for *all* pupils. This is always going to be the case simply because each individual pupil experiences your strategy differently and has a different *purpose* for exhibiting the type of behaviour that is causing you concern. When choosing strategies for improving motivation for learning and behaviour in the classroom, you need to have some idea about what 'drives' people into action. As a human being who may have struggled with motivation for certain imposed tasks, you will have a knowledge and understanding of what motivates you. You may be able to apply this knowledge to understanding the motivation of others. As human beings we share common *needs* that motivate us into action. You are likely to be aware of Maslow's theory of motivation (Maslow 1962), which refers to a hierarchy of human needs, with lower order basic physical needs having to be met if higher order needs such as self-actualisation are to be pursued. This theory allows us to understand that it is difficult for a pupil to be motivated to do school work if they are hungry, thirsty, tired or feel unsafe. However, Maslow acknowledged that the different levels of motivation could occur at any time in the human mind, such that our need to achieve could be motivating us even if we were tired, hungry or perhaps not even physically safe.

There is consensus within the field of motivation that, although different terminology is used, all humans need to achieve, to build positive relationships with others, and to have their increasing need for autonomy recognised and addressed (McLean 2009). In the classroom this translates into some key principles for motivating all pupils. Pupils need to:

1   feel they belong in the class and be involved
2   be able to achieve and experience a feeling of competence
3   be trusted and have a sense of independence.

Given these shared human 'needs', an enhanced emphasis on making a task 'motivational' would need to give particular attention to the following:

- The task is as relevant as possible to the needs and interests of the whole class (i.e. each person has something unique to offer and/or the task may require some collaborative endeavour).
- The task is achievable.
- The task review and feedback encourages pupils' own contribution to assessment or improvement.
- The teacher's choice of strategy should be influenced by which human 'need' they have decided should be addressed in order to influence pupils' behaviour. For example, if you feel that a pupil is shouting out and messing around in order to be valued and recognised by their peers, even if that risks being punished, then you will need to select a strategy that seeks to meet this need (i.e. to belong) in a more appropriate manner.

Although all pupils are considered to have these 'needs', the age of the pupils and the nature of the subject being taught will influence how the teacher balances the extrinsic factors (i.e. rewards and sanctions) and the intrinsic factors (i.e. the pupil's own will and skill) during the creation of 'motivational' learning activities.

Identifying learning behaviours associated with motivation

It is often easier for you to state the behaviour you *do not* want your pupils to exhibit than that which you *do* want to see. The following lists are not exhaustive but may help you to decide what behaviour(s) you want to target for development in your pupil(s) either to enhance learning or to 'replace' behaviour that is interfering with class and pupil learning.

Motivational learning behaviours associated with relationship with the curriculum

Learning behaviours you will need to encourage and/or teach/demonstrate:

- can plan a sequence of actions needed to complete a task
- can imagine what it feels like to succeed
- can write down, or verbalise what they have to do, what they can do, where they might need help, where to get that help from and how it will feel when they have finished
- has checked they have the equipment to do the task
- can get started – knows how to get self-started
- can re-tell instructions back to the teacher
- is able to say what they are trying to achieve
- is able to say how they plan to be successful
- is able to ask for help when necessary
- is able to ask questions
- can monitor how well they are doing towards the goal
- can set small steps and order them
- is able to look at previous work to understand how the current task may overlap
- is prepared to risk getting something wrong in order to move forward
- can say why they have to do the task
- can estimate how much effort it may take
- can verbalise choices they can make
- can ignore distractions.

Motivational learning behaviours associated with relationship with self and others in the class

This section provides examples of some *beliefs* and *thoughts* you need to promote in the minds of the class if you are going to meet the human needs outlined earlier that trigger motivation in your pupils (i.e. to belong, achieve and have some autonomy). This is not to say that you are not already doing this but it is important to give thought to how your behaviour, instructions and responses are being *interpreted* by your pupils. Sometimes all that is required is that you stress some of the *implicit* intentions of your teaching to make them *explicit* to those pupils who may be struggling with motivation for learning and as a consequence are exhibiting problematic behaviour. In considering the following list, think about any actions you might take in order to promote these thoughts and beliefs that underpin pupil motivation to get on with the required task or activity:

- 'I know what I have to do and am willing to have a go.'
- 'I have some control over my learning and behaviour.'
- 'These activities are real and useful.'
- 'I can be successful and achieve.'
- 'There are opportunities in class for 'rewards' and recognition.'
- 'If I try, but am not as good as others, my effort will still pay dividends and be recognised.'
- 'This is not going to be all boring; there will be something of interest (and 'fun') to look forward to.'
- 'If I decide to get involved with the task I will not risk failure, humiliation or social rejection.'
- 'It will not necessarily be easy but it will be worth it.'
- 'I don't have to work too long on my own and will have a chance to get actively involved.'
- 'My teacher thinks I am worth making an effort with and has some trust in me.'
- 'If I get stuck there are things I can do or people that will help.'

Identifying and selecting strategies: whole class

Many of the following strategies will be known and used by teachers reading this chapter. Not all of them can be used at any one time but it may be good to refresh and renew those that are already in use, or to reflect upon which ones might be particularly relevant to the classes and pupils you currently teach.

Strategies concerned with your manipulation of contexts and conditions in your classroom

- Aim to model motivated behaviour from the start in order to convey enthusiasm for the topic, a sense of purpose and direction, and anticipation of enjoyment and success. As with your planning for learning, high expectations for behaviour should be clarified and positively communicated to your pupils.
- Check that your lesson has included activities that meet pupils' core needs (i.e. to be able to succeed, to belong, to socialise with peers, and to have some control and independence). If there are aspects of the lesson that meet pupils' needs, they are more likely to be motivated.
- Make sure you, and your pupils, know the school's behaviour policy, sequence of sanctions and support mechanisms. You need to demonstrate that your main focus is on *learning*, not managing behaviour. For this you need to deal with behaviour efficiently, quietly and with confidence to avoid pupils distracting you, and them, from curriculum learning.
- Check for availability of any practical resources that may help to maintain pupil activity and the pace and flow of the lesson. This might include model answers, practical materials, spare basic equipment such as pens/pencils and a list of ideas or flow diagrams to support working through from start to finish.
- Check that pupil groupings do not overly risk the behaviour of those who are poorly motivated being reinforced by peers. Plan to make full use of positive peer influences.
- Check that seating arrangements suffice to support any intended collaborative activity.
- Ensure changes to the type of task run smoothly; otherwise pupils may use this as a delaying tactic that may serve to redirect their motivation away from the task.

Strategies linked to lesson delivery and assessment

- Build some aspects into the lessons that pupils perceive to be fun. There is consensus from research that pupils are more likely to be motivated if they perceive a lesson to be 'fun' as well as authentic and useful (Smith *et al.* 2005). The 'fun' bit is challenging but it has to be assumed that the pupils were not seeking fantastic entertainment but making a point that they were not motivated by too much didactic teaching and having to do 'exercises' (Littlejohn 2001).

- Be as clear with your *behavioural* objectives for the task as you have been with your *learning* objectives. Saying 'get on with your work' or 'work in groups' may not be specific enough for all pupils in the group. Specify some of the 'motivated' behaviours listed earlier that you expect to see.

- If feasible, do not start the lesson with too much teacher input. Expecting and planning for pupils' active involvement early on ensures a sense of 'getting on'. For example, instead of trying to convince the class that the topic has relevance and interest for them, suggest working in pairs or groups with a tight time frame to speedily list possible relevance and 'interesting bits'. This meets pupils' needs for peer interaction and affords opportunity for those who see no relevance for the lesson to have access to peers who are more successful in finding reasons to get on with their work.

- Be vigilant and consistent in rewarding ongoing appropriate behaviour – not just task success. Comment on the way pupils are going about the task generally so that an individual can 'pick up' what is required. For example you might say, 'Most of you have started by thinking about what you need to end up with – well done.' Formative feedback is very powerful for learning and is a central component of schools' Assessment for Learning approaches (Wiliam 2008); it applies equally to behaviour. Black and Wiliam (1999) found that constructive feedback also had a profound influence on pupils' motivation and self-esteem.

- Try to minimise the extent to which pupils' disruptive behaviour and non-compliance is rewarded by the peer group. Use peer assessment for behaviour as well as learning, stating criteria against which pupil judgements are made and making sure that the class is encouraged to report positively on each other.

- Try not to interrupt the flow of the learning activity when responding to undesirable behaviour. Make use of subtle approaches such as tactical ignoring, a long stare, a glance at the class rules, a verbal class rule reminder, etc.

- Build *choice* into the ways pupils can go about the task. This allows them to feel they have some control over their learning behaviour. For example, you might say, 'Some of you may prefer to start by looking at a model answer and then create your own, doing the bits you feel you can do . . . or you may want to do your own then check with the one in the book.'

- At times consult with the class on the best way to achieve the learning objective(s) that have been set. This allows the class to feel they have control over how they direct their motivation and an opinion that is listened to. It also affords pupils who have limited strategies the opportunity to hear and adopt those of others.

- Vary modes of presentation so that pupils' interest is held. IT has allowed lessons to be more engaging, albeit with more time demanded from teachers in preparing such inputs. Caution needs to be exercised so that pupils do not become passive recipients or too dependent on such inputs – hence the need for variation to secure ongoing pupil involvement. Asking pupils to respond to ongoing visually stimulating inputs by making written responses concerning, for example, key points, issues and debates or things to think about, can help to sustain active engagement, effective listening and processing behaviours.

- Vary conditions for working. Aim to use a mixture of individual and paired or collaborative tasks. This allows for interest to be sustained and meets pupils' needs and preferences for active engagement and collaborative work.

- Harness pupils' knowledge about their own learning. Once this information is brought into their conscious awareness, it can be used to improve motivation. For example, if you ask them to explain why they think they did not succeed in a task and they reply 'because I am not clever enough', it is unlikely that they will be motivated to continue. If they can see a surmountable reason why they failed, such as 'I was messing about with my friends so I did not put enough effort in,' they may be persuaded to try again. Placing emphasis on how learning behaviour differs between individuals, and getting pupils to apply their unique knowledge of their own learning to enhance their chances of success gives them the control and independence they seek. Explicitly thinking about learning is referred to as 'metacognition' and has a positive impact on pupil outcomes and motivation (Higgins *et al.* 2011). It plays a powerful role in improving learning, particularly for low-attaining pupils.

- The development of metacognition can also be encouraged by using assessment activities that ensure that pupils spend time 'thinking about how they are thinking'. The more pupils are aware of their thinking processes as they learn, the more they can control such matters as goals, dispositions and attention. Being in class allows them to discuss and compare how they and others learn. and to question assumptions they have made about their learning that is adversely affecting their motivation, for example: 'I am not going to try in school because I am not clever enough.'

- Motivation is fuelled by achievement. Setting appropriate learning objectives and designing tasks accordingly is crucial for motivating learning, and the same applies to behaviour. Conditions for assessment have to be manipulated so that all pupils can experience some success. Strategies include starting tasks with activities and outcomes that everyone can achieve. Easier questions may come first or there might be varying assessment options. For example, 'recognition' responses (multiple choice) are easier than 'generative' responses (essays, written answers, etc.). In setting goals and giving feedback, there is a need to distinguish between success that relates to *attainment* (as measured by externally prescribed age-normed levels) and success that represents *achievement* for the individual. Most pupils have made comparisons about themselves as learners relative to their peers but still need to experience personal success if their motivation is to be sustained.

- Take full advantage of opportunities for using a range of assessment approaches. These will include assessments that relate to both the outcomes prescribed for the individual pupil and for the group activity. This allows an opportunity for some pupils to experience more success through being a member of a 'team' and harnesses the power of peer influence.

- Consider carefully 'public' versus 'private' assessment outcomes – giving back marked work with feedback that can be accessed by the class group can be demotivating for a pupil who has not done well or those who do not want to be seen to have done well. Similar issues can apply to discussing predicted grades and setting personal targets in public.

- Pupils can be encouraged to become more in control of and independent in their learning if they are given ideas for getting started on a task. For example, they might be advised to:
  o   decide what bits they can do and start with those
  o   make a plan and do a bit of it
  o   think of how nice it will be when they have finished
  o   break the task down and reward themselves for keeping going
  o   ask someone to work with them
  o   plan it visually and tick off bits
  o   ask someone to read the text to them
  o   talk it through
  o   look back over previous work and find a task that was similar.

In looking at whole class strategies for improving pupil motivation for learning, it is important to note that motivation by its nature is variable. As mentioned earlier, lesson timings and topics obviously have an impact on motivation as does the class mix and pupil mood on entry to the lesson. Variations in motivation between and within lessons are inevitable and to be expected. These variations can inform changes that may be needed to contexts and conditions. Stable low motivation across all contexts would be a cause for concern. An acceptance of variation will serve to reduce negative teacher–pupil interactions (e.g. 'You could do this last lesson and were well behaved,' or 'It's a waste of my time and yours . . . '). Such interactions do not serve to increase motivation and risk the pupil leaving the class feeling negative about the teacher. It is not easy going for 'no grudges and fresh starts' with pupils who frequently don't work and mess about, but it is the recommended option.

Working with pupils who need a more individualised approach to motivational problems

Strategies identified in the previous section were intended for use with the whole class based on the aim of placing the improving of motivation for learning at the core of whole class behaviour management. This section takes a closer look at how you might develop your practice in working with those individual pupils where you need to reduce their motivation for behaving inappropriately and increase their motivation for classroom learning.

The starting point for applying the B4L approach to this group of pupils is to consider the *relationships* they have built up over time with curriculum, themselves and others (see Chapter 2). A few pupils may need the whole class strategies mentioned in the previous section delivered with more *intensity* or with closer *monitoring*. You may use their name to catch their attention, or you may specifically require them to make a response. If you have additional adult support, you may alert the adult to the motivational behaviours that you want to develop in the pupil so that there can be closer monitoring and reminding.

Identifying the purpose for the pupil of the negative behaviour

It is crucial to note that, no matter how strange, behaviour always has a purpose or function (LaVigna and Donnellan 1986). You may question why a particular pupil perseveres with behaviour that results in punishment, annoys peers and reduces their chances of getting any academic qualifications. But for the pupil the behaviour meets a need and serves a purpose. It is therefore self-judged as successful. For example, the pupil may tell themselves, 'I don't do any work in school and muck about but I have a better time than the geeks.'

At the level of practice, it can prove helpful to look at what needs are being met by the pupil's behaviour and then see if you can meet those needs in a way that will lead to more appropriate behaviour.

Asking yourself to what extent you feel that a particular pupil's behaviour can be attributed to insufficient attention being given to meeting their core human needs is a useful way of informing what feasible adjustments you could make to your classroom teaching that could improve the learning and behaviour of that pupil.

Table 3.2 describes how a focus on these needs can help to understand the reasons for a pupil's differing motivational behaviours.

It is important to give due regard to the *purpose* behind a pupil's behaviour. For some, particularly those at risk of behavioural problems, school is the one opportunity they will have to make choices about how to direct their motivation within a safe and supportive setting. If this opportunity is missed, then there is a risk that their behaviour problems will continue to develop beyond the school context and into their adult life. For some pupils, their behaviour may have had an original purpose but over time has become a habitual way of responding. For this reason, when teachers are seeking to improve motivation for behaviour, there is a need to accept the following:

- most behaviour change does not occur overnight; it will take time and patience
- behaviour change is best viewed as a gradual process with occasional setbacks
- difficulties and setbacks need to be reframed for both teacher and pupil as learning experiences, not failures.

Table 3.2 Identifying and meeting the pupil's need as a route to improving motivational behaviours

Needs that drive motivation	Resulting positive classroom behaviour	Resulting 'negative' classroom behaviour
To achieve and succeed	Will be energised to achieve learning goals set and get on with work.	Will put energy into behaviours that they decide are personal achievements i.e. successfully avoids lack of achievement being made public by refusing to start work.
To belong and be social	Works within the group setting so as not to annoy peers or teacher and may secure recognition and praise from others.	Seeks to be recognised within the group by 'being a laugh', 'playing up', 'winding up the teacher', etc. (Would this pupil have an identity if they were not known as a behaviour problem?)
To have some control and independence	Accepts some responsibility for own learning and progress. Monitors own work against given criteria for success, asks questions, suggests different/ better ways of doing a task, offers suggestions and ideas.	Motivation for control and independence directed towards non-compliance/refusal ('no one tells ME what to do', 'I'm NOT doing it, it's boring', etc.). Seeks to control pace and content of lesson through their own behaviour.

Strategies for redirecting or reducing motivation for 'negative' behaviour

Some strategies contained in this chapter may sound trite initially to a teacher faced with the competing motivations to get most of the class to stay on task while addressing the needs of a few pupils who are disruptive or disaffected. It is not easy and listing strategies does not seek to trivialise the issue of motivation for behaviour by offering any quick-fix solutions. As with previous strategy suggestions, the following list seeks to support you in identifying *what* strategies are likely to be most suitable for *which* particular pupils. It is not intended that you try to apply all strategies on a trial and error basis. You should instead apply what you have learned about motivation and behaviour to make an informed choice.

- Use changes observed in the pupil's motivation between and within lessons to identify conditions under which they are most motivated. Try to create at least *some* of the conditions that are motivating for that particular pupil in your lesson.
- Try to establish whether the issue is that the pupil does not have the necessary skills to do what is required of them or that they have the skills but have decided not to learn what is required. It may be helpful to liaise with your SENCO to explore whether the pupil has any underlying learning difficulty or difference such as speech, language and communication needs, dyslexia, an autism spectrum disorder or other form of special educational need (SEN). Some of the difficulties experienced by pupils may not be sufficient to warrant categorisation as SEN but they may nonetheless influence motivational behaviours and indicate that the pupil requires more targeted intervention.
- Reflect upon whether current rewards and sanctions are effective for that *particular* pupil. Check that sanctions are not being *experienced* as rewards (e.g. by being sent out of class the pupil escapes from an activity they dislike), and rewards *experienced* as sanctions (e.g. the pupil finds public praise or personal comment embarrassing).
- Find opportunities to have time with the pupil or a small group to challenge their 'thinking' about their motivational behaviours. These include how they think about the link between success and their own ability and effort (Weiner 1985) and whether they have an internal or external locus of control (see Chapter 2).
- Be alert for behaviours that reflect low self-esteem such as negative self-reference statements and work avoidance, or behaviour that serves to mask low self-esteem (e.g. over-confidence or being loud).
- Check that work is set with a level of difficulty that is slightly above the pupil's current ability, gradually raising expectations as learning progresses so that effort is needed but does not exceed pupil capacity.
- Monitor relationships with peers. If the pupil is someone who is rejected, seek to use collaborative curriculum tasks that have clear roles and responsibilities in order that peer relationships are controlled.
- Be very clear about what behaviour you expect to observe. For example, for some pupils, 'I want to see you getting on with your work' is not specific enough to avoid ambiguity and it gives an excuse for non-compliance.
- Consider seating the pupil with motivated peers so that motivation is 'caught' from these role models.

- Keep the pupil's tasks short and, accepting that motivation cannot be sustained without purpose and achievement, impose start times and end points. However, try to do this in such a way that the pupil thinks that they have planned their work. For example, you might say, 'Do you think that 5 minutes would be long enough for you to finish these answers? That would mean working quicker than some but I think you can do it.'

- Consider supplying visual time plans for the lesson so that the pupil can see end points and tick these off when done. Making a detailed list of every action (e.g. 'Fill in name, date', etc.) may support the pupil to feel they are getting off to a good start.

- Consider having a peer buddy motivator who works with the targeted pupil; agree with them the motivational behaviours that they both want to develop. Parallel self-starting is often easier than going it alone.

- *Always* use language that creates positive self-belief. Start the sentence with affirmation. For example, you might say, 'You can do this. Do you think the best way is . . . ?' rather than 'If you work hard you will . . . '

- Specifically recognise and reward the motivational *behaviour* rather than the outcome.

- Give very detailed formative feedback about motivational behaviours and their impact on task outcomes.

- Identify and target any specific metacognitive strategies that you think will enable the pupil to improve their learning behaviour and study skills.

- Give the pupil responsibilities so that they experience trust in their competence. Peer tutoring is powerful but there is a need to make sure that the pupil with the motivational problem is not always the tutee. Although an unmotivated pupil might normally prefer this role, it is possible that their motivation could be triggered by feeling that they had a useful role in another pupil's learning.

- Take due regard of the pupil's views on motivation (Smith *et al.* 2005) by finding out more about them in terms of what they would choose to do in their spare time and what is perceived by them to be 'enjoyable and fun'. Listening to their views is important even if it is not feasible to take them on board in practice.

- Seek to address the pupil's view that too much is going on in their head by giving them some tasks that are quite repetitive and easy as starters. A multiple-choice means of assessing how much the pupil has learned is easier and quicker for the pupil than if they have to generate their own answers.

- Seek to tackle issues of personal motivation through non-emotional means by using autobiographies or biographies about keeping motivated towards goals in the face of adversity, etc. This allows for objective discussion of motivation and behaviour issues through depersonalisation. The pupil may be much better able to comment on and address a person's motivation if that person is not them.

As with all other lists of strategies given in this chapter, these are only suggestions based on an understanding of the personal and contextual variables that have an impact on a pupil's motivation in the classroom. As such they provide a source of ideas rather than a prescription for practice. They will need to be rigorously evaluated against the purpose you want them to serve in bringing about changes to pupil motivation. If not, you will be continually searching for more and more strategies in the hope of finding the ones that suffice for the whole class. In spite of this pursuit, you will know that in reality no one strategy will be adequate for all pupils. They own their motivation and have the power to direct it as they choose.

Conclusion

Motivation is a powerful construct for teachers seeking to improve pupil behaviour and learning in schools. It allows us to explain why it is that individual pupils who are exposed to the same curriculum opportunities and teaching strategies often exhibit very different behavioural outcomes. Such differences affect both what individuals choose to direct their attention towards and the intensity and persistence of their behaviour.

The reality for teachers is that that they are seeking to improve motivation within a specific context. That context is one in which pupils are taught in groups with the purpose of achieving intended curricular outcomes. Consequently, a teacher's motivational strategies need to focus on motivating pupils to learn and achieve curriculum outcomes that they have not chosen. Within such a context, pupils are not always going to enjoy the learning activities, nor would they choose to engage in them if alternatives were available. Teachers therefore have to manipulate the classroom conditions and context that have an impact on motivation. In schools, motivation lies at the heart of developing independence and resilience in that it is concerned with the way pupils initiate, proceed and persevere through to an end point. Teachers are under pressure to constantly improve pupil performance and schools are judged accordingly. Teachers cannot do this alone. As they go through schooling, pupils need to increasingly develop their intrinsic motivation so that they put in the required effort needed to learn, behave and achieve.

The core issue is that the freedom individuals have to direct their own motivational energy in school will serve eventually to limit or enhance their life chances. The group setting of the classroom, alongside the structure and discipline within schools, does provide the context and conditions that can support individual pupils to learn from others and reappraise their own motivations for their behaviour. Schools also provide an opportunity for individuals to achieve and be valued. This in turn fuels the 'will' and the 'skill' that underpins improved motivation for behaviour change.

The B4L approach promoted in this chapter aims to synthesise school systems and strategies that motivate pupils to either concentrate on their learning or conform to the school's behaviour rules. Motivation is judged by the behaviour that teachers observe and the development and direction of these behaviours are at the core of the B4L approach. Improving motivation for learning and decreasing motivation for engaging in problematic behaviour does not lend itself to quick or easy solutions. Motivation is not something that a pupil has or does not have. The B4L approach recognises and uses the fact that the behaviour of each individual in the class is a response to the dynamic and reciprocal interaction of social, emotional and cognitive factors (i.e. what the pupil is doing, thinking and feeling).

Motivation is needs led. Teachers can only infer what those needs are from their pupils' behaviour. Pupil needs are individual in that they arise from the unique experience of that individual. Pupils also have common needs that, however conceptualised or written about, relate to their need for achievement, their need to belong and be valued, and their need for autonomy. If both teacher and pupil strive to meet these needs, then motivation for the behaviours that facilitate learning in group settings should increase.

Chapter 4

Personal style and self-management

Introduction

The Teachers' Standards set out 'a clear baseline of expectations for the professional prac-tice and conduct of teachers and define the minimum level of practice expected of teach-ers in England' (DfE 2011a: 1). As such they provide reassurance to all key stakeholders that there is a considerable degree of consistency in relation to the knowledge, skills and understanding a teacher brings to the classroom and how they present themselves within the classroom and elsewhere. However, those who enter the teaching profession are individuals and, while a degree of consistency is achievable at the level of a set of com-mon standards met, it needs to be recognised that teachers will have what Government guidance (TA 2012) refers to as a 'personal style'. This guidance states:

> Trainees should have developed their own personal style for managing behaviour. Knowledge of generic behaviour management systems and techniques is essential; the way they are used depends on the attributes of individual teachers and the con-text in which they are teaching.'

> (TA 2012: 1)

The importance of self-management is also acknowledged within the statement that teach-ers 'should be able to manage their own emotions when they are teaching' (TA 2012: 1). This chapter combines personal style and self-management on the basis that individual teachers do not experience these as separate areas. They need to manage the interplay between the personal attributes and dispositions they bring to the classroom and the values and behaviour they are required to demonstrate within their professional role. How the teacher manages the fusion of personal style and professional role will have an impact on the way in which they form relationships for learning in their classroom. In supporting teach-ers in recognising and managing their personal style, this chapter applies the Behaviour for Learning conceptual framework to the teacher. The underlying premise is that the teacher's personal style and self-management can be explored and understood through reference to the three interdependent relationships – with self, with others and with the curriculum.

The behaviour for learning perspective on personal style and self-management

Personal style

A teacher's personal style is an umbrella term that seeks to explain the individual dif-ferences that we observe between teachers in the way that they enact their professional role. There is always likely to be public, professional and political debate about what constitutes an appropriate and effective personal style for teachers. However, what is important when looking at personal style in relation to behaviour is how pupils experience and adapt to their own class teacher and any differences between teachers in their school setting. It is possible to use the Behaviour for Learning framework to understand the elements influencing a teacher's personal style (see Figure 4.1).

In summary, Figure 4.1 conveys the following ideas:

- There is the body of professional knowledge and skills that can be thought of as the curriculum content related to professional learning about pupil behaviour. In this chapter, this is conceptualised as the teacher's relationship with the behaviour curriculum.
- There is a set of skills and characteristics that influences how the teacher relates to their pupils. This is conceptualised as the teacher's relationship with others.
- There is a set of 'within teacher' factors that influence how the teacher experiences, interprets and responds to classroom events. This is conceptualised as the teacher's relationship with self.

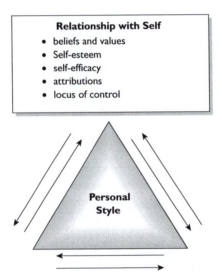

Relationship with Self
- beliefs and values
- Self-esteem
- self-efficacy
- attributions
- locus of control

Personal Style

Relationship with Others
- Recognises the implications for practice of the difference between personal and professional relationships
- Understands implications of reciprocity in forming effective relationships
- Understands the importance and impact of appropriate positive relationships
- Is able to understand behaviour from the pupil's perspective and the purpose it serves

Relationship with the Curriculum
- Knowledge of generic behaviour management systems and techniques, including effective use of praise, application of rewards and sanctions, routines
- Skills in delivery, including effective use of voice, eye contact and movement
- Knowledge of the school's systems and an understanding of the need for consistency and coherence in implementation
- Knowledge and understanding of strategies for dealing with challenging behaviour

Figure 4.1 The teacher's behaviour for learning triangle

The interdependent nature of the three relationships means that, for example, confidence in managing behaviour, which we would view as a relationship with self issue, could be increased by identifying and mentally rehearsing positively phrased corrections (see Chapter 7) to use in response to predictable classroom behaviours. Strengthening the teacher's relationship with the behaviour curriculum therefore has an impact on a relationship with self issue. Similarly, a personal belief that pupils learn to behave through punishment might cause a teacher to be resistant to a suggestion that incorporating more praise into their practice might be helpful. In this case a relationship with self issue, in the form of a personal belief, influences the willingness to engage with a particular strategy.

Self-management

Implicit within the term 'self-management' is the view that the teacher takes responsibility for maintaining a relationship with self that has a positive impact on the experience and behaviour of their pupils. Inevitably, as a relationship that reflects the inner workings of another's mind, an individual's relationship with self can never be fully understood. For the purposes of conceptual modelling, we have represented this relationship in terms of the teacher's beliefs and values, self-esteem, self-efficacy, locus of control and attributions. Self-management, we would suggest, involves developing sufficient awareness of these elements in order that they can be managed in a way that allows the teacher to be effective in their professional role and maintain their emotional health and well-being.

Understanding the teacher's relationship with self

It is necessary to spend at least some time exploring the question, 'Who is this *me* that I take into the classroom and present to my pupils?' (McGuiness 1993: 47) rather than sidestepping the influence of 'self'. In starting by looking at the teacher's relationship with self, it is an acknowledgment that this is the relationship that is likely to be the most influential component of their personal style. The relationship we have developed with ourselves and bring to the classroom has been developed over time and reflects how we have made sense of our experiences up until this point. As such, when you go into the classroom you are likely to make an interpretation of your experiences that fits with your own beliefs about yourself and others. For example, if you believe that your own success to date can be largely attributed to the effort you have made, you are likely to think that if you try hard enough you will be able to manage the behaviour of all your pupils. It may take time for you to accept the reality view that, while a good teacher can exert considerable *influence* over behaviour, they will not be able to *control* the behaviour of every individual they encounter, however hard they try. Unless this more realistic perspective is given credence, it may result in personal feelings of frustration and failure. Teachers necessarily have to balance retaining their individuality with being sufficiently flexible to adapt to the demands of the professional arena in which they have placed themselves. Self-awareness and the willingness to adapt are essential to the maintenance of a positive relationship with self.

As with your pupils, the relationship you have developed with yourself has an impact on your behaviour. In this section of the chapter, we consider key components of the teacher's relationship with self in order to raise to a level of conscious awareness those unique characteristics and traits that are likely to have an impact on your style of teaching and response to behavioural issues.

Underlying beliefs and values

Although a distinction can be drawn, both beliefs and values can be thought of as referring to what we hold to be true, how we think things ought to be and how people ought to behave. A teacher is likely to hold values and beliefs relating to pupil behaviour, including how pupils should behave towards adults, how behaviour is learned, and the causes and motives behind misbehaviour.

The decision by the authors of Key Stage 3 National Strategy Behaviour and Attendance Core Day 1 training materials (DfES 2003) to incorporate an introductory task inviting participants to reflect on common beliefs and values related to behaviour and attendance is significant in illustrating the influence of 'self'. We have used a number of the statements from this task in Activity 4.1.

Activity 4.1

Consider each of the statements in Table 4.1 and indicate your level of agreement.

Table 4.1 Beliefs and values related to behaviour (developed from DfES 2003)

Statement	Strongly Disagree	Disagree	Neither Agree nor Disagree	Agree	Strongly Agree
Good behaviour needs to be taught					
What you model is what you get – pupils learn by example					
Pupils learn to behave through seeing others receive sanctions					
More punitive regimes lead to worse rather than better standards of behaviour					
The more rules you have, the more opportunities there are for breaking them					
Pupils respond better to encouragement than punishment					
Pupils enjoy seeing others misbehave					
The pupil who *likes* to be in trouble has yet to be born					
Pupils nowadays have less respect for teachers					
Pupils learn best in ordered environments where boundaries are clear					
Pupils receive too many chances before school exclusion is used as a sanction					
It is everyone's right to feel safe and secure in school					
With rights come responsibilities – for staff and pupils					
If a teacher asks for help in relation to behaviour, it is a sign of weakness					
Every teacher needs help to manage behaviour at some point					

Beliefs and values and the implications for self-management

The point of an activity like 4.1 is not to attempt to condition your thinking but to encourage reflection on how particular beliefs and values may influence, for example:

- your decision making within the classroom, particularly when under pressure at the point when problematic behaviour is occurring
- your willingness to reflect on whether aspects of your own behaviour need to change in order to positively influence the pupil's behaviour
- your receptivity to alternative ways of responding that might be offered by colleagues or others
- your willingness to seek support when you encounter problematic behaviour.

Self-esteem

Generally (e.g. Coopersmith 1967; Lawrence 2006), self-esteem is conceptualised in terms of a difference between an individual's self-image and their ideal self. Ideal self can be defined as the individual's view of the characteristics and qualities they should ideally possess. You probably have a view of what an effective teacher is like; there may even be a person in your school or you have encountered whom you consider typifies the effective teacher. The content of policy and guidance documents and views of others whose opinions you consider count (such as Ofsted or your head teacher) may have influenced your view too. You will also have a view of your own characteristics and qualities. This is not an entirely personal appraisal; it will have been influenced by experiences and feedback from a variety of sources. If the gap between how you view yourself as a teacher (self-image) and your view of how you believe a teacher should be (ideal self) is large, then it could lead to quite low professional self-esteem.

Lawrence (2006) suggests that an individual has a global self-esteem as well as feelings of worth and unworthiness in specific situations. For example, you might have reasonably high social self-esteem – you may have a broad range of friends, you may know you can entertain people with a witty anecdote or two and you may have an active social life. You might have lower self-esteem in another area, such as your athletic, artistic or musical ability. Of course, you have a degree of choice in whether you take part in activities in these areas. As a teacher, the risk is that your professional self-esteem is a significant component of your global self-esteem. The additional hours outside the time you spend in contact with pupils will mean your role will take up a considerable proportion of your life. Because of this, the risk is that any difficulties you experience in this area start to have a pervasive effect on your global self-esteem.

Self-esteem and the implications for self-management

From the moment you start teaching, there will be threats to your self-esteem simply because you are taking your personally developed characteristics and attributes into the public and professional arena of the classroom. Teaching can undoubtedly bring numerous rewards when individuals and cohorts make progress either in relation to the curriculum or socially and emotionally. However, there will be occasions when pupils exhibit behaviour that will provoke feelings of irritation, frustration, incredulity, hurt, anger and sometimes even fear in a teacher. In order to protect yourself, it is important to strike a balance. A pessimistic outlook is unhelpful but so too is an idealised vision of what it is like to be a teacher. The following strategies might help in protecting your self-esteem:

- Re-appraise your ideal self. We are not, of course, suggesting that you should not have aspirations or seek to improve your practice. However, in terms of preserving your self-esteem as a teacher, it is important to make realistic and reasonable comparisons to address the distance between your self-image and ideal self. Consider whether the ideal is realistic at the moment. For example, the deputy head may be able to command silence simply by walking into the class and waiting. If you are a newly qualified teacher, you should look for specific behaviours you can emulate but you should also remember that the deputy head is probably well known to the pupils, has an established reputation, draws on several years of teaching experience and commands a degree of authority because of their role.

- Reflect on the validity of information you have used to construct your own self-image. We are not, of course, suggesting that you should have low expectations of yourself. However, if you are a teacher new to the profession, there will be things that you still need to learn and sometimes the things that you try will not work. The same is also true of more experienced teachers, but the key difference is that they are likely to have a broader range of successful experiences to set these difficulties against and so the threat to their self-esteem may be less. Explicitly focus on the aspects of your practice that are going well and where you can see improvements. In any formal or informal feedback on your teaching, take account of the development points but make a conscious effort not to over-dwell on any negative aspects.

- Remember that skills in group management are not a gift that a teacher either has or does not have (DES 1989). It should be expected and accepted that knowledge, skills and understanding will develop over time.

- Try to make judgements of your general worth based on sound criteria. These will include how well planned you were for your lesson, how enthusiastic you felt, pupil engagement, behaviour and learning outcomes. Although some colleagues may make judgements based on how long they or others have stayed working after school, time spent is not a valid measure of professionalism. A *good* senior leader will not make judgements about your professional practice based on such a crude indicator.

- Whatever the distance between your ideal self and self-image, try to *behave* as though there is none. Ask yourself, 'What would a confident teacher do in such a situation?' or 'What would be the resilient teacher's response?' The underlying assumption is that adopting such behaviours will influence the responses from others. This becomes reinforcing, leading to a deeper level of change. For example, a teacher might rehearse an assertive response to frequently encountered behaviours, try it, find that it works and, as a result of initial success, employ more strategies of this nature. Eventually the assertiveness, initially based on emulating specific behaviours, becomes more of a disposition.

- Set realistic targets for yourself. It is better to set a shorter 'to do list' for each day that you might succeed in completing rather than an ambitiously long one that will leave you feeling that you have failed when you do not complete it.

- Spend some time with people who are at the same stage of professional development as you. Being with, listening to and observing more experienced colleagues is undoubtedly valuable. However, you need to balance this by sharing experiences with other new teachers who are able to understand how you are feeling at this time.

- Because school takes up a large proportion of your day, any difficulties experienced in this area of your life can have an impact on your global self-esteem. In order to achieve a more balanced view of self-worth and efficacy, try to set aside some time in your day or week to engage in other activities that are not related to teaching and enable you to experience some success and enjoyment.

- Identify areas where devoting effort is likely to have a positive pervasive effect. There are probably many aspects of your practice, particularly as a new teacher, that you can improve. Working on all these may be unrealistic. Seeking advice from your mentor if necessary, try to identify the ones that will make the greatest impact.

Self-efficacy

Self-efficacy describes an individual's self-conception of performance capability (Emmer and Hickman 1991). Giallo and Little (2003) suggest that it is a multidimensional construct involving both efficacy expectations and outcome expectancy (Gibson and Dembo 1984). Bandura (1977) defined outcome expectancy as a person's estimate that a given behaviour will lead to certain outcomes, and efficacy expectation as the conviction that they can successfully execute the behaviour required to produce these outcomes. This has implications for practice. When teachers are considering advice and guidance on strategies and approaches related to behaviour, their degree of commitment to these is likely to be influenced by their belief:

- that, if implemented, these strategies and approaches have the capacity to contribute to better behaviour ('outcomes expectancy')
- in their own ability to employ these strategies and approaches ('efficacy expectation').

Doubts relating to either are likely to affect the degree of effort applied to implementing these strategies and approaches.

Efficacy and the implications for self-management

The following strategies might help in maintaining an appropriate level of self-efficacy:

- Rehearsing scenarios and strategies mentally or through role play, and familiarising yourself with the steps in the school's behaviour policy, can contribute to a feeling of preparedness. Giallo and Little (2003) suggest that the feeling of being prepared is essential in the development of an individual's confidence in their ability to execute a behaviour ('efficacy expectation').
- If you encounter a strategy or approach and you doubt its capacity to contribute to better behaviour ('outcomes expectancy'), spend some time exploring the evidence base rather than relying on your own intuition. Is there a range of people (e.g. colleagues, authors, researchers) who suggest this strategy or approach is effective?
- Put most effort into securing success. Bandura (1997) asserted that high self-efficacy is developed through the experience of success. When faced with a difficulty, try to bring to mind other similar situations in the past in which you were successful. A disadvantage for the new teacher over a more experienced colleague is that they may not have the same store of past positive experiences to draw on. In relation to the current situation, define the small changes you can make in your practice that are likely to be successful in taking you a step towards an outcome you view as desirable. This might be achieved by focusing on doing a few things better. For example, consistently adhering to the principle of a 5:1 ratio of rewards and sanctions (DfES 2005a; Dix 2007) can bring about improvements in classroom behaviour.

- Observe others who are similar to you (e.g. in age, gender, teaching experience) who, having experienced similar difficulties, are dealing effectively with a similar situation to the one you are trying to address. Bandura (1997) referred to the role of this kind of vicarious experience in developing high self-efficacy. The similarity is an important aspect – put simply, the underlying principle is 'If they can do it, so can I.' This is an interesting point for schools to consider because the usual approach is to provide opportunities for new teachers to observe more experienced colleagues.
- Associate with people who are encouraging and whom you believe have genuine faith in your ability to execute the action necessary to lead to a particular goal. Bandura (1997) considered social persuasion to be an important component in developing high self-efficacy. He suggested that the impact of the persuasive information on an individual's self-efficacy is often dependent on the prestige, knowledge, trustworthiness and credibility of the source.

Locus of control and attributional style

Every individual needs to feel that they have some control over what happens to them and what they do. The concept of 'locus of control' (Rotter 1954) can be thought of as a continuum that stretches from, at one end, a belief that whatever happens to us is entirely within our control (*internal locus of control*) to a belief at the other that whatever happens to us is entirely beyond our control (*external locus of control*) (Lawrence 2006). To be located at either extreme poses problems for the individual. If we believe everything is entirely determined by us, then every unfortunate chance event is constructed as a personal failing. If we believe everything is entirely determined by others, then we become passive victims of circumstance with a limited sense of personal agency. If a teacher adopts a view that the control of pupil behaviour is *entirely* a result of their actions, this is likely to be problematic because classroom events inevitably have an unpredictable quality.

The teacher is often working with 25–30 pupils who bring to the relationship a diverse range of behaviours and experiences. *Much* of the pupil behaviour encountered can be positively influenced by factors within the teacher's control and these are the factors to work on. Alternatively, if a teacher adopts a view that they have limited or no control over some pupils' behaviour, this is likely to adversely affect the effort and persistence they apply to their behaviour management strategies.

There is a considerable degree of overlap between the concept of an individual's locus of control and attribution theory. People have causal explanations for their own behaviour (intrapersonal attributions) and for other people's behaviour (interpersonal attributions) (Chaplain 2003). A teacher's style of attribution gives an indication of how much control they perceive they have had in relation to both positive and negative classroom experiences.

Some attributions will be internal, relating to the teacher's own choices and behaviour; others will be external, relating to factors such as luck, other people's behaviour or factors in the environment. Research (e.g. Croll and Moses 1985; Miller 1996; Tobe 2009) suggests that teachers tend to attribute misbehaviour to home and within-pupil factors more than they do to teacher and school factors (Tobe 2009). External attributions are liable to generate low self-efficacy, because the teacher feels there is no course of action available that they can successfully enact that will improve the situation. In its extreme form, this pattern could be regarded as 'learned helplessness' (Seligman 1975) where, when faced with a situation they perceive to be difficult, an individual gives up because they believe any change or progress towards any favourable outcome is beyond their control. The statements used in the survey that provided the data for Tobe's (2009) study contained a number that represented external attribution, including the following:

- Pupil misbehaviour is due to poor parenting skills.
- Pupil misbehaviour is caused by the child's innate personality/temperament.
- Pupils misbehave because there is an insecure attachment between themselves and their parents.
- Pupils misbehave because they are given too many rights.
- Pupils misbehave when they have a troubled home background.

(Tobe 2009: 10–11)

We are not claiming that these factors are beyond a school's influence, nor are we suggesting that teachers should disregard the multiple influences on pupils' behaviour. However, for a teacher experiencing difficulty with a class, group or pupil, over-dwelling on factors they can exert little if any influence over is unhelpful. If, for example, the teacher attributes a pupil's behaviour to the fact that their family life is chaotic, then this may lead them to feel they are helpless to facilitate any effective intervention. In contrast, if the teacher attributes aspects of the behaviour to the pupil's lack of experience of structure and predictability, this may lead them to recognise the potential to positively influence the pupil's behaviour through consistent use of the school rules and routines.

It is important for classroom teachers to attempt to place emphasis on factors over which they can exert some influence. These would include, for example, teaching and learning strategies and their style of classroom and behaviour management.

Locus of control and attributional style and the implications for your self-management

The following strategies might help you to feel more in control of your situation:

- An entirely external or entirely internal locus of control is problematic: balance is important. In any behaviour-related situation, reflect on your own actions and consider what you could have changed that might have prevented this developing or led to a better outcome for both you and the pupil. Take responsibility for those aspects you can positively influence but recognise too that sometimes some classroom behaviour exhibited by individuals will be the result of a combination of factors over which you have limited control.
- Your preparedness is something you can control. Plan for predictable classroom behaviours and identify preventative and reactive strategies and approaches. This helps to avoid the feeling that your behaviour is being driven by that of the pupils.
- When faced with a more significant behavioural problem, ask yourself some 'scaling questions'. Scaling questions are an important tool in solution-focused therapy but also featured in Behaviour and Attendance materials produced through the National Strategies (DfES 2004a). The usual starting point is a question like: 'On a scale of 1–10, where am I now, where 10 represents a time when the problem no longer exists or is within totally manageable proportions and 1 represents the worst the situation could be? If you placed yourself at a 4 on the scale, the subsequent questions might be:

  o   What is it that I am doing that has caused me to put myself at a 4 rather than a 3?
  o   What would it look/feel like at point 10? What would be happening?

- o   I've said I'm at a 4 now. What would need to be happening for me to put myself at a 5?
- o   What actions could I take that would move me from a 4 to a 5?
- o   What kind of support do I need in order to move to the next point of the scale?
- o   What point was I at last year/term/week?

The importance of these questions in the context of your locus of control is that many of them encourage you to think about the actions *you* can take in addressing the current concern.

- Focus on systematic problem solving rather than pinning false hope on quick-fix solutions to complex situations. Use of the Behaviour for Learning conceptual framework is one approach to systematic problem solving in relation to pupil behaviour, encouraging a focus on variables the teacher can positively manipulate.
- Plan for pressure. There will be times in the year when you will experience more pressure (e.g. report writing). You cannot avoid these times but you can take some control by trying to clear space for them. For example, you might ensure that during this period as many lessons as possible are based on familiar lesson plans, involve limited creation of any new resources and are based on activities that make more use of peer- or self-assessment to reduce the need for marking. When you have a choice, you might also try to avoid or limit other outside school commitments at this time.
- Remember that what you do when you are in the classroom will exert the greatest influence over pupil behaviour. Try to keep on top of the marking and anything else that will build up if not done. Having to devote time to clear a backlog will have an impact on your capacity to plan and prepare new and engaging lessons. Going into class underprepared will erode your feeling of control.
- Inevitably events will occur in school that are unanticipated and you will have to deal with them. This can lead to a feeling that events are controlling you and, however hard you work, you cannot regain control. Aim to redress the imbalance of control you are experiencing by making a list or realistic appraisal of 'What will be the outcome if I do not get this done in time?' Focus your efforts on those items on the list that will make the greatest impact or have the highest stakes attached. If you anticipate that you are unable to meet a deadline because of workload, do not leave it too late but aim to see if there is any room for negotiation – then you have engineered some control.

Relationship with others

As adults, teachers are likely to have an extensive personal knowledge of relationship building. They appreciate that relationships are reciprocal and dynamic, and that they require different styles for different purposes. Teachers bring to the classroom their personal experience of building, maintaining, repairing and ending relationships. Their professional role and the context and conditions of the school setting do, however, require an understanding of how relationships in school differ from personal relationships. It is important to look beyond the surface of the truism that teaching is all about relationships. There are key differences between 'school' and 'personal' relationships that have implications for practice. Some of these are now outlined.

Choice

Relationships in school are usually not chosen by the teacher or the pupils. The teacher is allocated a class or teaching group and the pupils are allocated to it. Ways in which you can help the relationship to work include:

- accepting professional responsibility to make relationships work, including those that are 'difficult'
- seeking information and support from staff who have previously taught the same pupils
- conveying through your words and actions that you like being with your pupils – this includes your general demeanour and simple things like smiling from time to time and greeting pupils on arrival
- working with departmental colleagues and/or the senior leadership team when classes are allocated, and looking at the balance of pupils in any one class group in terms of behaviour so that issues of feasibility can be highlighted.

Purpose

A main *purpose* of making relationships from the teacher's perspective is to enable the pupils to learn. Within this broad aim, there may be specific drivers such as ensuring pupils make good academic progress or achieve particular grades in national tests. In supporting these aims, the teacher may also require a relationship that is based on compliance and cooperation. The pupils may not share the same purpose. For some, the purpose of coming to school may, for example, be to socialise with peers and have some fun while fulfilling the statutory acquirement to attend. The relationship the teacher requires may limit these things. Ways in which you can help the relationship to work include:

- identifying and communicating what is expected from pupils in terms of *both* their social behaviour *and* the intended learning outcomes
- including opportunities where pupils can work collaboratively to take advantage of the learning resource and enjoyment factor offered by peers
- keeping a tight focus on learning and avoiding being distracted by pupils who try to get you off track or involved in long discussions about behaviour
- conveying to pupils the short and longer term relevance and potential benefits of what they are learning
- seeking regular feedback, through observation and enquiry, on how individual pupils are experiencing the class teaching
- exploring why certain pupils have responded as expected and others have not, and using this knowledge to adapt practice.

Duration

Neither party can readily choose to end the relationship. The limited exceptions include exclusion of a pupil by the school, the pupil truanting or the school accepting there is a clash of personalities and changing the pupil's class. Both parties need to accept that they are in the relationship for the long haul – usually at least one academic year. Consequently, it is important to work at maintaining the relationship, repairing it when necessary. Ways in which you can help the relationship to work include:

- knowing, understanding and consistently applying the school's behaviour policy – remembering to demonstrate that it is the pupil's *behaviour* that is unacceptable, not the pupil themselves
- ensuring that you make a distinction between those pupils who 'won't' behave (i.e. have chosen not to) and those who 'can't' behave (i.e. do not have the appropriate

behaviour in their repertoire) because this may have implications for your response, including the sanctions that it is appropriate to apply

- treating each day as a fresh start and not bearing grudges
- being stable and consistent – you are only human, but you should strive to ensure that fluctuations in mood, triggered by whatever factors, do not manifest themselves in how you relate to your pupils
- being prepared to apologise and clarify if you have misinterpreted a pupil's response or attributed their behaviour to a wrong cause (e.g. lack of effort)
- avoiding sarcasm and jokes about a pupil's behaviour; even if well-meant, jokes about an individual risk misinterpretation and can mar the relationship because of the discomfort the pupil may feel at being on the receiving end of such a remark, especially if in the public environment of the classroom
- avoiding any endorsement of, or involvement in, jokes made by others about a pupil, or self-deprecating remarks made by the pupil themselves.

Quantity

A teacher, like their pupils, has to make and maintain a number of relationships in any one school day. Ways in which you can help a relationship to work include the following:

- Be honest about what relationship style and strategies you can *feasibly* operate in the classroom. You cannot 'act' a relationship style over time – if you are not a humorous person, then beating yourself up because other teachers may be more popular is destructive; instead you should aim to acknowledge and maximise your own relationship strengths.
- Demonstrate that pupils are seen by you as individuals. Get to know something about each pupil as an individual – their name, their strengths and weaknesses, the types of learning they find easier and those they find more difficult, and what interests them in and outside school.
- Check that expectations for in-class behaviour are consistent across the school and ensure that these are clearly displayed within the classroom and articulated and reinforced during lessons. This enables the pupil to experience consistency.
- Make sure that you know and understand the support systems that are operating in the school and the procedures for communication (e.g. between pastoral and subject teachers) that affect individual pupil experiences. This allows you to be sensitive to a pupil's individual circumstances but it also reduces the opportunities for the pupil to manipulate differing expectations by, for example, falsely claiming that certain flexibilities over completing homework have been agreed by pastoral colleagues.

Group setting

Most of the time the teacher–pupil relationship is conducted in a group setting. This means it is public and the actions of both parties are seen and sometimes evaluated by others. For both the teacher and the pupil there is likely to be concern not just for how the other is experiencing the relationship but also how observers are viewing it. Consequently, both teacher and pupil may feel the need to preserve a public image. More positively, the group setting of the classroom is also a resource that the teacher has at their disposal. Ways in which you can help the relationship to work include the following:

- Be mindful of the crucial importance of being *fair* and consistent to all pupils. This includes not having favourites or over-focusing on those who are prone to misbehave.
- Notice, remark on and reward positive behaviour – including from those who behave well all the time.
- Use strategies such as take up time and the ignoring of secondary behaviours (see Chapter 7) to allow pupils the opportunity to save face when complying with your verbal correction of their behaviour.
- Be prepared to follow up issues after the lesson or to call the pupil to one side rather than becoming engaged in a public interaction where your behaviour and that of the pupil is more likely to be affected by an awareness of an audience.
- Do not expose a pupil's weaknesses or personal information to the rest of class – speak to them quietly one to one or after class if necessary.
- Use the group as a resource for learning and for promoting positive relationships through activities that target collaboration and cooperation, such as paired and group work, peer assessment and appropriate use of competition.
- Use proximity, eye contact and gesture to show *individual* pupils that you have noticed what they are doing (good or bad). Aim to 'catch them' showing good learning behaviours.
- Use descriptive positive feedback (as opposed to just 'Good' or 'Well done') so that others in the group understand what the required behaviours are (see Chapter 6).
- Use the group to negotiate difficulties. For example, you might say, 'Some people are not handing homework in on time – what can we do about this?'
- Use the group as a source of information for others. For example, you might say, 'What do you do if you get stuck with your work? How did you go about remembering?' This allows those pupils who do not have many problem-solving strategies to try out those used by peers with a broader repertoire.
- Recognise friendship groups and take strategic decisions (e.g. seating plans) based on whether learning is likely to be enhanced or not by pupils sitting with friends. With older pupils it may be possible to directly explore the issue that different group or team compositions are better for different purposes. This is a way of enabling them to recognise that the person they choose to socialise with may not be the best person to work with.
- Try to make a special effort with those pupils who do not attract attention and who risk being ignored throughout the school day.
- Seek to depersonalise relationship problems via the curriculum by using examples from literature, films and TV, current affairs and history. Role play or, for younger children, puppets can be used to demonstrate positive social behaviours or, if a negative scenario is acted out, as the stimulus for a problem-solving discussion. These types of de-personalised approaches allow individual pupils to reflect on behaviour and relationships without feeling emotional or defensive.

Competing pressures

Pupils, particularly by the time they reach secondary school, may feel competing pressures between the need to relate positively to the teacher and the need to relate positively to their peers. Ways in which you can help the relationship to work include the following:

- Examine how positive correction (see Chapter 7) and the sanctions system are being experienced by pupils. What is it that makes some pupils seek attention from their peers at the expense of receiving sanctions from their teacher? Are the sanctions used for messing about with peers effective? (For example, do others admire pupils who are sent out of class?)
- Examine how positive verbal feedback and the rewards system are being experienced by pupils. Do well-behaved pupils get less attention? Does receiving public positive attention attract negative labels such as 'boff' or 'geek'?
- Recognise the desire to socialise and, rather than resisting this, provide some opportunities for pupils to work with peers. Successful group working can be rewarded with increased opportunities to work in this way so that pupils can spend time with peers and still achieve.
- Use examples to demonstrate the juxtaposition and value of effort/work *and* friendships (e.g. sports teams, friendship groups that work hard and achieve, special interest groups).
- Ensure tasks offer a suitable level of challenge for pupils. In the face of work that is experienced as too difficult, other priorities such as off-task chatter may hold greater appeal and represent a welcome distraction. The same may be true of work that is experienced as too easy, or boring in its repetitive nature.
- Protect the rights of pupils by responding firmly to those who make nasty comments about others; the group must feel safe and protected from such comments and be reminded of the impact of their own behaviour on others.

Power

A teacher is nearly always going to be outnumbered by their pupils. However, most pupils understand and broadly accept the expectations of the teacher–pupil relationship and tacitly agree to allow the teacher to exercise certain rights during the lesson, while at the same time forgoing some of their own. For example, the teacher can speak publicly and control communication but if pupils wish to speak publicly the teacher is permitted to decide when this is appropriate and may ask the pupil to wait. If the pupil needs to speak to a neighbour, they are expected to do so quietly (Robertson 1996). Pupils do have the power to make teachers' lives very difficult if they are not willing or able to make the tacit agreement to cede certain rights to the teacher.

French and Raven's (1960) work may help to explain why most pupils are prepared to tacitly cede control to the teacher. They suggested there were five bases of power, which can be applied to teachers:

1   *Legitimate power* – teachers, by virtue of their adult status generally and their role as teachers specifically, hold legitimate power.
2   *Reward power* – teachers can reward pupils with praise and other signs of approval.
3   *Coercive power* – teachers can threaten and impose sanctions, and show other signs of disapproval.
4   *Referent power* – teachers have the ability to influence others' behaviour because they are liked, admired and respected as individuals.
5   *Expert power* – teachers' expert power relates to their ability to influence others' behaviour because of recognised knowledge, skills or abilities.

(Olsen and Cooper 2001; Lunenberg 2012)

Legitimate, *reward* and *coercive* powers can be viewed collectively as position powers. *Referent* and *expert* powers are personal powers (Olsen and Cooper 2001) because they relate to personal qualities and skills. The teacher needs to use these different sources of power wisely. They cannot rely exclusively on their position powers but must seek to exert influence through expert and referent power. Ways in which you can help the relationship to work include the following:

- Seek a *balance* between a strong leadership style (authoritarian) and a cooperative leadership style. Pupils are adaptable, but extremes and unpredictable fluctuations of relationship styles are problematic.
- Demonstrate enthusiasm and knowledge within your subject area – this is your 'expert power'.
- Adopt the principle of being friendly but not the pupils' friend. Build your 'referent power' by being friendly, approachable, interesting and interested, but recognise that ultimately the purpose and nature of the relationship is different from that of social relationships.
- Exercise your 'reward power' through positive feedback and other signs of approval.
- Make fair and consistent use of your own and the school's 'legitimate' and 'coercive' powers to impose agreed sanctions when necessary.
- Do not use power to secure compliance but to secure improved learning behaviour.
- Give choices rather than ultimatums.
- Show respect to pupils by, for example, listening, keeping agreements or promises (marking dates, etc.), being on time, being fair, being considerate and not assuming things about them based on hearsay, home background or reputation.
- Admit you are fallible when necessary if a pupil does not respond as required – for example, 'I may not have explained that clearly.'
- Look for opportunities to involve pupils in decision making.
- Look at workload and other demands on pupils from their perspective – even if you do not have the power to make changes, you have the power to empathise.
- Explicitly explore rights and responsibilities within the teacher–pupil relationship. Both parties have rights and responsibilities.
- Use literature, films, TV, politics, current affairs and history to make explicit the link between power and responsibility.

Relationship with the curriculum

In the context of this chapter, the teacher's relationship with the curriculum relates to the body of knowledge and skills that enables them to foster and maintain positive patterns of behaviour in their pupils and respond effectively when misbehaviour occurs. In terms of teacher training and continued professional development, we can think of this as a curriculum for behaviour. It is a subset of the teacher's broader relationship with the curriculum that encompasses their knowledge, skills and understanding related to their subject, the curriculum and pedagogy.

Much of this book is concerned with supporting the development of those aspects of a teacher's practice that could be considered as forming the curriculum for behaviour. In this section of the chapter, we deal with a number of other elements that could be construed as part of the curriculum for behaviour but are not covered elsewhere.

Use of voice

The teacher's voice is arguably their most valuable asset because it is the means by which they communicate with most pupils, not only transmitting information but also influencing the mood, atmosphere and emotions within the classroom.

Getting the volume right

Teachers need to be audible. The pupils at the back of the class need to be able to hear just as well as those at the front. This is achieved through projection rather than volume (Zwozdiak-Myers and Capel 2005). Some new teachers assume they need to speak louder than they actually do. If the reason for speaking loudly or even shouting is to give instructions over the top of the noise in the classroom, then there are other issues to address related to gaining and maintaining group attention. An appropriate volume needs to be employed that allows the whole class to hear but is not too loud. Talking too loudly can also make it difficult to use subtle changes in tone of voice to convey meaning.

Sometimes it can be the feeling of talking to a mass rather than individuals that causes teachers to rely on volume rather than projection. To overcome this feeling, one approach that can be helpful is to focus on a series of individuals at different points around the room and especially those sitting nearer the back. Select an individual in your mind, look at them, making eye contact if possible, and for a very brief time speak as though you are talking directly to them. As you would in normal conversation, look for their subtle reactions as you are talking that show they are hearing what you are saying. Then choose another person to direct your attention towards. You are likely to find that by connecting with individual pupils in this way you will naturally project your voice.

If in doubt about your voice reaching the back of the room, either ask pupils to indicate that they can hear you or, if you feel this may convey an unhelpful lack of confidence in your abilities, invite a teaching assistant or other colleague to sit at the back and listen. The aim, O'Flynn and Kennedy (2003) suggest, is for the teacher to keep their voice soft and gentle for normal working as this has a calming effect on pupils and is conducive to creating a good working atmosphere. Remember that loud teachers tend to have loud classes (Zwozdiak-Myers and Capel 2005).

The volume will, of course, vary to suit the type of lesson and the type of activity. Clearly, the kind of voice used to give an instruction or introduce an activity to a group of 30 will be different to the voice that you would use when speaking to a small group or an individual.

Pitch

As a general rule, deep voices sound more serious and significant whereas high voices are more exciting and lively (Zwozdiak-Myers and Capel 2005). A voice with a lower pitch can create a sense of importance because it is likely to be perceived as more authoritative and confident than a high-pitched voice. Dropping the pitch of your voice can add weight to what is being said whereas raising the pitch can lighten the tone. A lower pitched voice can be raised more easily to command attention, whereas raising an already naturally high-pitched voice may result in something similar to a squeak that does not carry the same weight (Zwozdiak-Myers and Capel 2005). Clearly some people have higher or lower pitched voices than others and, although we all naturally vary this as part of normal everyday conversation, it is important to be aware of your natural pitch and its implications for practice. If you know you have a tendency for your voice to become higher pitched when feeling under pressure or anxious, consciously try to lower your voice slightly at these times.

Pace of speech

The pace of speech used when addressing a class needs to be a little slower than that used if conversing with friends (Visser 2006). Balance is important. If a teacher talks too quickly, then pupils are likely to miss key elements of what is being said, but if the pace is too slow they will lose interest. Pace needs to be flowing but not too predictable. Variations in the pace of speech can be used to convey different meanings and emotions. For example, speeding up the pace of speech can be used to show excitement, slowing it down can emphasise a point or convey the gravitas of the situation.

Anxiety or nervousness tend to increase an individual's pace of speech so in situations that may provoke these feelings it is important for the teacher to monitor how quickly they are speaking (Visser 2006). As well as potentially making it more difficult for pupils to take in what is being said – especially if they too are stressed or anxious – the increase in pace can convey a lack of confidence.

Teacher movement and use of space

A lot of minor pupil misbehaviour can be prevented or addressed by the teacher's movement around the classroom. At a preventative level, circulating around the class can contribute to a teacher's overall 'withitness'. 'Withitness' was a phrase coined by Kounin (1970) to describe the teacher's ability to convey to pupils that they were aware of what was going on in all parts of the room. At a reactive level, if a pupil is engaged in some minor off-task behaviour, simply moving to their area of the room or pausing momentarily by them in the course of routinely circulating can be enough for them to realise that their behaviour has been noticed without the need for the teacher to say anything.

In order to use teacher movement effectively, some consideration needs to be given to the room layout so that there are no areas that can only be reached by a very circuitous route. If seating plans are used, it is also possible to take into account the positioning of pupils the teacher may need to reach more often. However, care should be taken to avoid implicitly creating a 'naughty' table or area of the room.

A question to consider is how much teacher movement is desirable. While pupils are engaged in independent or group work, circulating around the room is, as already suggested, a useful way of conveying 'withitness' but it should not be experienced by pupils as the teacher patrolling, looking for trouble to quash. Instead, the circulating should be a part of supporting learning, with the teacher stopping to check how pupils are getting on with the task, responding to questions from individuals and so on. The way in which the teacher interacts at these points also conveys important messages. O'Flynn and Kennedy (2003) suggest that looking at the pupil's work and squatting down to their level is not threatening whereas looking down at the pupil from above can be unsettling.

Ideally, the teacher should avoid getting locked in one place for an extended period of time, but when this is unavoidable – for example, when a pupil needs more detailed guidance on the task – continue to scan the class (Brophy 1996). 'Withitness' can then be conveyed by occasionally commenting from this position on something happening elsewhere in the room. The comment may be on something positive, an instruction to a group or an individual or, when necessary, a positive correction of behaviour (see Chapter 7). This technique is also applicable when working with a focus group for an extended period of time.

Teacher movement when addressing the whole class needs to be managed carefully. The right amount of animation maintains interest but too much can make the teacher appear like a caged animal at the zoo (Neill and Caswell 1993) and cause the pupils to act like spectators at a tennis match, their heads turning from side to side watching the teacher's movement, potentially at the expense of taking in what is being said. It is helpful to identify an approximate spot where you stand to give important whole class messages, because just your location in this position can help to cue the pupils in non-verbally to the fact that something important is about to be said to which they are expected to listen. This will help to support additional verbal (e.g. 'Ok, class 5, facing this way and listening now, thanks') or non-verbal (e.g. the use of a rain stick) markers (Neill and Caswell 1993) used to gain group attention.

Self-awareness is important. If you find addressing the whole class an anxiety-provoking activity and in these situations your response to the anxiety is to pace around or generally fidget, then it may be better to sit on the edge of your desk so that this movement is restricted (Neill and Caswell 1993). This can help to convey greater confidence.

Gaining group attention

Barnes (2006) suggests that common problems for new teachers are signalling effectively that they want class attention and, having called for it, making sure this attention is given before continuing.

In gaining the attention of the class you have a choice. You can use a verbal or non-verbal signal. Non-verbal signals to gain whole class attention have the advantage that you do not have to raise your voice. Examples include countdowns on an interactive whiteboard, rain sticks and taught sequences of hand gestures that pupils copy as soon as they notice the teacher making them. Whistles are appropriate for outdoor locations and some indoor sports activities, but we would not recommend them for classroom use – you are trying to reduce the noise, not add to it.

If you decide to use a verbal method, then ensure that in the call for attention you keep the instruction brief and to the point. For example, you might say, 'Ok, Class 5, facing this way and listening now, thanks.' Alternatively, you might prefer 'Everybody stop. Things down, and look this way' (Barnes 2006: 17). If there is a lot of noise, you can say the first two or three words loudly (but not shouting) and then drop the volume for the remainder. If you remain loud, there is no reason for the pupils to quieten to hear what you are saying.

Most pupils will probably give their attention at the verbal or non-verbal signal but there may be some who do not. This reflects Barnes' (2006) second commonly encountered problem of ensuring attention is given before continuing. The teacher has a choice in this situation. Having called for class attention they can wait for it silently. This can work, but generally only when most pupils are already giving their attention. If more than a few are not giving their attention, then something needs to be said because the chances are that these pupils are so engrossed in what they are doing (which positively could be the task, or less positively off-task chatter) that they have not noticed that the teacher is waiting. At this point a variation on the original request for attention can be given (e.g. 'Class 5, I need to see *everyone* facing this way and listening now, thanks'.) Barnes (2006) makes the important point that, while waiting, the teacher should avoid responding to questions from individuals. If the teacher gets drawn into something else in this way, it undermines the message that they are waiting for attention. If necessary, the teacher can use a non-verbal gesture of signalling with the palm of their hand facing the pupil concerned that they do not want any questions at the moment.

Unless it really is just one or two in a sea of virtual silence, avoid the temptation to target straight away those pupils who are not giving their attention. The risk is that you end up reeling off a long list of names and lose the attention of those who were ready. Instead, direct positive comments to individuals who are ready to listen. Ideally select pupils who are in close proximity to those who are still not giving you their attention. For example, a primary teacher might say 'Kirsty, I can see you're sitting up ready to listen.' Similar comments could then be directed to one or two other pupils, possibly more, in the hope that those who are not currently giving their attention adjust their behaviour. As others do give attention, a positive comment can be directed at them as well. The aim of this strategy is to keep the attention on those who have complied and at the same time reduce the number who are not yet ready to listen. Once the number has been reduced, then individual directions can be given, such as 'John, I need you to be facing this way and listening now.' It is difficult for all but the most determined of pupils to keep talking against a background of silence so such direction may not even be necessary.

Barnes (2006) makes an interesting point in not ruling out the use of hand clapping. We would suggest this should be used sparingly because it adds noise to the situation and does not represent a form of communication we tend to use in normal human relationships – most of us would be given short shrift if we did this to gain our partner's attention! However, in the context of an individual relating to a large group, a hand clap preceding or accompanying the phrase 'And stop (single hand clap) . . . everybody facing this way' can be helpful. Repeated hand claps need to be used with caution. Barnes (2006) is precise in suggesting that, if using multiple hand claps to gain attention, this should be one clap per second. This time interval allows the clapping to sound controlled and measured.

Conclusion

This chapter has presented a teacher's personal style as the dynamic interaction between their professional knowledge about pupil behaviour, a variety of 'within teacher' factors and a social dimension conceptualised as the teacher–pupil relationship. 'Within teacher' factors such as beliefs and values, self-esteem, self-efficacy, locus of control and attributional style are unique to the individual teacher. Self-management is about developing awareness of these factors and actively managing them, based on recognition of how they might affect classroom practice.

Part of developing your overall resilience as a teacher is recognising that you cannot predict and control every individual's behaviour. What we have described in this chapter as the curriculum for behaviour is something over which you can exert some control by building your capacity in this area over time. This will involve securing your knowledge of the well-established principles of good practice in behaviour management and developing awareness of, and confidence in, your own personal style.

It is a truism that teaching is all about relationships. In this chapter, we hope to have encouraged closer scrutiny of the nature of the pupil–teacher relationship by exploring some of the key differences between this and a typical social relationship. With this knowledge, the teacher is better placed to understand how the teacher–pupil relationship is likely to be experienced by pupils, and ways in which to positively influence this.

Chapter 5

School systems and frameworks for managing behaviour

Introduction

This chapter is concerned with the nature and purpose of whole school systems and their influence on classroom practice. The overriding purpose of whole school systems is to secure an environment in which every pupil can benefit from the learning opportunities on offer. Effective whole school systems provide a stable, safe and predictable environment for staff and pupils. It is important that you have a good knowledge of whole school systems and your responsibilities within these. When considering whole school systems from a behaviour for learning perspective, the emphasis is on how individuals experience and interpret procedures and practices that have been designed for the whole school population.

The need for a whole school approach to managing behaviour is well established within Government guidance (e.g. DES 1989, DCSF 2009a, DfE 2014b). In its emphasis on whole school approaches to behaviour and discipline, the Elton Report (DES 1989) represented a major shift regarding the management of behaviour in schools (Hallam and Rogers 2008). Although the Elton Report (DES 1989) is recognised as influential in its strong reinforcement of the need for a whole school approach and its consideration of the factors that shape this, the existence of school policies concerning behaviour was been noted much earlier (e.g. Galloway *et al.* 1982; Upton 1983; Docking 1987). Since the Elton Report, recognition of the importance of adopting a whole school approach to pupil behaviour has been a feature of Government guidance.

A school's behaviour policy is central to defining the whole school approach. The requirement for schools to have a behaviour policy is firmly established in legislation (e.g. Education Act 1997; School Standards and Framework Act 1998; Education and Inspections Act 2006). Current Government guidance (DfE 2014b: 3) requires schools 'to ensure they have a strong behaviour policy to support staff in managing behaviour, including the use of rewards and sanctions'. By law, schools are required to set out measures in their behaviour policy that aim to:

- promote good behaviour, self-discipline and respect
- prevent bullying
- ensure that pupils complete assigned work
- regulate the conduct of pupils.

(DfE 2014b: 4)

It is important to recognise that a school's behaviour policy is just a document and the extent to which the approaches outlined within it are genuinely whole school is dependent on its contents being workable and followed by individual members of staff.

The current Teachers' Standards require teachers to 'establish a framework for discipline' but also to operate 'in accordance with the school's behaviour policy' (DfE 2011a: 8). The additional guidance issued by the current Government and intended to strengthen teacher training in relation to behaviour reinforces this point. It states that trainees should ' . . . be able to adapt their practice to fit with the school behaviour policy and should understand that consistency is an essential component of managing behaviour' (TA 2012: 2).

When joining a school, a teacher, particularly one who is in the early stages of their career, will be expected to adhere to the current policy. Behaviour policies should be reviewed periodically and this process should ideally capture the perspectives of all stakeholders, thus providing an opportunity at some point for them to influence the content. In some schools, the ethos is such that the senior leadership team welcomes suggestions of changes and observations about the effectiveness of aspects of the policy at any time. Even though you may not currently be able to change the behaviour policy that you work with – and indeed may not wish to – it is important to develop an understanding of the generic key components of most schools' behaviour policies and the thinking behind these. This will help you not only to predict how pupils may experience and interpret these components, but also to anticipate and prepare for potential difficulties in applying the policy within your classroom. This understanding will be helpful, too, when you move to another school with a different policy or, as you move on in your career, perhaps take on a senior leadership team role that involves your taking decisions about the direction of policy.

School behaviour policies differ, but there are certain principles and components that are common to many. This chapter explores these in the context of the principles of the behaviour for learning approach.

Key components of an effective whole school approach

There is some consensus between the previous Government (DCSF 2009a) and the current Government (DfE 2014b) over the aspects of school practice that, when effective, contribute to the quality of pupil behaviour. These are:

1   a consistent approach to behaviour management
2   strong school leadership
3   classroom management
4   rewards and sanctions
5   behaviour strategies and the teaching of good behaviour
6   staff development and support
7   pupil support systems
8   liaison with parents and other agencies
9   managing pupil transition
10   organisation and facilities.

This list was originally put forward within the Steer Report (DfES 2005a). This report was produced by a team consisting of head teacher Sir Alan Steer, twelve other professional practitioners, a DfES adviser and an Ofsted adviser. The role of the group was to identify key practical proposals to help raise standards of behaviour and discipline.

What you can expect to find in a school behaviour policy

Although changing legislation inevitably influences aspects of the content, a typical school behaviour policy is likely to cover these broad areas:

- A statement of the principles that underpin the policy
- A code of conduct for pupils setting out the expectations of behaviour
- Promoting and rewarding good behaviour
- Addressing poor behaviour through the use of disciplinary sanctions
- Acknowledgement of the school's legal duties under the Equality Act 2010 in respect of both safeguarding and pupils with special educational needs (SEN)
- Arrangements for monitoring and reviewing the policy.

Some school policies are more detailed than others – for example, covering specific topics such as the confiscation of pupils' property and 'regulating pupils' conduct and disciplining them for misbehaviour outside school premises' (DCSF 2009a: 23). Current guidance on the use of reasonable force (DfE 2013a) also advises that it is good practice to set out in the behaviour policy the circumstances in which force might be used.

There are considerable variations between individual schools in their approaches to behaviour and, importantly, in the extent to which the individual teacher has responsibility for determining the class-based steps of the policy.

Your responsibility as part of a team

As previously indicated, as a member of the school team you will be expected to adhere to the school's policy and use appropriate channels to convey any concerns or difficulties you have, rather than unilaterally varying from it. This is important in ensuring pupils experience a high degree of consistency. As we explore in more depth later, it is important to interpret consistency in terms of the predictability and stability of the pupil's experience, rather than as responding to behaviour in an identical manner for all pupils.

For primary school pupils, the typical model of one teacher for the year ensures some consistency, but they will encounter other teachers and adults in assembly, the corridor, the playground and, in some schools, for subjects that are taught by specialist teachers or where setting is used. Pupils will also move to a new class the following academic year. A significantly different set of expectations and approaches to behaviour may be problematic as pupils struggle to adapt to these. To take a simple example, if one teacher has been generous in the distribution of rewards but the next teacher gives far fewer, then a pupil has to make sense of this. Some may understand that it is the result of teacher difference, but, potentially more harmfully, others may interpret it personally as meaning that they are not performing as well in their behaviour or learning as they were previously.

In secondary schools, variations in expectations and approaches to behaviour may be more problematic. Pupils may encounter four or five teachers a day. It is important that expectations and approaches to behaviour are broadly similar. As well as the lack of predictability and stability caused by significant variations and experienced by all pupils, some pupils may directly question a teacher as to why they are enforcing a rule or expectation when another does not. A typical line might be 'But Mr Smith lets us.' Such lines are usually not delivered by pupils as a neutral observation on variations in practice between teachers, but instead suggest through their tone a degree of unfairness and unreasonableness that, unless the teacher can manage their own feelings in response, can lead to an escalation of the incident. We will return to this point in Chapter 7, but for readers who are cherry picking their way through the book we will just say at this stage that a useful response to reduce the risk of escalation is 'Maybe he does. In this lesson I'd like you to . . .' This technique is sometimes referred to as partial agreement (Rogers 2011).

As a final note on the need to adhere to the school policy, should your practice be questioned by a parent/carer, pupils or possibly another professional, it is far easier for senior colleagues to support and, if necessary, defend you, if you have acted in line with the policy and the values and principles that underpin it.

The caveat in this general endorsement of the importance of a team approach is that clearly, in encouraging you to adhere to policy, we are not advocating unquestioning compliance with practices that you recognise as ethically, morally or legally wrong. Although rare, there have been examples within health, social care and educational settings of a culture of abuse developing that staff, either actively or through their silence, have been complicit in maintaining. Individuals have responsibility to voice their concerns and take appropriate action.

A framework for managing behaviour: rules, rewards and sanctions

For many years, national policy and guidance has encouraged a framework for managing behaviour in schools based on rules, rewards and sanctions. In endorsing the need for a whole school approach to behaviour the Elton Report stated:

> We consider that the best way to encourage good standards of behaviour in a school is a clear code of conduct backed by a balanced combination of rewards and punishments within a positive community atmosphere. Establishing a whole school behaviour policy is an important step in that direction.
>
> (DES 1989: 99)

This led to the formal recommendation 'that schools should strike a healthy balance between rewards and punishments and that both should be clearly specified' (DES 1989: 100).

Commenting on school rules, the Elton Report also established some key principles regarding their formulation that are still relevant today:

> The number of rules should be kept to an essential minimum, and only include ones which the school will enforce. The reasons for each rule should be obvious. Obscure, arbitrary or petty rules discredit the whole code. The distinction between rules which are a direct application of fundamental principles, such as an absolute ban on physical violence, and administrative regulations, such as the name tagging of clothes, should be made quite clear. Wherever possible rules should be expressed in positive terms: for example 'take care of the building' rather than 'don't write graffiti'.
>
> (DES 1989: 100)

The Elton Report's message regarding the balance between reward and sanctions was reiterated in the Steer Report (DfES 2005a) in its 'Principles and practice – what works in schools' section:

> In schools with good standards of behaviour, there is a balance between the use of rewards and sanctions. Praise is used to motivate and encourage pupils. At the same time, pupils are aware of sanctions that will be applied for poor behaviour.
>
> (DfES 2005a: 18)

Within the Labour Government's *School Discipline and Pupil-Behaviour Policies* (DCSF 2009a), two sections entitled 'Promoting and rewarding good behaviour' and 'Punishing poor behaviour – use of disciplinary sanctions' made it clear there was an expectation that rewards and sanctions would form a central part of a school's policy. In considering the use of rewards and sanctions, it is important to note the ratio between the two. A common recommendation (e.g. DCSF 2009a) for classroom practice is a 5:1 ratio of rewards to sanctions. The need to keep a strong focus on positive behaviour at whole school level is also supported by the Elton Report's comment that 'Our evidence from visits, confirmed by research findings, suggests that schools with a negative atmosphere will suffer more from bad behaviour than those with a positive one' (DES 1989: 89).

Although a much briefer document than its 2009 counterpart, the current Government's guidance on behaviour and discipline in schools (DfE 2014b) suggests that, in developing the behaviour policy, the head teacher should reflect on rewards and sanctions along with the nine other key aspects of school practice the Steer Report (DfES 2005a) had suggested contributed to improving the quality of pupil behaviour. In light of past recognition of the need for a balance between rewards and sanctions and the importance of the 5:1 ratio, an interesting feature of the current Government's guidance (DfE 2014b) is the lack of any suggestion of the rewards a school might use but a list of ten possible sanctions.

The Teachers' Standards also require teachers to use 'praise, sanctions and rewards consistently and fairly' (DfE 2011a: 8–9) and guidance intended to improve teacher training for behaviour suggests trainees should 'know how to apply rewards and sanctions to improve behaviour' (TA 2012: 2).

Reflecting the guidance over the years, rules, rewards and sanctions tend to form the operational core of most schools' behaviour policies and for most readers these are likely to represent the aspect of the policy's application with which they are most directly involved during their day-to-day practice. In stating this, however, we would not want to ignore the importance of parts of the school policy covering, for example, the teaching of social, emotional and behavioural skills (see DfES 2005c, 2007) or the systems of support available for pupils whose behaviour is not ameliorated by the rules, rewards and sanctions.

There are variations in the responsibility given to classroom teachers for developing the rules that apply in their classrooms and the class-based rewards and sanctions. Some schools have quite a prescriptive set of stages the class teacher is expected to go though in the classroom before a pupil encounters higher level sanctions. Similarly, a teacher might be expected to record merits that lead to a head teacher's award or some other commendation. In other schools, classroom teachers may be left largely to their own devices in determining their classroom discipline plan. In some schools, there may be a common set of rules displayed in all classrooms; in others, the teacher will have the responsibility for formulating these, although typically there will be an overall school set that any class rules would be expected to reflect. The teacher's responsibility may be to express these in a more age-appropriate way for particular year groups.

The behaviour for learning perspective on rules, rewards and sanctions

The framework of rules, rewards and sanctions is intended to provide a stable, safe and predictable environment where all pupils are encouraged to develop a positive relationship with the curriculum, themselves and others. The overarching principle determining the compatibility of any framework of rules, rewards and sanctions with the behaviour for learning approach is the extent to which these elements at least protect and, when possible, enhance the three relationships and foster the development of positive learning behaviours.

A point we stress throughout this book is that it is important to keep in mind the principle that individuals experience and interpret events individually. It is therefore necessary to be realistic in what can be achieved by a combination of rules, rewards and sanctions necessarily constructed on the principle of a best fit for the majority. For example, Canter and Canter (1992) suggested that their influential Assertive Discipline approach is effective with 90–95% of pupils. Similarly, Mosley and Sonnet (2005: 73) acknowledged that there will be a small number of children who are 'beyond being able to respond to, or benefit from, the normal proactive motivational procedures used in the Golden Time incentives system'. It seems likely that, whatever whole school system is adopted, it will not be effective for all pupils. It would be possible to expend a lot of energy continually changing the behaviour policy with the unrealistic aim of trying to develop a policy that fits everybody. Effective behaviour policies seek to encompass as many pupils as possible but recognise the necessity of having supportive measures in place for those who fall outside this.

Behaviour policies are successful because the experience and interpretation of many individuals are, of course, not totally unique; there will be some commonalities in the rewards pupils find rewarding, the sanctions pupils experience as aversive, and the expectations of behaviour to which pupils are willing and able to adhere. This is what allows us to formulate whole school approaches that work for the majority. The reasons behind some pupils' differing interpretation and response to rewards and sanctions may include the following:

- What as adults we consider to be rewarding may not be experienced as such by a pupil. Being singled out for praise, for example, may be embarrassing for some children and consequently they may exhibit less of the behaviour that gained the praise.
- What as adults we consider to be aversive may not be experienced by the pupil as such. For example, receiving negative attention from an adult may be experienced as preferable to receiving none.
- The pupil's view of the person giving a reward or sanction may influence its impact. The reward or sanction may mean more or less to the individual depending on whether they like or respect this person. Pupils may also have a perception of the rewarder's or sanctioner's view of them. Relationships therefore are important.
- The pupil's reflection upon the experience of being rewarded or sanctioned is likely to influence their response. They may interpret a reward as undeserved or patronising, or view a sanction as unfair.

- There may be many other rewarding or punishing factors present besides the ones a teacher is controlling. For example, while the teacher may use ignoring as a response to attention-seeking behaviour, it may be the attention of peers that is more important to the pupil.
- Rewards and sanctions are reliant on the pupil having the required behaviour in their repertoire. Some pupils may not have reached this point developmentally; others may not have learned this behaviour and it may require teaching. Just as with a difficulty in learning, there is a need to ask ourselves whether the pupil knows what to do, knows how to do it and whether they have had enough practice at doing it before 'we simply ascribe dubious motivation and rush into rewards and punishments' (Faupel *et al.* 1998: 8).
- The current behaviour may be serving a purpose for the individual that means it is too valuable to relinquish for a reward or sanction. An example might be a pupil who fears failure misbehaves to avoid starting a task, thus protecting their relationship with self.

Although for most pupils thoughtful application of the school's behaviour policy will be sufficient, for some it may be necessary to try to understand the interpretation that they are making. This can be done through careful observation over a period of time, as well as talking to them about their behaviour in order to gain some insight. Just as we might talk about personalising or differentiating learning, we sometimes have to respond differently to individuals in relation to behaviour.

Any practice or approach encouraged through the school's behaviour policy should not be to the detriment of any one of the three behaviour for learning relationships. For example, a reward that contained an element that a pupil experiences as humiliating or embarrassing would risk having an impact on relationship with self. Care should also be taken if a pupil is required to complete a curriculum task as a sanction, because this might risk undermining their relationship with that curriculum area if they come to associate it with punishment. For this reason, we would suggest that staying in at break time, lunch time or an after-school detention to complete work should be framed as a logical consequence resulting from non–completion of the task in the allotted time. It should not be an arbitrarily imposed sanction such as requiring the pupil to complete a page of maths because they were talking in assembly or have consistently infringed a uniform rule.

In terms of learning behaviour, it would be difficult to claim that every practice or approach actively promotes this. However, attention needs to be given to whether positive learning behaviours are being discouraged or negative learning behaviours promoted by any aspect of policy. For example, if the regime is such that pupils perceive that making a mistake in a curriculum area will be attributed to a lack of concentration, poor motivation or lack of effort and result in a reprimand or sanction, it could undermine risk taking, creativity and the recognition that effective learning involves making errors and learning from these.

Formulating rules

As the Elton Report noted, it is advisable to frame rules positively. There are three main reasons for this:

1   A positively expressed rule provides information on the expected behaviour.
2   If we tell someone *not* to think of something, they will probably, at least momentarily, think of that thing. If pupils are going to momentarily think of something, then it would be better that it was the required behaviour. The rule might therefore be 'We use respectful language' rather than 'Do not swear'.
3   A positively expressed rule helps a teacher to frame their correction positively (see Chapter 7) because they only need to formulate a sentence around the wording of the rule.

From a behaviour for learning perspective, positively phrased rules reflect the principle of keeping a focus on those behaviours that are necessary for learning in a school environment.

There is not complete consensus on the need to only express rules positively. Rogers (1990, 2011) for example, suggests a rule should specify what is and what is not acceptable. Illustrating this point, he suggests, a teacher might say 'We walk quietly in the classroom; we do not run' (Rogers 1990: 98). The area of agreement, however, is the need to lead with the positive direction.

Rules should be few in number and restricted to those that protect the rights of all members of the class, including the teacher and other adults. Hook and Vass (2002) suggest there are at least four basic rights:

1   The teacher's right to teach
2   The pupils' right to learn
3   Everybody's right to safety (physical and psychological)
4   Everybody's right to be treated with dignity and respect.

As Hook and Vass (2002) argue, it is important that rights are linked with responsibilities. For example, although the pupil has the right to be spoken to with respect, they also have the responsibility to speak to others in this way. In formulating the rules, it is necessary to distinguish between behavioural requirements that relate to the protection of rights and those that are simply concerned with the smooth running of the classroom. The latter are important but can be thought of as 'regular practices that we should proactively teach students (rather than tell then assume they know) to make events run smoothly' (Hook and Vass 2002: 49). For example, a teacher might establish routines for entering and exiting the classroom, accessing classroom resources or the problem-solving process to be followed when stuck with an aspect of a task. The distinction between rules and routines is not rigid but thinking in these terms will be helpful in keeping the list of rules reasonably short. There is no reason why a teacher should not display reminders of the routines separate from the rules, or even develop a 'sub-set' of rules that apply to a particular area of the classroom (e.g. the book corner) or particular activities (e.g. group work) if this is felt to be helpful. The main point, however, is that, whatever else exists, pupils are aware of an overarching concise set of class rules that protects rights. Rogers (2011) reports encountering classrooms with twenty or more rules on the wall. It is unlikely pupils would remember all these.

For younger children in particular, a visual reminder of a rule, such as a cartoon drawing or a photograph, can be helpful in supporting the written version. If a visual reminder is used, we would suggest this should depict the rule being followed rather than broken, because the purpose is to provide guidance on the *required* behaviour. This is particularly true if the reason for the visual reminder is to support pupils who may have difficulty in reading the written rule.

Developing routines

We have already made reference to routines as distinct from rules. In a class of thirty, and a school of several hundred pupils, there need to be accepted ways of carrying out regularly occurring activities. Below are some examples:

- Entering the room: in some schools, the routine is that pupils line up outside the classroom; in others they may come straight in. There may be particular expectations of what they do when they come in. This is also a routine.
- Hats, coats and bags: as a routine, pupils may be expected to take off hats, scarves and any other outer clothing, and deposit bags either beside their desk or in some other designated location.
- Lining up to leave the room: the key elements in this routine might be pushing in their chair, lining up without touching or talking to others, and facing the front of the line.
- What to do when stuck on a piece of work: the teacher might establish a set of self-help strategies pupils are expected to use before asking for their help.
- Entering a lesson after it has started: some pupils will join a lesson late because of, for example, a doctor's appointment. Others will be late for no particular reason. The routine relates to what the teacher expects them to do on arrival. For example, do they go straight to their desk, or should they make their arrival known to the teacher and give a reason for their lateness?
- Signals used by the teacher to gain whole class attention: the teacher may have a particular means of gaining attention that signals to the class that they are expected to stop what they are doing, face the front, and listen for directions.
- Contributing to class discussions: the expectations may vary from lesson to lesson. It may not be appropriate in some lessons to adhere to the more traditional approach of pupils putting their hands up to contribute. Pupils can learn multiple routines but it is important to remind them of the one that applies in a particular lesson or even at a particular point in the lesson.

You may be able to think of some other routines, and of course the type of routine needed will vary according to age group. Essentially anything that needs doing on a regular basis can be viewed as a routine with specific ways of doing it established. The key point, however, is that the routines are made explicit to pupils, taught and reinforced.

Clear routines help the school and the classroom to run smoothly. Like rules, they help to create an orderly and predictable environment in which individuals are less likely to make behavioural mistakes simply because they do not know what is expected.

The use of rewards

Some reward systems are based on teachers and other adults giving a reward that has value in its own right to the individual. Other schools operate systems where a reward given to an individual or group contributes towards an individual, class or house total that will eventually lead to a higher reward. There is a variety of rewards commonly used in schools. These include:

- verbal or non-verbal indication of approval of the behaviour
- positive referral to (usually) senior staff
- stickers and stars
- raffle tickets
- merits and house points
- certificates
- celebration assemblies
- special privileges
- 'Congratulations' and 'Good news' postcards home
- personalised letters to parents
- positive phone calls home.

Rewards that engage support from parents can act as a powerful incentive but it does need to be remembered that, for a variety of reasons, not all parents will provide this support. For some pupils, the receipt of the reward from their teacher may still have value even though they do not get the added value of parental approval that the approach is intended to trigger. For others, the presumption of parental approval being available may provoke negative feelings about the reward, about their relationship with their parent and possibly about their teacher for not recognising their circumstances.

The use of raffle tickets typically involves these being given to pupils as a reward with a draw being conducted, perhaps at the end of the week, and prizes awarded. Pupils need to have a basic grasp of probability at the level of recognising that gaining more tickets increases the chance of winning. The frustrating element for some pupils may be that they receive a lot of raffle tickets but win nothing, whereas a pupil who gained just one was drawn as the winner. Older pupils may simply accept that this is an inevitable characteristic of a raffle, but younger children may feel that it is unfair.

The approach of referring pupils who have behaved well to a senior member of staff is helpful in overcoming the general perception that this is where you are sent for misbehaviour. It helps to send a message that members of the senior leadership team are interested in hearing about good behaviour and so fits with the general principle of placing the emphasis on the positive. At the level of individual experience, it is important to remember that, for some younger pupils in particular, referral to the head teacher or other member of the senior leadership team, even for a positive reason, may be daunting. The point of a reward is that it should motivate the pupil to continue demonstrating the behaviour that has led them to achieve it. While we would want to support the pupil to overcome their fear, if the thought of going to see the head teacher or going into the Year 6 class that the deputy head teaches to receive the reward fills them with dread, then the reward is probably not that motivational. We could apply the same considerations to rewards given publicly in assemblies. For some older pupils, a different issue may emerge. Some secondary aged pupils may be embarrassed about being seen to go to a member of the senior leadership team as a result of good behaviour or being given a reward publicly – or at least embarrassed to give any indication that this approval means anything to them. Although practically, schools have to devise their overall system of rewards based on the principle of the 'best fit' for the majority, for individuals for whom the standard rewards do not appear motivational it is important to try to understand how these are being interpreted and experienced.

The use of sanctions

As previously suggested, the level of responsibility an individual teacher has for developing their classroom discipline plan varies between schools. Some readers may be working in schools where there is a series of prescribed steps they are expected to follow, usually starting with a verbal warning, whereas others will be expected to formulate class-based sanctions that lead to defined stages beyond the classroom. There is a variety of sanctions that schools have used over many years. These include:

- verbal or non-verbal indication of disapproval of the behaviour
- removal from the group (in class)
- withdrawal from a particular lesson or peer group (e.g. by sending to another class or another location specifically intended for this purpose)
- withholding participation in an activity or event that is not an essential part of the curriculum
- referral to (usually) senior staff
- withdrawal of specific privileges
- carrying out a useful task in the school
- a variety of forms of detention
- a fixed period of internal exclusion
- a fixed period of external exclusion
- permanent exclusion.

Only the head teacher can decide to exclude a child permanently or impose a period of external fixed term exclusion. Therefore, these are sanctions that the classroom teacher needs to be aware of as part of the whole school policy but is not responsible for issuing.

We would suggest that whole class sanctions should always be avoided. It is unlikely that a school's behaviour policy would include such an approach as one of its recognised sanctions. The Elton Report (DES 1989) was clear that the practice of punishing whole classes is always seen as unfair by pupils and the resulting grievance is likely to be damaging to the school atmosphere. One of the report's 138 formal recommendations was that head teachers and teachers should avoid this practice (DES 1989). More recently, guidance issued under the Labour Government stated that schools should 'avoid whole group sanctions that punish the innocent as well as the guilty' (DCSF 2009a: 31).

Launched in the immediate wake of press coverage (e.g. *The Guardian* 2014) of then Secretary of State Michael Gove's wish for a return to 'traditional' punishments for school misbehaviour, current Government guidance (DfE 2014b) provides the following examples of sanctions:

- a verbal reprimand
- extra work or repeating unsatisfactory work until it meets the required standard
- the setting of written tasks as punishments, such as writing lines or an essay
- loss of privileges – for instance the loss of a prized responsibility or not being able to participate in a non-uniform day (sometimes referred to as 'mufti' days)

- missing break time
- detention including during lunch-time, after school and at weekends
- school based community service or imposition of a task – such as picking up litter or weeding school grounds; tidying a classroom; helping clear up the dining hall after meal times; or removing graffiti
- regular reporting including early morning reporting; scheduled uniform and other behaviour checks; or being placed 'on report' for behaviour monitoring
- extra physical activity such as running around a playing field
- in more extreme cases schools may use temporary or permanent exclusion.

(DFE 2014b: 8)

Many of these suggestions reflect the range of sanctions schools have been accustomed to using for some time. Of particular note are those that were given greatest prominence in the reporting of the apparent return to 'traditional' punishments – namely, litter-picking, running around the field and writing lines. Not only are these recommendations anachronistic, they are also unhelpful in fostering and maintaining the positive teacher–pupil relationships that secure good behaviour in schools. Viewed from the perspective of a pupil's relationship with the curriculum, it is difficult to see why, when schools are attempting to promote positive attitudes to physical activity and writing, it is thought to be a good idea to construct these as punishments. Perhaps the most important question is why it is even perceived to be necessary to set out these sanctions within official guidance. After all, Ofsted data suggests that behaviour is good or outstanding in around 90% of schools (Ofsted 2011) and the 'great majority of children and young people enjoy learning, work hard and behave well' (Ofsted 2005: 3), while in an NFER survey of over 1,600 teachers 95% felt behaviour was acceptable or better in their own schools (NFER 2012). Based on these statistics, most pupils would seem to be responding to methods already employed. For those who do not, these suggested 'traditional' punishments may be experienced as deliberately antagonistic and simply act as further confirmation of what many of them may have already believed about teachers, schools and authority. The Government would do well to heed two warnings from the Elton Report:

- 'Schools which put too much faith in punishments to deter bad behaviour are likely to be disappointed.' (DES 1989: 98)
- 'Punitive regimes seem to be associated with worse rather than better standards of behaviour.' (DES 1989: 99)

From a behaviour for learning perspective, the important point to consider in relation to any sanction imposed is the individual's interpretation. For example, the pupil who finds the playground environment unpleasant may not be overly concerned about the loss of their break time. For some, exclusion from school may be experienced as a reward rather than a sanction, even though it may have a longer term detrimental impact. Likewise, the issuing of detentions that do not actually happen because of unclear lines of responsibility among staff will not be experienced as a sanction.

Sanctions, consequences or punishment?

The terms 'punishment' and 'sanction' are used interchangeably in general policy and guidance related to behaviour (e.g. DCSF 2009a; DFE 2010, 2014b). However the Teachers' Standards (DfE 2011a) and the additional guidance intended to improve teacher training for behaviour (TA 2012) are consistent in using the term 'sanction'. The term 'consequence' does not appear in policy documents issued by the Coalition Government, but it did feature a number of times in the Labour Government's *School Discipline and Pupil-Behaviour Policies – Guidance for Schools* (DCSF 2009a) alongside reference to punishment and sanctions. The document also concluded with a sequence of tables listing 'the rights and responsibilities of schools, pupils and parents in ensuring an orderly climate for learning' (DCSF 2009a: 60).

Although it is included in current Government guidance, the term 'punishment' has unhelpful connotations. It suggests a strong element of retribution, of making the person experience something unpleasant because of what they have done. It does not have strong connotations of learning from your mistakes or learning better ways of behaving or relating to others, except in the sense possibly of learning not to commit the same offence again because something unpleasant will befall you *if* caught. In an environment such as a school that is concerned with learning in the broadest sense, we would have to question whether this is a sufficient aspiration.

In schools, the term 'sanction' tends to be used more widely. As a term it conveys a stronger sense that the school as an organisation has a defined range of penalties it can impose as a necessary part of its role in regulating the behaviour of large groups. It is a less emotive term and may also be helpful in creating some distance between the current approaches used in schools and those of the past such as corporal punishment. Although we might make this distinction, at the level of a literal definition, the sanction imposed is simply the punishment for the behaviour.

The term 'consequence' has some merits in terms of the thinking it attempts to promote in pupils. The terms 'sanction' and 'punishment' imply a concern primarily with the actions on the part of the school. In contrast, referring to a consequence is intended to place the pupil in a position of exercising some control, albeit within the parameters of a choice defined by the teacher, over what happens to them. The longer term aim is that this contributes to an understanding and belief on the part of pupils that the actions they choose to take influence what happens to them. It reflects the general principle that will extend into adult life that every time we make a choice there is a consequence. Rewards and sanctions are both consequences that result directly from a pupil's behaviour (Hook and Vass 2002). A pupil may, for example, choose not to treat another pupil with respect by using verbal 'put-downs', thereby infringing a rule. Equally, pupils are making positive choices when they get on with their work, cooperate, talk politely to adults or ignore distractions.

A distinction can also be made between natural and logical consequences. Natural consequences are those that result without any teacher intervention. For example, if a young pupil refuses to put on their coat at break time on a cold day, the consequence is that they will feel cold. However, the teacher does have a role in ensuring that the natural consequences of the behaviour are not physically or psychologically harmful to the pupil (Hardin 2008). If a child in a Reception class resists wearing their coat on a cold day, the teacher might give them the choice of going outside with their coat on or staying in at break time. If the pupil was in Year 6, the teacher might feel more inclined to let the pupil learn from their own experience of the natural consequence of feeling cold. It may be more difficult to identify the risk of psychological harm and intervene. If, for example, a pupil spreads rumours about others or discloses confidences shared by friends, then a

Table 5.1 Differences between punishment and logical consequences (from Galvin 1999: 86)

Punishment	Logical consequences
May be perceived as arbitrary	Are related to the misbehaviour
May tell the pupil he/she is bad	Express the reality of the social order without necessarily conveying a value judgement
Focuses on what is past	Are concerned with past and present behaviours
Expresses anger	Are based on logic not retaliation
Is associated with threat (open or concealed)	Ensure responsibility is assumed by the individual
Demands obedience	Lead to an active teaching process
Is negative and short term	Teach ways to act that will lead to more successful behaviour

natural consequence may be that they become increasingly socially isolated as their peers tire of this. Although the consequence is natural, most schools would recognise the need to intervene in some way to change this socially self-destructive behaviour.

Logical consequences are those that the teacher or school determines rather than being the obvious result of a pupil's own acts (Meyerhoff 1996). The concept of logical consequences – as opposed to simply consequences – is based on the work of Dreikurs and Grey (1968). The insertion of the word *logical* implies a degree of connection between the misbehaviour and the consequence. As Galvin (1999) argues, this increases the likelihood of a pupil learning from the choice they made and reduces the chance of their shifting the focus onto the teacher's behaviour by, for example, viewing it as unfair. Table 5.1 puts forward a number of distinctions between punishment and logical consequences.

An example of a logical consequence would be requiring a pupil to complete a task at break time because they have wasted time during the lesson. As we will discuss further in Chapter 7, the teacher would typically have moved through a sequence of steps before reminding the pupil of this as the consequence if they continue with whatever behaviour is currently distracting them from the task. However, if the teacher had instead required the pupil to write lines, pick up litter in the playground or run round the field (DfE 2014b), this would not be logical. Although referring to logical consequences in his earlier work (Rogers 1990), prolific writer on behaviour, Bill Rogers, has more recently (e.g. Rogers 2011, 2012) used the term 'related consequences'. The underlying principle is the same: there is an attempt as far as possible to demonstrate some connection between the behaviour and the consequence. Drawing on Albert (1996) and Nelsen *et al.* (2000), Hardin (2008) put forward the '5Rs of logical consequences' (see Table 5.2).

The suggestion that a consequence should be equal in proportion and intensity to the misbehaviour needs some qualification because in isolation it could be misinterpreted as advocating 'an eye for an eye' type of approach. The suggestion from Hook and Vass (2002), like Canter and Canter (1992) before them, is that the relationship between choices and consequences needs be one of inevitability rather than severity. In other words, it is not how severe the consequence is that makes the difference but the fact that this consequence happens every time this behavioural choice is made. As we discuss in Chapter 7, we should not equate inevitability with immediacy.

As the criteria provided by Galvin (1999) suggests, the argument that the proponents of the term 'consequences' would no doubt make is that by adults using this term it

Table 5.2 The 5Rs of logical consequences (Hardin 2008)

Related	A consequence should be logically connected to the behaviour. The more closely related to the consequence, the more valuable it is to the student.
Reasonable	A consequence should be equal in proportion and intensity to the misbehaviour. The purpose is for the students to see the connection between the behaviour and the consequences, not to make them suffer.
Respectful	A consequence should be stated and carried out in a way that preserves a student's self-esteem. It addresses the behaviour, not the character of the student.
Reliably enforced	A consequence should follow misbehaviour. Threats without action are ineffective. Consistency is the key.
Revealed	A consequence should be revealed (known) in advance for predictable behaviour such as breaking class rules. When misbehaviour occurs that was not predicted, logical consequences connected to the misbehaviour should be established.

separates the approach from commonly held beliefs regarding the purpose and nature of punishment. Realistically, we are in a policy context where the terms 'punishment' and 'sanction' are more commonly used (e.g. DfE 2014b), but the principles in Table 5.2 can and should be applied whether we are talking about punishments, sanctions or consequences. School leaders and those teachers with greater autonomy in establishing their own classroom discipline plan may like to read the arguments put forward (e.g. Dreikurs *et al.* 1998, Galvin 1999, Hardin 2008, Rogers 2011) and consider whether adopting the term 'consequence' is likely to be beneficial.

From a behaviour for learning perspective, the following are the key points to note about the principles in Table 5.2.

- There is an emphasis on self-efficacy. The pupil is encouraged to recognise that what they choose is instrumental in determining the outcomes for them.
- The focus is on the choice made rather than the individual. The consequence and the implied disapproval are of the act, not the person. Although we cannot *guarantee* how every individual will interpret and experience the consequence, this affords *a degree* of protection to the individual's relationship with self.
- A degree of protection is afforded to the teacher–pupil relationship. The consequence is the result of a choice made within a known framework. It is not the result of animosity, frustration or simply the teacher having an off day.

The notion of choice and consequence is not without its critics. It can be argued that realistically the only choice offered is 'behave or else!' (Curwin and Mendler 1989, Porter 2007). Porter (2007) argues that effectively responsible behaviour is defined as little more than doing what you are told, with 'good choices' being those that the teacher approves of. Kohn (1996) is similarly critical suggesting that a pseudo choice is offered with very little opportunity for pupils to make meaningful decisions. He argues that, although the claim is that pupils are being taught to be responsible, in reality they are being taught to be obedient. The choice, Kohn (1996) asserts, may be experienced as little more than obey or suffer.

Exploring notions of consistency

Consistency is generally accepted as a key principle of behaviour management but it is important to move beyond the simple notion of a need to be consistent and interrogate the meaning. We would suggest consistency needs to be understood in two ways. First, that the teacher is experienced by pupils as *the same* from one day to the next. For example, the pupils should not find the teacher positively correcting or imposing sanctions in response to certain behaviours on one day but totally ignoring these the next. Clearly the teacher is a human being and will have fluctuating moods influenced by both school and personal factors, but this should not be reflected in their approach to classroom discipline. For the pupils there needs to be predictability and stability. Second, the teacher needs to be consistent on issues. Therefore, if a pupil engages in a piece of behaviour that infringes the rights of another, this should *always* be addressed. However, *how* it is addressed with a particular individual may need to vary and be based on the teacher's judgement of how best to impress upon that pupil that the current behaviour is unacceptable, and to direct them towards the alternative behaviour that is required.

The extract below is taken directly from the Disability Rights Commission's *Code of Practice for Schools* and illustrates why a simple interpretation of consistency as meaning responding in an identical way to all pupils could be problematic.

> At the end of a lesson, homework is written on the board. A pupil with dyslexia is unable to copy it down in the time. He is given a detention for not doing his homework.
>
> - Is this less favourable treatment for a reason related to the pupil's disability?
>   The reason for the detention is the failure to do the homework. This relates to his inability to write it down in the time available, which is a part of his disability.
> - Is it less favourable treatment than someone gets if the reason does not apply to him or her?
>   The treatment that he received has to be compared with the treatment that other pupils received who had done their homework. They were not being given a detention.
> - Is it justified?
>   There was a general assumption on the part of the teacher that all the pupils would be able to write down the homework in the time at the end of the lesson. It is unlikely that there is a material and substantial reason to justify the less favourable treatment. In addition, it is likely that there are reasonable adjustments that could have been made . . . for example, more time could have been provided. The detention is likely to amount to unlawful discrimination.
>   (Disability Rights Commission 2002: 46–7)

The way the scenario is unravelled may seem complex, particularly the line that requires comparison with the treatment of those pupils who had done their homework. However, our intention in providing this example is not to frighten or confuse readers but to illustrate the importance of predicting how individuals are likely to experience classroom events, including in this case the requirement to copy down the homework quickly and the issuing of detention when the homework was not done. An indiscriminately operated blanket policy of giving a detention for failure to hand in homework is at the root of the problem in this scenario. As Stobbs notes, 'The most common way for schools to discriminate is by applying a blanket policy – policy that is applied in the same way to all children but puts disabled children at particular disadvantage compared with children who are not disabled' (Stobbs 2012: 19).

Your school will be expected to comply with the Equality Act 2010 and part of this compliance involves schools considering how its policies, including the behaviour policy, reflect their duty under the Act not to discriminate against a pupil or prospective pupil by treating them less favourably because of their:

- sex
- race
- disability
- religion or belief
- sexual orientation
- gender reassignment
- pregnancy or maternity.

(DFE 2013b)

It is hoped that some of the general issues associated with the imposition of sanctions will have been resolved by the school, and the behaviour policy may already include guidance on avoiding discrimination. Operating in line with this policy should offer you some protection.

Critical perspectives on rewards and sanctions

One concern sometimes expressed about the use of rewards and sanctions is that they rely largely on extrinsic motivation. In other words, the pupil exhibits the behaviour in order to receive the reward or avoid the sanction. The associated concern is that the behaviour may not transfer to contexts where the rewards or sanctions are not available. The aspiration should be that the system of rewards and sanctions contributes to personal development so that more positive patterns of behaviour are internalised by the pupil and become an established part of their repertoire of behaviours. The parallel hope is that some intrinsic motivation will develop based on a belief in the benefits of these behaviours both for the individual and society in general. Arguably it is this aspect that it is often left mainly to chance. It is important to recognise that rewards and sanctions are first and foremost a management tool reflecting the school's need to maintain an orderly, disciplined environment. As large institutions that require the collecting together of groups of 20 or 30 pupils in classes, and sometimes hundreds in assemblies (Thomas 2005), it would be difficult for schools to function effectively without ways of keeping order.

Whether learning about behaviour also takes place is largely dependent on the interpretation individual pupils make of their experiences of the policy. These experiences can be mediated through dialogue, which is why in the chapters that follow we emphasise the importance of the teacher ensuring that the pupil understands why they have received a reward or sanction and, in the case of the latter, the alternative behaviour required. Schools can also make a positive impact on behavioural learning through direct and incidental teaching of social, emotional and behavioural skills (e.g. DfES 2005c, 2007).

Those such as Kohn (1996, 1999), who write from a humanist perspective, are critical of the use of rewards and sanctions, considering both to represent forms of coercion.

Drawing on Rogers (1951) and Rogers and Freiberg (1994), Porter (2007: 127) suggests that the humanist perspective is based on a view that 'All children want to learn skills that are useful in their lives and therefore, when adults do not threaten them with punishment or bribe them with incentives, they will be motivated in school and will make constructive choices'. In a summary of humanists' claims regarding the destructive and ineffective nature of external controls, Porter (2007: 133) suggests that:

> The administration of rewards and punishments is educationally *ineffective*, as consequences focus children's mind on what *they* will get out of behaving in a particular way, whereas egalitarian discipline wants them to focus on the effects of their behaviours *on others*. The result is that, when students do comply with coercion, they do so in their own interests, not others', which will not teach them right from wrong.

The humanist claim that Porter reports goes beyond our earlier suggestion that the use of rewards and sanctions to establish patterns of behaviour may leave longer term personal development to chance and portrays these methods as potentially counterproductive. Within his critique, Kohn draws parallels with learning when considering the contribution to personal development:

> My argument is that the quest to get students to act appropriately is curiously reminiscent of the quest to get them to produce the right answers in academic lessons. Thus, the constructivist critique, which says that a right-answer focus doesn't help children become good thinkers, also suggests that a right behaviour focus doesn't help children become good people.
>
> (Kohn 1996: xv)

Activity 5.1

Consider the following quotes. The first comes from Kohn's (1999) book *Punished by Rewards: The Trouble with Gold Stars, Incentive Plans, A's, Praise and other Bribes*. The second comes from Wheldall and Merrett's (1989) guide to their positive teaching approach.

> What rewards and punishments do is induce compliance, and this they do very well indeed. If your objective is to get people to obey an order, to show up on time and do what they're told, then bribing or threatening them may be sensible strategies. But if your objective is to get long-term quality in the workplace, to help students become careful thinkers and self directed learners, or to support children in developing good values, then rewards, like punishments, are absolutely useless.
>
> (Kohn 1999: 41)

> Because rewards and sanctions are important parts of the Positive Teaching repertoire, the charge of bribery is sometimes levelled at our approach. This glib charge is easily challenged since bribery usually means to give someone an inducement in advance to do something immoral or illegal! In Positive Teaching praise and rewards are, essentially, given following appropriate behaviour which is in the pupil's long-term interests. To call such behaviour bribery makes as much sense as saying that teachers have to be bribed for working with a monthly pay cheque!
>
> (Wheldall and Merrett 1989: 16)

- Which perspective most closely represents your view? Why?
- Do you think Kohn is right to liken rewards to bribery or do you accept the distinction made by Wheldall and Merrett?
- Do you think there is any difference between Wheldall and Merrett's desire to promote 'appropriate behaviour which is in the pupil's long-term interests' and Kohn's objective of helping pupils become careful thinkers and self-directed learners and support them in developing good values?

Although there are criticisms (e.g. Kohn 1996, 1999; Porter 2007) regarding the use of rewards and sanctions, these form part of the generally accepted approach to managing behaviour presented in Government guidance documents (e.g. DFE 2014b). It is probably also true to say that rules, rewards and sanctions represent the mainstay of most schools' behaviour policies, albeit with some variation in individual school systems.

Conclusion

The school's behaviour policy is a key document in supporting your management of behaviour within the classroom. It is important that your practice fits with and follows the policy. It is likely that in most schools you will encounter the behavioural trinity of rules, rewards and sanctions although there will be variations in the framework for discipline employed. From a behaviour for learning perspective, the important consideration is the compatibility of any framework with the principle of at least protecting and, when possible, enhancing the three relationships (with self, with others and with the curriculum) and fostering the development of positive learning behaviours. Any practice where a potential detrimental effect on these relationships for learning could reasonably be predicted should be avoided.

For most pupils, most of the time the framework of rules, rewards and sanctions will suffice – indeed we would go as far as to suggest that there are many pupils who would actually behave well regardless of whether there were rewards and sanctions on offer. Ultimately, however, behaviour policies cannot realistically be expected to work for all pupils because they are designed for groups but experienced and interpreted by individuals. Continuously changing policy to attempt to capture those who fall outside it is likely to prove disappointing. A policy that is necessarily designed on the basis of the best fit for the majority cannot take account of every individual's personal interpretation and experience of it. An effective whole school approach will offer overall consistency but respond flexibly and supportively to those pupils whose behaviour is 'not ameliorated by the behaviour management techniques usually employed in the school' (DfES 2001: 53).

The best advice on rules, rewards and sanctions could be summed up as have them, know them, make them known to pupils and use them consistently but recognise the limitations. The next two chapters look in more detail at the use of positive feedback, rewards, positive correction and sanctions in your classroom.

Chapter 6

Effective use of positive feedback and rewards

Introduction

The need for teachers to focus on positive behaviour is well established in national guidance on behaviour. The Elton Report made the point that evidence gathered from literature and through the enquiry itself suggested that teachers should 'emphasise the positive, including praise for good behaviour as well as good work' (DES 1989: 72), and make sparing and consistent use of reprimands and sanctions. The point that praise should be available for behaviour as well as academic learning was reinforced by the Steer Report's (DfES 2005a) observation that, while many schools had excellent systems to reward good work and behaviour, there were some that relied on sanctions to enforce good behaviour but neglected the use of appropriate rewards.

Reflecting the consistent message of the need to recognise and reinforce positive behaviour, guidance on school discipline and pupil behaviour policies issued by the Labour Government stated: 'It has long been established that rewards are more effective than punishment in motivating pupils. By praising and rewarding positive behaviour, others will be encouraged to act similarly' (DCSF 2009a: 27).

The document also suggested that a rewards/sanctions ratio of at least 5:1 was an indication of a school with an effective rewards and sanctions system. The origins of this suggestion are not entirely clear, although the DCSF document attributes it to the Elton Report. Whatever the origins, the ratio reinforces the message that there is a need to place emphasis on recognising and acknowledging positive behaviour through the use of praise and other forms of reward.

The current Teachers' Standards (DfE 2011a: 8–9) require teachers to 'establish a framework for discipline with a range of strategies, using praise, sanctions and rewards consistently and fairly'. This chapter encourages you to think beyond the simple and generally accepted need to 'be more positive' and consider how praise and rewards can be provided effectively in line with the principles of the behaviour for learning approach.

Positive feedback and reward in the context of the behaviour for learning approach

From a behaviour for learning perspective, the purpose of praise and rewards (and the positive correction and sanctions discussed in the next chapter) is to foster the development of positive learning behaviours. For many pupils the standard diet of rewards and sanctions, together with an eclectic mix of other routine practices, achieves this (or at least does not hinder it). Inevitably for some, it does not. The B4L approach explicitly recognises this and, through the core and extended use described in Chapter 1, provides a means of responding, either by a more explicit focus on the desirable learning behaviours or by targeting one or more of the behaviour for learning relationships.

Within the B4L approach, praise is conceptualised as the provision of verbal encouragement that is focused on the learning behaviours exhibited. It can be thought of as the provision for the pupil of feedback on their behavioural performance. For this reason and some others we explore in the next section, our preference is for the term 'positive feedback' rather than 'praise'. When a reward is given, we would always expect positive feedback to accompany it so that the pupil still receives information on their performance. Positive feedback can contribute to the pupil's relationship with self by letting them know that their positive learning behaviours have been noticed and are valued. It is important for a teacher to recognise and respond differently to the exceptions, but most pupils, like adults, will like to hear when they have done something well.

When a teacher feeds back positively, it also has a potential impact on the pupil's relationship with others. Even in an interaction with a pupil over their compliance with a basic expectation, the positive feedback does not just relate to the behaviour: it conveys a message about the teacher–pupil relationship. For example, when a teacher acknowledges that a pupil has remembered their planner, they are also implicitly affirming to them 'I do notice when you get things right'. Such an interaction lets the pupil know that they are in a relationship with a teacher who recognises and values their efforts, rather than a relationship that is based on fault finding and criticism.

However, although many pupils may experience positive feedback in this way, a note of caution should also be sounded here. The pupil's relationship with others does not just include their relationship with their teacher. Adopting a B4L approach involves selecting and evaluating strategies rather than expecting to follow a recipe for best practice. For some pupils, their relationship with peers may be damaged by receiving positive feedback or a reward from the teacher because to be seen to gain teacher approval is not desirable. Consideration therefore needs to be given to the way in which feedback is given. For example, it may need to be given more privately or in a depersonalised way.

Finally, the positive feedback can also provide reinforcement of the learning behaviours associated with the pupil's relationship with the curriculum. For example, the teacher might positively recognise the pupil's personal organisation or their problem-solving strategies when they encountered a difficult part of the task.

Positive feedback rather than praise

Although 'praise' is the term that is in common usage (e.g. DfE 2011a, 2014a; TA 2012) our preference is for the phrase 'positive feedback'. We would argue that, when the term 'praise' is applied in an educational context, it needs to be understood as referring to positive feedback. If praise is interpreted in the more conventional, publicly accepted sense, there is an implication that the act that attracts it is of a significant magnitude to be deserving of a high level of approval, admiration or commendation. We might, for example, hear on the news of a member of the public praised for their quick thinking and bravery in an emergency situation. This person is very different from a pupil who has, for example, remembered to put their hand up rather than calling out, or has remembered to bring the right equipment to a lesson. We believe that this is why some teachers find it difficult to accept the idea of praising pupils; it seems incongruous to *praise* a pupil for conforming to basic expectations, especially those that many others routinely follow. However, giving *feedback* on performance is something teachers do regularly and necessarily in relation to learning. We would suggest that we need to think in terms of *feedback* in relation to behaviour as well. With older pupils in particular, using a phrase like 'Fantastic, John, you've remembered to put your hand up' may seem insincere to the praise giver, the praise receiver and the observers. However, in the same situation we could say, 'John, thanks for waiting, how can I help?' This provides positive feedback on performance and conveys, in a low-key way, that the teacher notices when a pupil demonstrates the required behaviour.

What do we know about effective positive feedback?

O'Leary and O'Leary (1977, cited in Brophy 1981: 12) indicated that teacher praise must have the following qualities to function effectively as reinforcement:

1   Contingency: the praise must be contingent on performance of the behaviour to be reinforced.
2   Specificity: the praise should specify the particulars of the behaviour being reinforced.
3   Sincerity/variety/credibility: the praise should sound sincere. Among other things, this means that the content will be varied according to the situation and the preferences of the student being praised.

In a seminal piece of work on the use of praise by teachers, Brophy (1981: 12) drew on a range of studies, including O'Leary and O'Leary's (1977) work, to make the distinctions between effective and ineffective praise shown in Table 6.1.

Brophy (1981) was referring to all uses of praise, not just in relation to behaviour. Informed by Brophy's suggestions, we would stress the following key points when using positive feedback to promote the development of learning behaviour:

• Feedback to individuals is provided within the context of a whole class approach where desirable learning behaviours are known, explicitly referred to and regularly reinforced.
• Phrase the feedback so that it is descriptive, providing information to the pupil on the learning behaviour they have exhibited that has drawn this positive attention. In the case of public positive feedback, this also allows other members of the class to hear information about the desirable learning behaviours.
• The feedback can be purely descriptive (e.g. 'John, I can see you are sitting up ready to listen') but if there is an evaluative element (e.g. 'Well done') it should form only a small proportion of the message.
• If a teacher just uses the evaluative element (e.g. 'Good', 'Fantastic', 'Well done') without a descriptive component, they are missing an opportunity to convey information to the pupil concerned and, if publicly given, others too about the desired learning behaviours.
• Positive feedback needs to be available for effort, improvement and achievements in both learning and behaviour.
• Within the positive feedback, any reference to the reasons for success should relate to factors the pupil can influence (e.g. their effort, sustained attention to the task) on future occasions.

Table 6.1 Effective and ineffective praise (Brophy 1981: 26)

Effective Praise	Ineffective Praise
1 Is delivered contingently	1 Is delivered randomly or unsystematically
2 Specifies the particulars of the accomplishment	2 Is restricted to global positive reactions
3 Shows spontaneity, variety and other signs of credibility; suggests clear attention to the student's accomplishment	3 Shows a bland uniformity, which suggests a conditioned response made with minimal attention
4 Rewards attainment of specified performance criteria (which can include effort criteria, however)	4 Rewards mere participation, without consideration of performance processes or outcomes
5 Provides information to students about their competence or the value of their accomplishments	5 Provides no information at all or gives students little information about their status
6 Orients students towards better appreciation of their own task-related behaviour and thinking about problem solving	6 Orients students towards comparing themselves with others and thinking about competing
7 Uses students' own prior accomplishments as the context for describing present accomplishments	7 Uses the accomplishment of peers as the context for describing students' present accomplishments
8 Is given in recognition of noteworthy effort or success (for *this* student) in relation to tasks	8 Is given without regard to the effort expended or the meaning of the accomplishment (for *this* student)
9 Attributes success to effort and ability, implying that similar successes can be expected in the future	9 Attributes success to ability alone or to external factors such as luck or easy task
10 Fosters endogenous attributions (students believe that they expend effort on the task because they enjoy the task and/or want to develop task-relevant skills)	10 Fosters exogenous attributions (students believe that they expend effort on the task for external reasons – to please the teacher, win a competition or reward, etc.)
11 Focuses students' attention on their own task-relevant behaviour	11 Focuses students' attention on the teacher as an external authority figure who is manipulating them
12 Fosters appreciation of and desirable attributions about task-relevant behaviour after the process is completed	12 Intrudes into the ongoing process, distracting attention from task-relevant behaviour

- Positive feedback should not be used in a way that is likely to be experienced as manipulative, insincere or 'all technique and no substance'.
- Positive feedback should not be 'overblown' – remembering basic equipment is worthy of positive acknowledgement (e.g. 'Good to see you've remembered your . . . ') but more than this may be experienced as patronising or insincere.
- Don't mix positive feedback with negative feedback. Human nature is to dwell on the negative component even if this only represents a small proportion of the overall

message. For example, if your aim is to reinforce settling to the starter activity, you would avoid a statement like 'You got on really quickly with the starter, it's such a shame that you . . .'

- Avoid the 'giveth and taketh away' approach of saying, for example, 'You've worked really hard today . . . for a change' or 'I see you've remembered your planner . . . at last'.

Remembering to give positive feedback

The Elton Report (DES 1989) contained the comment that 'in some schools a pupil can only get attention in one or other of two ways – by working well or behaving badly' (DES 1989: 99). Although 25 years old, this is still an observation that it is important to consider as a teacher in terms of monitoring and evaluating both the overall classroom climate you are creating and the experience of individuals within your class.

We have already covered one reason why some teachers may find it difficult to be more positive in the classroom. It may be that praising a behaviour that could reasonably be considered a basic expectation seems unnecessary. It is hoped that focusing on the notion of positive feedback will help in reconciling such concerns by drawing a parallel with the approach we would use to encourage learning. Canter and Canter (1992), the originators of the Assertive Discipline approach, put forward another argument as to why it may be difficult for teachers to remember to focus on and acknowledge positive behaviour. They had found through their observations that 90% of teachers' comments to pupils regarding behaviour were negative. Canter and Canter (1992) explained this by using an anxiety scale. They suggested that at 0 the teacher's anxiety is so low that they are probably asleep, 100 on the scale represents a panic attack and 50 the normal anxiety level within the classroom. If a pupil loudly disrupts or refuses to do as they are asked, then the teacher's anxiety level rises. Canter and Canter (1992) argued that there is a physiological reaction to a perceived threat that prompts the teacher to act to lower the anxiety that is currently causing a degree of discomfort. The action might be a verbal reprimand or the threat or imposition of a sanction. The physiological response when pupils are behaving well may be a drop in the teacher's anxiety level. As Canter and Canter (1992: 61) put it, 'There is no voice in your head telling you to do something immediately. No panic. No sense of urgency.' The suggestion in some texts (e.g. DfES 2005a; Dix 2007) that there should be a ratio of at least five positive comments to every negative comment is helpful as a reminder that may compensate for what Canter and Canter (1992) suggested is a natural tendency to react strongly to misbehaviour but give insufficient attention to positive behaviour.

Although ratios provide a quantitative means of monitoring teacher positivity within the classroom and reinforce the important message that teachers should focus more attention on the positive, it should be recognised that not all positive feedback necessarily carries equal weight. Positive feedback from someone who is important to the pupil and whose opinion they respect is likely to be more significant. The quality of the existing teacher–pupil relationship is therefore an important variable. A single piece of positive feedback from someone with whom you have a good relationship and whose opinion you respect may carry more weight than several pieces of positive feedback from someone for whom you have little regard.

Activity 6.1

This activity is intended to give a broad indication of your positivity within the classroom. Because you know this, you may be more positive than you would normally be. This is a known effect and does not matter – as with pupils who seem to behave well when they are being observed, it at least shows the behaviour is in your repertoire!

- Draw a seating plan of your class, ensuring that under each pupil's name there is space for recording. Have an additional box somewhere on the paper headed 'Comments to the class or groups'.
- Ask a colleague with whom you have a good relationship to observe one of your lessons.
- On the classroom plan, your colleague should use a simple code to record under a pupil's name any comments you directed to them. The code should cover:
    o positive behaviour-related comments
    o negative behaviour-related comments
    o positive learning-related comments
    o negative learning-related comments.

The same four categories should be used for 'Comments to the class or groups'.

- Before the observation you should agree on how certain interactions will be recorded. For example, some learning-related comments will simply be instructional. You may agree that these will be excluded, you might have an additional neutral category or you could decide that any comment that is not negative should be recorded as positive. In the next chapter, we talk about positive correction. For example, you might say, 'John, facing this way, thanks' as an alternative to 'John, stop turning round'. Although the wording is positive, this is still responding to unwanted behaviour, so you might decide this sort of comment is still classed as 'negative behaviour related'. Remember, however, that this is not a statistical exercise, nor is it intended that you should compare yourself with anyone else, so absolute consistency in recording is not required. It is just helpful to the observer to have some idea in advance of how to record these examples when there might be an element of doubt.
- Look at the results of the observation. Consider questions such as:
    o What is the balance between the different categories of comment overall?
    o How many positive behaviour-related comments did you make compared with negative behaviour-related comments?
    o Are there some individuals who received no comments of any kind from you?
    o Are there some pupils who received only negative behaviour-related comments from you?

(continued)

(continued)

> o Does the plan reveal sections of the room where most of the comments were negative behaviour-related comments?
> o Are there gender differences reflected in the distribution of the different types of comment?
>
> • Of course, one reaction when you see that a pupil has received a number of negative behaviour-related comments might be that this was the result of the behaviour they chose to exhibit. This may be true but, if we think in terms of relationships and what it is like to be the pupil, there would be a concern if the only interactions with adults they experienced lesson after lesson and day after day were of this nature. There would be a need to consider carefully how positive aspects of the pupil's learning and behaviour, however small, could be identified and remarked upon.

Tailoring praise to individuals

As adults we may assume positive feedback to be, as its name suggests, a positive experience for pupils. The underlying principle is that, if a required behaviour is positively reinforced by something that the pupil finds rewarding, they will be more likely to exhibit that behaviour again in the future. If this is a major purpose of providing positive feedback, then it makes sense to attempt to deliver any positive comment in a form that the pupil prefers and is likely to experience positively.

Public or private positive feedback

Some pupils prefer public acknowledgement; others prefer their positive feedback to be low key and one to one. The choice of strategy for reinforcing behaviour needs to be based on a prediction of how the individual is likely to experience it. If they experience public positive feedback as embarrassing and/or a threat to their social standing within their peer group, then their interpretation may be that it is not positively reinforcing at all.

Depersonalising positive feedback

We have already touched on the possibility that some pupils may find it difficult to accept praise, and suggested that a stronger emphasis on the descriptive component within positive feedback may help. However, an alternative for those pupils who experience difficulty in accepting even the types of comments that include just a positive inference is to depersonalise the positive feedback. For example, as an alternative to singling out an individual, a teacher could say, 'This group's worked well together. I liked the way you all took turns using the equipment. That's good collaboration.' Or 'I'm pleased to see everyone on this table's settled down and got their equipment out.' The hope would be that the individual pupil would make the connection themselves that this positive comment applied to them as much as the others.

Reducing the evaluative component even further

As we have indicated, effective positive feedback involves a descriptive element that gives the pupil information on the behaviour they have exhibited that has gained this positive attention. The evaluative element of the message (e.g. 'Good', 'Well done'), if one is included at all, represents quite a small proportion of the message. Some pupils may find it particularly difficult to accept positive feedback that contains any evaluative component. For example, a pupil with low self-esteem might find it hard to accept a comment such as 'Well done, you kept your cool and put forward your argument when others in the group disagreed with you', or 'Well done, you were sharing really nicely', because such strong positive messages may not fit with how they view themselves. Coopersmith (1967) suggested that individuals, when confronted with evidence they are better or worse than they themselves have decided, generally resolve any dissonance between this evidence and their own view of themselves in favour of their customary judgement. The pupil may, for example, attempt to resolve the experienced dissonance between their customary judgement and a positive evaluative comment by attributing externally (e.g. the teacher is just saying it but doesn't really mean it) or by taking some action (e.g. destroying their work or misbehaving) that attracts peer and adult reactions more consistent with their own view of themselves. As an alternative strategy the teacher could use a solely descriptive comment such as 'You settled really quickly to the starter today'. It would be more difficult for the pupil to reject this because it is simply a statement of fact and contains less of an implication that an evaluation is being made.

Positive feedback to the whole class

Following the principle of five positives for every negative will help to maintain a more positive atmosphere within the classroom. In the next chapter we will cover positive correction as a way of ensuring that, even on those occasions when you need to address unwanted behaviour, you can do so in a way that keeps the focus on the required behaviours. There will be times, however, when it is appropriate to provide some positive feedback to the class as a whole. Similar principles apply to those when providing positive feedback to individuals. Keep the focus on a description of the behaviour and frame the evaluative comment in terms of its effect on you. For example, at the end of an activity you might say, before moving on to the next activity or further instructions, 'I'm really pleased with how well you all listened while other people were feeding back on their experiments.' Such a statement indicates the effect on the teacher ('I'm really pleased') and the learning behaviour (listening while others fed back). However, we do not want to over-complicate this process or imply that it should be treated in a formulaic way. At the close of the lesson, a secondary teacher might simply say, 'Good lesson today, everybody. Look forward to seeing you next week.'

This is not overblown praise that says the pupils were brilliant or fantastic simply for doing what was required of them; it simply acknowledges that their individual contributions made it a collectively successful, and possibly enjoyable, experience.

Making effective use of rewards

Schools vary in the extent to which the class teacher is afforded the opportunity to develop their own class-based system of rewards. In some schools, there is a whole school system to which teachers are expected to adhere. For example, in a primary school a teacher might be expected to give out merits that, once a certain number is reached, lead to a head teacher's award. It is important that you find out your own school's system and work within it.

A taxonomy of rewards

The positive feedback already discussed is a form of reward. We would also include non-verbal signals of approval such as a smile or a thumbs up. A range of rewards commonly used by schools are listed in Chapter 5. Here, however, we move on to consider some of the principles associated with the effective use of rewards. It is useful to consider first where particular forms of reward fit within an overall taxonomy of rewards:

- Intrinsic rewards: an intrinsic reward is the most educationally desirable kind of reward. By intrinsic reward, we mean the kind of pleasure and satisfaction that a pupil gets from the work they are engaged in.
- Experience of success or making progress: this is the feeling of satisfaction experienced when a task is completed successfully or steps towards the end goal are achieved.
- Other people's praise or approval: this can be verbal, such as the positive feedback we have talked about in this chapter, or non-verbal, such as a smile.
- Preferred activities: in general, the opportunity to engage in a preferred activity will serve as a reward for engaging in a less desired activity.
- Token rewards: these include things such as house points, stars and stickers. They are referred to as tokens because they have no value in themselves, but represent something else that is valued. Sometimes the value of the token is that it represents success or another person's approval. As we have previously suggested, tokens may stand alone or be part of a system where a certain number of tokens collected leads to a particular reward.
- Tangible rewards: these include things such as sweets, small toys and vouchers with financial value.

(based on McPhillimy 1996)

As is perhaps immediately evident, applying the notions of intrinsic reward and the experience of success or making progress is more difficult when thinking about pupil behaviour. Intrinsic reward needs to be interpreted as demonstrating particular behaviours based on the understanding that it is right and proper to behave in this way rather than because a reward is on offer. We could, of course, debate at length what right and proper means and for whom, but for simplicity we will make the assumption that there are some generally accepted expectations in society of how people should behave towards each other and that adhering to these requires individuals to balance their own needs with those of the wider community.

The experience of success or making progress within the taxonomy of rewards is a little easier to relate to behaviour and certainly the positive feedback we have talked about in this chapter is a helpful means of contributing to this. However, behaviour is often evaluated in terms of the reduction or cessation of certain misbehaviours. While this is a form of progress, a key principle underpinning the B4L approach is that we should draw more parallels with learning. Typically with learning we focus on and encourage through positive feedback the development of and eventual mastery of skills. We should do the same for behaviour; if we can do this, then it is possible for the pupil to recognise their progress in this area.

With regard to tangible rewards in the taxonomy, we would suggest that teachers should think carefully and consult with colleagues about whether this approach is appropriate and necessary. Having attractive pencils or rubbers on offer as a reward when a pupil reaches a certain number of points may not cause too much concern, but offering sweets, for example, could be in conflict with the school's healthy eating policy. We are aware of a number of secondary schools that use shopping vouchers, cinema tickets or theme park tickets as part of their reward system and presumably find these effective motivators. We would suggest that the use of such high-level tangible rewards is not an approach to be adopted unilaterally by an individual teacher – not least because every so often a story hits the press about the use of such approaches. Typically such stories are not positive, name the school and go along the line of questioning why pupils are being given shopping vouchers, cinema tickets or theme park tickets just for turning up and behaving themselves.

McPhillimy (1996) makes the point that the higher level of rewards, such as intrinsic rewards, are educationally preferable. This is an interesting point to consider because most school systems are characterised by forms of token reward. However, an important aspect of the taxonomy of rewards is that often different levels of reward are used simultaneously. For example, if a pupil is given the opportunity to engage in a preferred activity as a result of maintaining attention on a less favoured task for a period of time, or awarded a sticker, the teacher can supply some positive feedback that helps the pupil to recognise what they have achieved. Although intrinsic motivation may be the aim, we would suggest that some supplementary extrinsic motivation in the form of positive feedback or a reward will not diminish this for those who are already functioning at this level. As we have remarked previously, in the context of a relationship it is simply a way for the teacher to indicate that they still notice and appreciate the pupil's efforts. Similarly, if positive feedback focused on learning behaviour is used (rather than bland praise) and accompanies any rewards given, we believe this does not reduce the chance of pupils developing intrinsic motivation. By providing this type of feedback, the teacher mediates the learning from the experience of receiving the reward. For some individuals, the positive feedback and rewards may be important in maintaining a level of behaviour that allows them to start developing intrinsic motivation as they come to realise that getting their work done, not getting into trouble and the more positive relationships they are able to build bring their own benefits.

Some rewards are simply standalone indicators of approval. For example, a young child might be given a sticker. Others, such as the example given previously of a merit system that leads to a head teacher's award, are based on the idea of working towards a longer term goal. With younger children in particular, a consideration may be whether they are able to connect several events for which they have received a token with a head teacher's certificate given out later. No doubt most individuals would be pleased to receive the certificate, just as they were to achieve the merits that led to it, but whether they necessarily appreciate that the string of merits is an indication they have behaved consistently well and are therefore deserving of the head teacher's certificate may be questionable. There is a case for directly teaching pupils what the different stages of a system such as this represent. Ideally, we would like the pupil to be able to give a developmentally appropriate answer to the question 'What did you get that for?' if asked about their reward.

Taking away rewards once given

Rewards that have been given should not be taken away from groups or individuals if a subsequent piece of misbehaviour occurs. The reason is that the positive behaviour happened and was deemed worthy of positive recognition at that time; to remove the reward effectively wipes out the significance of that event. There may be a temptation, with a whole class system such as the collecting of marbles in a jar (Canter and Canter 1992), to take away marbles for the misbehaviour of individuals in an attempt to capitalise on both an individual's sense of responsibility to the group and peer group pressure motivated by the eventual reward on offer. Two questions arise; the first is whether it can be guaranteed that the individual feels any responsibility to the wider group. Indeed, the pupils whose behaviour often causes the greatest concern for teachers are those who seem unable or unwilling to predict the effects of their actions on other people. The second question relates to the issue of the peer group pressure that it is typically assumed will occur. The hope may be that peers will have a quiet word with the pupil along the lines of 'Hey, come on, you're making it bad for the rest of us.' We have to ask ourselves whether this is a realistic expectation. Kohn is sharply critical of systems that mean the misbehaviour of individuals can delay or prevent the class from accessing a whole class reward in an attempt to encourage peer group pressure, suggesting, 'This gambit is one of the most transparently manipulative strategies used by people in power. It calls forth a particularly noxious sort of peer pressure rather than encouraging genuine concern about the well-being of others' (Kohn 1999: 56).

At this point we should highlight one approach that represents an exception to the principle that rewards, once given, should not be taken away. Some primary readers may be working in schools that operate the Golden Time system put forward by Mosley and Sonnet (2005). They present Golden Time as part of a whole school approach so, if it appeals to you as a method to use in your own classroom, we would advise reading *Better Behaviour through Golden Time* (Mosley and Sonnet 2005) to ensure you understand how the surrounding elements are intended to work together. In summary, under this system all children start the week with the same number of minutes of Golden Time each. If they infringe one of the Golden Rules, a minute of Golden Time is deducted. At the end of the week, pupils are able to engage in one of usually a range of Golden Time activities on offer. Those who have lost minutes of Golden Time through the week have to wait for this period of time before they can join the Golden Time activity. For younger children, this system may be operated on a daily basis rather than over a week because they may not be able to make a connection between behaviour early in the week and the reduction of their Golden Time at the end. This system appeals to some teachers because it gets around the concern sometimes voiced that pupils who behave well most of the time do not get rewarded. However, this should not be interpreted as licence to do nothing else; Mosley and Sonnet (2005: 47) suggest 'we need to praise to the skies the child who keeps the Golden Rules all day, every term' and include some copiable Golden Time certificates in their book to support this. Under this system, the pupil who consistently behaves well gets a reward in the form of their full amount of Golden Time. Mosley and Sonnet (2005) suggest that it is important for those who have lost minutes of

Golden Time to be able to see the activity they would have engaged in if they had chosen to heed the warning given before the loss of minutes. The recommendation is to use a sand timer so that the waiting pupil can see the time passing. Mosley and Sonnet argue that this has an almost hypnotic quality and is preferable to a watch or clock that may be 'indecipherable to a child who is hot with emotion' (Mosley and Sonnet 2005: 44). If you are contemplating using this system, it is important to consider the management implications of potentially having several pupils waiting for differing amounts of time before starting their Golden Time activities. Some pupils will experience this as intended and compliantly reflect on the fact that had they made different choices they could now be engaging in the Golden Time activities others are enjoying. Others may experience and interpret the period of waiting differently and the reminder of what they are missing may fuel resentment and anger. Mosley and Sonnet (2005) provide some guidance on what to do with pupils whom they class as 'beyond' Golden Time, so again we would recommend you read their book if you are considering this approach.

Consistency between colleagues in the use of rewards

When starting in a new school, try to gain an understanding of how readily rewards are given by other teachers. This will enable you to gauge how frequently you should give rewards and what they should be given for. You may, of course, disagree with what you see and feel that pupils need rewarding more or less frequently. However, it is important to recognise that pupils will make interpretations of any deviation. For example, in a secondary school, if copious rewards are given in English but very few in Maths, this potentially raises questions for pupils in terms of whether the rewards relate in any meaningful way to their performance in these lessons or are just a reflection of individual teachers' personalities. In a primary school, if the pupils are used to receiving frequent rewards in Year 3 but move to Year 4 and find they do not get as many, it may raise the question for some of whether they personally have become worse in their learning or behaviour.

It is difficult to remove entirely the subjective element in the use of rewards, but schools and individual departments can benefit from scenario-based staff development activities that explore what the response would be in a particular situation. The key points to explore through such activities are:

- the methods used before formal rewards to acknowledge and reinforce academic and behavioural effort, improvement and achievement
- use of the school's formal rewards system to acknowledge and reinforce academic and behavioural effort, improvement and achievement.

Monitoring the distribution of rewards in your class

Activity 6.1 provides a snapshot of the use of positive feedback but it is probably not an exercise that it is feasible to repeat often. Nevertheless, it is important to informally self-monitor who you are directing positive comments towards and who receives primarily negative comments or possibly no comments at all. It is easy to fall into a pattern where it is the same pupils who receive the positive comments all the time and the same pupils who receive the negative or corrective comments. Inadvertently, a relationship is built between the teacher and pupils based on these interactions, and there is even a risk that the teacher may over-focus on those who misbehave and end up picking up on minor behaviours that from other pupils might not be noticed.

The distribution of formal rewards is easier to monitor. If some form of recording is not already built into the system, we would suggest that you find some means of keeping track of the pupils to whom you are giving rewards. It is important to monitor in relation to, for example, ethnicity, gender, special educational needs and disability, and to take appropriate action when distribution implies that there may be some bias (DCSF 2009a).

As we have previously suggested, rewards should indicate what is valued by accompanying them with positive feedback, but unless you monitor the distribution there is a risk that you inadvertently convey messages about *who* is valued.

Conclusion

Through our experience, we would suggest that schools and individual teachers are now better at positively acknowledging pupils' behaviour than when the Elton Report (DES 1989) made its comment that pupils could only get attention by working well or behaving badly. However, it would be rare to come across a teacher who praises or rewards pupils *too* much. As we have intimated within this chapter, the reason why there is still a degree of reticence may be the implication in the use of the word *praise* that this needs to be fulsome, glowing and possibly gushing. This naturally triggers thoughts about whether we should be expected to or need to praise pupils for complying with basic expectations. Praise within the behaviour for learning approach is reframed as positive feedback and should be viewed in terms of a form of encouragement focused on the learning behaviours exhibited. It is intended to protect and enhance the pupil's relationship with self, relationship with others and relationship with the curriculum by providing information on behavioural performance. It is for these reasons that we advocate that rewards are also accompanied by positive feedback.

There will be some pupils who seem unmoved by positive feedback and rewards or even actively reject them. This should not be surprising, given that individuals experience and interpret positive feedback *as individuals*. It is important to recognise that not all pupils find the same types of reward motivating and so it may be necessary to consider how a rewards system that broadly works for the majority needs to be adapted for individuals. This might require giving the positive feedback more privately or depersonalising it. The pupil themselves might be able to provide some information on what they would like to happen when they have done something well. Asking them should therefore be included as an option when trying to problem solve, if the usual combination of positive feedback and rewards appears to offer little appeal.

Chapter 7

Effective use of positive corrections and sanctions

Introduction

This chapter can be seen as the sister to the previous chapter on positive feedback and rewards. Schools have been encouraged over many years through Government guidance documents (e.g. DES 1989; DCSF 2009a) to maintain 'a healthy balance between rewards and sanctions to encourage positive behaviour' (DCSF 2009a: 9). The Coalition Government's current guidance continues to reflect the need for both elements, requiring head teachers and governing bodies to 'ensure they have a strong behaviour policy to support staff in managing behaviour, including the use of rewards and sanctions' (DfE 2014a: 3). However, the document makes no reference to a need for the balance to be healthy and is itself firmly skewed towards disciplinary sanctions.

This chapter is based on the principle that strategies come before sanctions. It provides guidance on the language teachers can use in response to the more commonly occurring, predictable behaviours before considering how the sanctions available to a teacher can be applied effectively. Emphasis is placed on framing corrections positively, keeping a focus on the required behaviour.

However well it is done, responding when a pupil misbehaves is reactive, but this is not a term we use in a pejorative sense. The Elton Report was clear that 'Reducing bad behaviour is a realistic aim. Eliminating it completely is not' (DES 1989: 65) and so it is certainly necessary for teachers to know how to react to incidents of misbehaviour. However, it is also important to have regard for Kounin's seminal research in which he found that desist techniques for dealing with misbehaviour 'are not significant determinants of managerial success in classrooms' (Kounin 1970: 71). The implication is that, while teachers need to be competent and confident in the use of a range of strategies to respond to individuals who misbehave, there reaches a point of diminishing returns. Ultimately, becoming better at desist techniques, where *better* is interpreted as simply meaning knowing *more* strategies and applying these well, is unlikely to be the major contributory factor in securing and maintaining more positive learning behaviours within the classroom. It is important, therefore, to view the development of a language for correcting behaviour and the effective imposition of sanctions in the context of a broad range of other factors that contribute to and maintain more positive patterns of behaviour within the classroom. These include the planning and organisation of the lesson and the general quality of the teaching, as well as the use of positive feedback and rewards discussed in the previous chapter. As earlier chapters have explained, the development of learning behaviours is underpinned by three relationships of which one is the relationship with the curriculum. Current guidance for providers of teacher training on the knowledge, skills and understanding that trainees will need in order to be able to manage their pupils' behaviour is prefaced by the comment that:

> It is important to note that good teaching is the most effective way to get good behaviour. Teachers who plan and teach dynamic, stimulating lessons based on sound assessment and excellent subject knowledge are likely to experience fewer difficulties with behaviour.
>
> (TA 2012: 1)

From its inspection of schools, Ofsted (2011: 12) has also indicated some correlation between the quality of teaching and behaviour, reporting that 'where teaching is good pupils' behaviour is usually at least good as well'.

Positive correction and sanctions in the context of the behaviour for learning approach

This chapter seeks to provide a range of practical strategies for responding to misbehaviour that are compatible with the principles of the B4L approach if delivered in the intended spirit. They are intended to offer protection to the pupil's relationship with self and relationship with others (in particular with the teacher). The following points provide some guiding principles:

- The language used by the teacher is respectful.
- 'Put downs' and de-valuing terms should be avoided.
- The behaviour is the problem, not the person.
- Language, strategies and sanctions aimed at embarrassing the pupil in front of their peers should be avoided.
- Corrections and directions should be phrased positively to provide the pupil with information on the required behaviour.
- Language, strategies and sanctions used should encourage reflection and emphasise the pupil's choice in determining alternative outcomes.
- Use of the curriculum as a sanction should be avoided, unless 'logical', such as catching up on work missed as a result of behaviour.
- The aspiration should be that language, strategies and sanctions used contribute to the pupil learning more than just not to behave in this way in order to avoid punishment.

Within the behaviour for learning approach, the purpose of behaviour management is to promote learning (Powell and Tod 2004; Ellis and Tod 2009). This principle extends to the use of positive correction and the imposition of sanctions. Accepting this view supports teachers in keeping a clear focus on both the purpose and nature of any interaction with the pupil related to behaviour. A focus on learning prompts a number of considerations about the delivery of positive correction and sanctions:

- How can we apply the principles of curriculum learning to behaviour?
  In curriculum learning, the focus is typically on what a pupil needs to start doing or do more of in order to make progress in the subject rather than what they need to

stop doing or become less bad at. The same approach can usefully be applied when thinking about behaviour. Later in this chapter there is consideration of how to phrase correction positively in order to place emphasis on the required behaviour, rather than focusing on the unwanted behaviour.[1]

- What do the pupils learn from the behaviour that the teacher models?
  Managing emotions is one of Goleman's (1995) five domains of emotional intelligence and is incorporated within the SEAL curriculum (DfES 2005c, 2007). If this self-regulation is seen as necessary to develop in pupils, then it would seem reasonable that teachers model this in their interactions with pupils. If teachers get excessively angry or aggressive, particularly over relatively small issues such as failure to bring equipment or talking out of turn, it is questionable how this fits with developing in pupils the ability to manage how they express emotions, cope with difficult feelings and employ strategies for expressing their feelings in a positive way (DfES 2005c, 2007). What are pupils expected to learn about self-regulation if their teacher gets angry – whether real or feigned for impact – over a forgotten planner or textbook? Of course some pupils exhibit behaviour where to feel anger in response to their actions is entirely justifiable. Even with such incidents, there is a responsibility upon the teacher to model appropriate management of their feelings. A similar argument can be applied to the use of sarcasm, verbal put-downs and attempts to embarrass the pupil in front of their peers. While such methods may, on occasions, achieve some success in stopping the unwanted behaviour, they neither model nor foster positive human relationships. Indeed many teachers would rightly be concerned if any of their pupils demonstrated these behaviours towards others.

- How does the focus on learning affect disciplinary priorities?
  The timing and nature of a teacher's response should be informed by the extent to which the current behaviour has an impact on the development of pupils' learning behaviour. Pupils can still learn while wearing caps, trainers or make-up, nor does skirt length, the lack of a tie or the failure to do up a top button impair cognitive functioning. Although this may seem an obvious statement, many teachers expend a lot of time and energy on these matters. The suggestion, of course, is not that teachers should let these issues go; indeed it is important that they do adhere to policy on these matters because to fail to do so can make life more difficult for colleagues who do attempt to enforce the school rules. However, if the priority is learning, then it needs to be recognised that none of these uniform-related infringements, in themselves, impede this. The teacher therefore has a choice in *when* and *how* to address the issue, perhaps by giving one simple direction (e.g. 'John, cap off, thanks') or a rule reminder (e.g. 'John, you know the rule, coats off in class') as the class settle into their seats and then, if the individual remains non-compliant, pursuing this one to one once the rest are engaged in the lesson.

General considerations

Before exploring specific strategies related to positive correction and sanctions, it is important to consider a range of general principles and practices.

Plan for predictable behaviour

A survey conducted to inform the Elton Report (DES 1989) asked teachers to identify the behaviour they experienced over the course of 1 week in October 1988. Responses were returned by approximately 3,600 primary and secondary teachers. From this data, the Elton Report established that teachers had to deal most frequently with incidents of low-level disruption but more significant incidents of physical or verbal aggression towards staff were rare. This is a message that has regularly been reiterated (e.g. DfES 2005a; Ofsted 2005).

Activity 7.1

Look at Table 7.1, which sets out the results from the Elton Report (DES 1989) showing the percentage of teachers indicating that they had to deal with different types of pupil behaviour during their classroom teaching over a 1-week period.

Table 7.1 Percentage of primary and secondary teachers indicating they had to deal with different types of pupil behaviour during their classroom teaching over a 1-week period (based on DES 1989: 242)

Type of pupil behaviour	Reported frequency with which dealt with during lessons:			
	At least once during week		At least daily	
	Primary (%)	Secondary (%)	Primary (%)	Secondary (%)
Talking out of turn (e.g. by making remarks, calling out, distracting others by chattering)	97	97	69	53
Hindering other pupils (e.g. by distracting them from work, interfering with equipment or materials)	90	86	42	26
Making unnecessary (non-verbal) noise (e.g. by scraping chairs, banging objects, moving clumsily)	85	77	42	25
Physical aggression towards other pupils (e.g. by pushing, punching, striking)	74	42	17	6
Getting out of seat without permission	73	62	34	14
Calculated idleness or work avoidance (e.g. delaying start to work set, not having essential books or equipment)	67	87	21	25
General rowdiness, horseplay or mucking about	60	61	14	10
Verbal abuse towards other pupils (e.g. offensive or insulting remarks)	55	62	10	10

Type of pupil behaviour	Reported frequency with which dealt with during lessons:			
	At least once during week		At least daily	
	Primary (%)	Secondary (%)	Primary (%)	Secondary (%)
Not being punctual (e.g. being late to school or lessons)	53	82	11	17
Persistently infringing class (or school) rules (e.g. on dress, pupil behaviour)	50	68	13	17
Cheeky or impertinent remarks or responses	41	58	6	10
Physical destructiveness (e.g. breaking objects, damaging furniture or fabric)	16	14	1	1
Verbal abuse towards you (e.g. offensive, insulting, insolent or threatening remarks)	7	15	1	1
Physical aggression towards you (the teacher)	2.1	1.7	0	0

- How do the frequencies match with your own experiences?
- The list of behaviours is about 25 years old; are there any behaviours that you would add?
- Approximately how frequently do you encounter these?

Because we have some idea of those behaviours that are likely to occur with a degree of regularity, it makes it possible to plan for them. We would suggest taking some of the known frequently occurring behaviours and using the advice offered later in this chapter on positive correction in order to generate and rehearse either mentally or with friends or colleagues what you would say. This rehearsal will help to build confidence so that when such behaviour occurs you are more likely to react calmly and assertively.

Frame correction positively

Positive correction is not a strategy in itself; it is an overarching term used by Rogers (e.g. 2007, 2012) and within National Strategy documents (e.g. DfES 2003, 2004a) to capture the idea that teachers should seek to frame their correction and direction positively when misbehaviour occurs. A positive correction might, for example, be 'Stacey, facing this way, thanks'. We could contrast this with what could be termed a negative correction, such as 'Stacey, stop turning round'.

Framing corrections in terms of the required behaviours helps to keep the atmosphere of the classroom positive, unlike the frequent use of statements beginning or containing

'don't', 'no' or 'stop'. If we accept the Elton Report finding that 'schools with a negative atmosphere will suffer more from bad behaviour than those with a positive one'
(DES 1989: 89), then there is an obvious rationale to this approach. At the level of individual pupil experience and the general climate for learning, the classroom can become a
depressing environment if the air is filled with a continual stream of negatively expressed
messages, even if they are directed towards other pupils. If you have not looked at it yet,
we would draw your attention to Activity 6.1 in the previous chapter, which provides
a means of reviewing your positivity. There is also an argument that, if the required
behaviour is stated, this is the image that a pupil brings to mind, rather than the unde-
sired behaviour (Hook and Vass 2002). We have already made the point in relation to
the development of classroom rules in Chapter 5 that if we tell someone *not* to think of
something they will probably, at least momentarily, think of that thing. The same principle applies when verbally intervening when misbehaviour occurs. If pupils are going to
momentarily think of something in response to our intervention, then it would be better
that it was the required behaviour.

As we suggested earlier, it can be helpful to plan for the more predictable occurrences
and rehearse a response. Pupils will, for example, call out, leave their seat without permission and argue back. Framing corrections positively requires thought and practice
because it may not be intuitive. Taking the example of the pupil who calls out, the natural teacher reaction might be to say, 'Don't call out' or, if this is a regular occurrence and
the source of some frustration, even, 'Don't call out. How many times do I have to tell
you?' Positively framed alternatives as a response to this predictable occurrence include:

- 'Hands up without calling out, thanks . . . '
- 'Remember our class rule for asking questions.'
- 'Hands up so I can see your voice.'
- 'I can hear questions; I can't see hands up.'
- 'I get concerned when several of you call out . . . we end up not able to hear anyone.'

These examples are suggestions from Rogers (2011). From a behaviour for learning perspective, it is necessary to recognise that these interactions with pupils occur within the
context of a relationship and, as such, cannot be reduced to the level of a script or recipe.
As a reader looking at these suggestions, it is likely that you will have a reaction to them
based on imagining both yourself saying them and your pupils hearing them. While the first
two examples have a general utility that is difficult to argue with once we have accepted the
need to frame responses positively, the next three may raise issues. For example, you may
not feel you could deliver the line 'Hands up so I can see your voice' credibly because it
may not fit with your style and personality as a teacher. For some pupils, such as those on
the autism spectrum, this line might be problematic because it does not make sense when a
literal interpretation is applied. The fourth example, 'I can hear questions; I can't see hands
up', is also problematic in this respect. Its strength is that it is depersonalised – it does not
target anyone specifically – but it does require that pupils understand it beyond its literal
level as a descriptive statement and recognise the implication that they should put their
hands up rather than call out. The strength of the fifth example, 'I get concerned when
several of you call out . . . we end up not able to hear anyone', is that it is a form of 'I' statement. In other words, it starts by describing the effect on the teacher and the wider effect
on others. Like the fourth example, it does rely on pupils recognising the implication that

they need to change their behaviour in response. This aspect could be addressed by adding the action necessary to address the situation. For example, the teacher could continue with 'I'd like you to remember to put your hands up.' While there is a lot to commend this type of statement, the potential problem is the length. There may be some pupils who cannot cope with the amount of words in this instruction.

Awareness of an increased range of positive correction strategies may contribute to developing the confidence and competence that many trainees and qualified teachers seek in relation to the management of behaviour. However, the risk is that teachers become attracted to techniques and place their faith in the magic of the method. In other words, it would be possible for a teacher to arm themselves with a stock of lines acquired from, for example, Bill Rogers (e.g. 2011), Hook and Vass (2002) and National Strategy documents (e.g. DfES 2003, 2004a) without fully grasping that:

- although the adoption of these forms of language can contribute to the development of more positive relationships, the line is always delivered within the context of an existing relationship, which may be good, bad or indifferent, and this will influence how it is received
- the teacher needs to be able to deliver the line credibly, in a way that fits with their own personality and values
- the teacher needs to be able to select and adapt the line for different learners
- the pupil will have a reaction to the line and we need to be responsive to this – we cannot expect any interaction to follow a rigid script
- these lines will not work every time with every pupil; the teacher is simply increasing the likelihood of a more positive outcome more often through this good practice.

Adopt a 'least to most intrusive' approach when positively correcting

The DfE (1994a) offered the advice that:

> Interventions have to be carefully judged by teachers, using their knowledge of individual pupils or class groups, and doing no more than is needed to secure the desired change in the pupil's behaviour; as over-reaction may provoke unnecessary escalation of an already difficult situation and seriously limit the teacher's subsequent room for manoeuvre.
>
> (DfE 1994a: 14)

The missing element from this otherwise sound advice is that, by starting with the *lowest* level of intervention necessary to settle the behaviour, the teacher is minimising disruption to teaching and learning for the class as a whole. By intervening in a low-key manner, the teacher avoids becoming involved in a protracted, often very public interaction over behaviour that can have an impact on the pace and flow of the lesson and prove distracting to other pupils. To take an example, if the behaviour could be settled by the teacher simply carrying on with their lesson introduction to the class but moving to briefly stand near a pupil who is talking to their neighbour, then this would be preferable to a verbal instruction to face this way or stop talking. Rogers (e.g. 1997, 2007, 2012) conceptualises the notion of starting at the lowest level necessary to settle the behaviour as the 'least to most intrusive' approach. Figure 7.1 depicts this approach in visual form

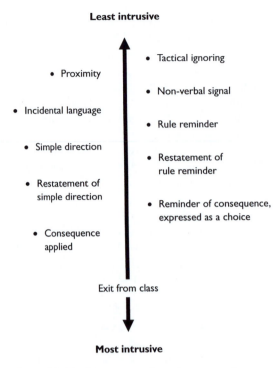

Least intrusive

- Proximity

- Tactical ignoring

- Incidental language

- Non-verbal signal

- Simple direction

- Rule reminder

- Restatement of
  simple direction

- Restatement of
  rule reminder

- Consequence
  applied

- Reminder of consequence,
  expressed as a choice

Exit from class

Most intrusive

Figure 7.1 The least to most intrusive approach

linked to a number of strategies discussed in this section of the chapter. This is not meant to be prescriptive – it is, for example, debatable whether *tactical ignoring* is less intrusive than *proximity*. Rather, the example is intended to convey the idea that the teacher needs to consider a gradual and graded set of strategies that they might employ.

Some strategies

This part of the chapter moves into a consideration of some examples of the strategies that could be employed within a least to most intrusive framework. The list is not exhaustive, nor are all the strategies as presented necessarily applicable to all age groups, although it is usually possible to adapt them based on the underlying principles.

Tactical ignoring

Tactical ignoring is a technique referred to by Rogers in a number of publications (e.g. Rogers 2011, 2012). It involves consciously deciding not to directly address a particular behaviour. The technique of ignoring the behaviour is underpinned in part by the assumption that teacher attention (even if negative) may act as a form of reinforcement that serves to sustain the behaviour. Care should be taken not to over-service behaviour with undue attention, but it should be recognised that teacher attention may be of little consequence compared with peer attention or approval (Wheldall and Merrett 1989).

Tactical ignoring is useful for minor off-task behaviour where the teacher is confident that the pupil will re-direct themselves to the task in hand without adult intervention. Tactical ignoring can be combined with the technique of praising the pupil as soon as it is noticed that they are demonstrating the required behaviour. This helps to show that the teacher is interested in positive behaviour and that engaging in such behaviour gains attention.

Proximity praise

Proximity praise is used in conjunction with tactical ignoring. Again, mainly useful for low-level misbehaviour, it involves tactically ignoring the pupil's misbehaviour while commenting positively on a pupil nearby who is demonstrating the required behaviour. For example, if Kerry is turning round talking, the teacher might say to another pupil near to her, 'Naomi, I can see you're facing the front ready to listen.' The premise is that Kerry will hear what the required behaviour is and adjust her own behaviour accordingly. The technique is made more powerful if, as soon as Kerry demonstrates the required behaviour, the teacher directs some positive feedback towards her.

With a primary aged pupil, two assumptions underpin the use of the proximity praise technique – that teacher approval matters to the pupil and/or the pupil has not noticed what the required behaviour is. At secondary level, it is likely that for a lot of pupils peer group approval will matter more than teacher approval, and so hearing somebody else receiving positive feedback may not provide sufficient motivation for a pupil to adapt their behaviour. This strategy therefore tends to be relevant in those cases where the judgement is that the pupil has just not noticed that the teacher is waiting for attention and hearing the required behaviour stated is a sufficient prompt.

Non-verbal signals

Most teachers already use a range of non-verbal signals. The 'teacher look' is one common example. This typically involves slightly prolonged eye contact, often coupled with a pause in speech, to indicate disapproval. There are numerous other examples:

- Raised eyebrows, pointing at the clock or at written expectations on the walls all have the capacity to prompt pupils to address their behaviour, while representing a low level of intrusion on the part of the teacher (Galvin 1999).
- Perhaps more commonly in primary classes, a teacher might put their finger to their lips to convey the need for quiet.
- If a pupil is frequently turning round, the teacher might catch their eye and make a rotating movement with their hand to indicate the need to face the right way.
- A thumbs-up signal can be used to convey approval and is likely to be understood as such by most pupils.
- The teacher raising their own hand can act as reminder to a pupil who calls out that they need to put their hand up.
- The teacher extending their arm horizontally with fingers pointing upwards and palm facing the pupil can be used to block a pupil's verbal interruption or as a signal to wait.

Many of these techniques are intuitive. Most pupils would understand their meaning without being told in advance. In highlighting the use of non-verbal signals as a specific strategy, Rogers (1997) also suggests that teachers can develop what he terms *privately understood signals* to be used with individuals or the class. These are signals where the meaning would not necessarily be clear without some prior explanation. Rogers (2007) gives the example of four fingers extended downwards to represent the four legs of a chair. This 'four on the floor' gesture offers a more positive alternative to repeated requests to sit properly.

Incidental language

Incidental language (Rogers 2011) involves the teacher making a casual observation with the implied meaning that the pupil or pupils address the issue. We have already given the example of 'I can hear questions; I can't see hands up.' Another example would be the teacher who, walking past a group, comments, 'it's a little noisy over here' or 'one or two people are talking a little too loudly'. The major strength of this technique is that it depersonalises the correction. However, as previously suggested, it needs to be used with some thought because some pupils, such as those on the autism spectrum, may apply a literal interpretation and not pick up on the implied need for action.

Simple direction

A simple direction (Rogers 2011) involves stating to the pupil the behaviour that is required. An example would be 'John, back in your seat, thanks.' Using the pupil's name helps to alert them that there is an incoming message. This cueing in of the pupil is important because they can sometimes find themselves in trouble either because they have not heard the first part of the instruction and have consequently not done as asked, or they have not had the processing time to stop what they are currently doing, think about, understand and comply with the direction quickly enough for the teacher. Putting a pause after the pupil's name and before giving the direction will help in gaining and sustaining attention (Hook and Vass 2002; Rogers 2007). Most pupils will respond to their name by giving eye contact. As Hook and Vass (2002) point out, sometimes it will be necessary to say the pupil's name more than once. The example would therefore become 'John . . . John . . . back in your seat, thanks.'

Rule reminders

Most schools and classes have a range of rules displayed (see Chapter 5). A clear, positively expressed set of rules opens up a range of positive, correctional language for the teacher. Rule reminders (Hook and Vass 2002; Rogers 2007, 2011, 2012) can take a number of forms. It is possible to say, for example, 'John, remember our rule for asking for help' or 'John, we put our hands up to ask for help'. In both cases the purpose is to minimise any dialogue so that the teacher is not distracted from other priorities such as taking questions from other pupils who have put their hands up. When the teacher wants the pupil to verbally rehearse the rule, they might phrase the rule reminder as a question such as, 'John, what's our rule for asking for help?' As explored in more detail later, you would only pose the question if you judged that at this point in the lesson you could afford to open up dialogue. If, for example, the interruption came as you were part way through an explanation to a focus group, then a straightforward ruler reminder expressed as a statement may be better.

Question and feedback

Questions generally invite an answer – even rhetorical ones if the listener does not appreciate the rhetorical nature. A key principle should always be not to ask a question if you do not want an answer. A question invites a pupil to engage in dialogue and as such is more intrusive than, for example, a simple direction or rule reminder. Galvin (1999) advises teachers to beware of the 'why' question and instead focus on 'what'. For many pupils explaining 'why' they did something is very difficult and the answers they give are likely to range from very limited (e.g. 'I dunno') through to sometimes vacuous, but socially useful, expressions of guilt (e.g. 'I was messing about when I should have been working') and convoluted accounts of events that attribute blame to a range of sources. Galvin (1999) suggests instead questions such as:

'What are you doing?'

'What should you be doing?'

'What did we agree about that?'

'What's the rule?'

'What do you need to do?'

'What do you think about what you're doing now?'

'Is that reasonable or fair?'

'Will that work be finished by breaktime?'

(Galvin 1999: 80)

It would be possible to question the utility of some of Galvin's suggestions. For example, 'Is that reasonable or fair?' asked of the pupil in relation to their misbehaviour conveys a strong message that the expected answer is 'No'. For the pupil to recognise this and respond accordingly is quite an important social skill but may carry little real meaning in terms of accepting that their actions were unreasonable or unfair. In discouraging the routine and frequent use of 'why' questions, it is important to recognise that pupils' explanations for events do contain important clues about their causal attributions that can inform interventions. The key message would therefore be that the frequent use of *why* questions (e.g. 'Why haven't you finished your work?', 'Why are you messing around?') as a behaviour management strategy for the classroom has limited utility. However, within a supportive dialogue with a pupil that is intended to explore the way in which they interpret situations, asking *why* is likely to be very necessary.

Hook and Vass (2002) and Rogers (1997) take the use of questions a stage further than Galvin (1999) and describe a technique that can be summarised as *question and feedback* based on a framework of questions. Question and feedback involves the teacher asking an open question such as 'What are you doing?' Common responses are likely to be 'Nothing' or 'My work' but in some cases the pupil might give a longer explanation. As with all techniques, the teacher's personality is a factor. The key to this technique is the ability to ask the initial question in a neutral manner, react calmly to the responses and to steer the focus back to learning. If as an individual, a teacher feels that they cannot do this, then this technique is not for them. With this caveat in mind, the following two examples illustrate how this technique can be very effective:

Example 1

Teacher: 'What are you doing?'
Pupil: 'Nothing.'
Teacher: 'What should you be doing?'
Pupil: 'My work.'
Teacher: 'Ok, so what's the next thing you need to do?'

Example 2

Teacher: 'What are you doing?'
Pupil: 'My work.'
Teacher: 'Ok, so what's the next thing you need to do?'

In both examples there is the possibility that the pupil may respond to the teacher's last question by saying that they do not know. In this case the teacher is able to return to a learning focus and explain. If, however, the pupil gives a response that indicates that they do know what to do, the teacher can simply say something like, 'Ok, so if you get on with that now and I'll come back in a few minutes and see how you are getting on.' Again, the dialogue and the teacher–pupil relationship have returned to a learning focus.

In most cases pupils will recognise the implication within 'What are you doing?' that the teacher has noticed exactly what they are doing and will reply 'Nothing' or 'My work'. However, as we have indicated, we are not working to a script. Some pupils may reply with a comment such as, 'I was only talking to Terry' or 'I needed to get something from my bag', or even the very honest 'I was just messing about'. The teacher is still able to follow this with the question, 'What should you be doing?' and then use the sequence outlined in examples 1 and 2. Alternatively, the teacher might decide that partial agreement, outlined later, is the more appropriate strategy to use.

Choice and consequence

A common message in relation to behaviour management is that pupils make choices about their behaviour (e.g. Canter and Canter 1992; Hook and Vass 2002; Dix 2007; Rogers 2011). They may, for example, choose not to treat another pupil with respect by using verbal 'put-downs'. This infringes a rule and there is a consequence for this choice. We have explored some of the thinking behind the idea of choices and consequences in Chapter 5. The language of choice:

- allows the teacher to focus on the behaviour rather than the pupil's character
- puts the responsibility for the behaviour on the pupil

- conveys the implicit message that a different choice was possible and will be possible in the future
- focuses attention on the pupil's choices, separating them from the behaviour of others
- depersonalises the interaction, conveying implicitly the message 'This is not a personal attack, you have chosen not to follow the rules and I am applying the appropriate sanction.'

(adapted from Dix 2007)

Consequences will vary according to the circumstances but are usually offered at the more intrusive end of the least to most intrusive hierarchy. It might be, for example, that the teacher says to a pupil, 'If you choose to carry on talking then you will need to work by yourself.' It is debatable whether the actual words 'choose' or 'choice' need to feature within every interaction of this nature. Over used, these can sound rather clichéd and more about technique than relationships. Arguably, choice is conveyed just as well in a statement like 'You either need to finish the work now, or you'll need to stay in at break time to complete it.' To emphasise the point, this could be followed with 'It's up to you' or 'It's your choice'. The key point is that the statement, whether specifically using the words 'choose' or 'choice' or not, conveys to the pupil that there is an alternative outcome that their behaviour can determine. These principles apply whether the consequence is an action such as moving to work in a different seat, a sanction or a referral to a senior member of staff.

Some further considerations

The preceding section outlined a range of strategies. There are a number of other points to consider when using these approaches.

Take up time

When directing or correcting a pupil, it is important to allow *take up* or *thinking* time (Hook and Vass 2002; Rogers 2011, 2012). The teacher might, for example, employ a simple direction like 'Put your mobile away, thanks.' The pupil, in putting the phone away, is effectively showing to the teacher and to their peers that they are accepting the teacher's authority over them. For some pupils this may represent a loss of face. To remain standing over the pupil awaiting compliance can exacerbate this feeling because the pupil needs to comply under the teacher's gaze and inevitably with other pupils watching to see what will happen. Allowing take up time avoids this. It involves the teacher issuing the direction and then moving away to talk to another pupil or attend to something else. It gives the pupil the opportunity to process the request, which is important for some, and then to take the decision whether to comply or not, out of the spotlight of teacher and peer attention.

As well as the benefits for the pupil in terms of allowing them to save face by not having to comply so publicly, take up time is also beneficial for the teacher. When the teacher moves away they, of course, remain vigilant with regard to whether the pupil has complied with the direction or not. If the pupil has complied, then the teacher can decide when to go back and engage in a positive interaction about the task or behaviour to show that the relationship is still intact. If the pupil has not complied, then, having moved away from the interaction, the teacher is in a far better position to take a considered decision about the next action necessary than if they were standing over the pupil awaiting compliance.

Tactical ignoring of secondary behaviours

Sometimes pupils will exhibit a *secondary behaviour* (Hook and Vass 2002; Rogers 2007, 2011, 2012) in response to a positive correction by a teacher. Typically these are behaviours with an irritating or provocative quality. They convey a degree of minor resistance, implying 'I'm doing it, but grudgingly'. For example, the pupil told to put a mobile phone away in their bag might comply but 'tut' or make a mumbled comment while doing it. Having the mobile phone out during a lesson can be thought of as the primary behaviour and is the behaviour that the teacher originally set out to address; the tutting or mumbled comment is the secondary behaviour. Some pupils may be consciously or subconsciously using secondary behaviours as a way to deflect attention from the primary behaviour. By attending to the secondary behaviour, the teacher is effectively both succumbing to this agenda and reinforcing the diversionary use of secondary behaviour as a successful strategy. Other pupils may be using it as a face-saving strategy to show either the teacher or their peers that although they are complying they are offering some resistance. Limiting this minor face-saving strategy may provoke some pupils to offer greater resistance as a means of preserving face, or contribute to resentment of the teacher for putting them in this position where they have to publicly totally capitulate.

The *default* position should be to ignore the secondary behaviour. There will be times when professional judgement, based on knowledge of the pupil and the context, determines a different response. The most obvious example is if the secondary behaviour is of a level that means that it assumes the status of a primary behaviour and has to be dealt with. There may be other occasions however. The key point is that the teacher should not simply be *reacting* to secondary behaviours. When unsure, the default position is to ignore, keep the focus on the primary behaviour, and follow up the secondary behaviour later if it is a cause of concern. If the secondary behaviour is of concern, then it is usually better to call the pupil aside at the end of the lesson 'for a quick word' and address the issue privately and calmly. When we make this point in training sessions, often somebody will ask whether by not dealing with the secondary behaviour others in the class will think the pupil has been allowed to get away with it or that they can behave in the same way. There are a number of points to make in response to this. We are only referring to the *secondary* behaviour; the pupil has complied with the direction in relation to the *primary* behaviour. There will be very few pupils, if any, who will mentally note the teacher's apparent non-response to the pupil tutting, mumbling something under their breath or following the instruction a little grudgingly as a weakness or an opportunity to capitalise upon later. The benefits for the teacher of *not* getting involved in a prolonged discussion and interrupting the pace and flow of the lesson outweigh the minimal risks of copycat behaviour. If a teacher does decide to follow up the secondary behaviour and take the pupil to one side at the end of the lesson, this is likely to make more of an impression on the individual and the class than the necessarily limited discussion they would be able to have at the time the secondary behaviour occurred. From the perspective of the pupil's relationship with self and relationship with others, the secondary behaviour needs to be viewed as a clue to how they are experiencing the initial correction; they are showing that they need to save face in front of their peers or protect their own self-image by offering a little resistance. Tackling them at the time might push them into more of this behaviour based on these needs. Taking them to one side removes the audience and so reduces the need to engage in behaviours to save face. It also reduces availability of these behaviours because to be effective they usually need some form of audience to play to. From the perspective of the other pupils, word will get round that the particular pupil has been kept back. We believe the vernacular among pupils is 'He's getting done' or 'He's gonna get done now', and so the significance of this occurrence is not lost on the rest of the class and may be afforded more status than the more entertaining interaction that may have ensued had the teacher tackled the secondary behaviour in the lesson.

Partial agreement

The implicit assumption so far within this chapter is that the pupil accepts the positive correction – even though they might not respond to it, in which case the teacher will need to consider their next step on the least to most intrusive scale. Some pupils, however, will argue back. Partial agreement (Hook and Vass 2002; Rogers 2011) is a helpful technique in this situation. When pupils argue back, the temptation may be to challenge this rather than keeping the focus on the behaviour the initial interaction was intended to address. For example, a teacher, observing that a pupil is failing to get on with the task because they are talking, might say, 'Michael, the writing needs to be finished by break. If you carry on talking, then you will need to stay in and complete it.' From the teacher's perspective, this is a reasonable reminder of the consequence if the behaviour continues. However, the use of a particular strategy, whatever its good practice credentials, cannot guarantee the pupil's response. Michael might respond with 'I wasn't the only one talking; why don't you tell them?' Partial agreement involves framing a response that acknowledges the concern expressed but re-states the original message. For example, the teacher might say something like 'Maybe you weren't the only one, but at the moment I need you to get on quietly. I'll keep an eye on the others.' Hook and Vass (2002) argue for the additional consideration of the meaning conveyed by 'but' in this sentence, instead preferring the word 'and'. 'But', they suggest, implies disagreement because it usually prefaces a counter perspective.

This technique is also useful when pupils draw attention to the apparent inconsistent application of the school rules by colleagues. For example, when directed to follow a seating plan, a pupil might say, 'Mr Smith lets us sit where we like'. Partial agreement can be used here as a way of the teacher avoiding being drawn into justifying their right to implement a seating plan, publicly criticising a colleague for not following school policy or reacting with an aggressive response like 'I don't care what happens in Mr Smith's class; in my class you sit where I tell you.' Using partial agreement, the teacher could instead say something like 'Maybe he does . . . (small pause to allow the pupil to recognise that the teacher is not going to argue or confront) . . . In our class we have a seating plan, so I'd like you to sit there.' Depending on the pupil and the situation, it might be appropriate for the teacher to offer, 'If you are unhappy with where you are sitting then we can talk about it at the end of the lesson.' This sort of offer would be particularly applicable if the pupil was raising an issue of unfairness or favouritism. If the issue is genuinely important, they will be willing to give up a little of their own time to have their views heard.

Delivering blanket messages

Up until now the assumption has been that the behaviour to be addressed is restricted to a small number of pupils to whom positive corrections can be delivered individually. Sometimes, however, the behaviour is more widespread and it will be necessary to stop the class to reinforce the expectations of behaviour. This needs to be handled carefully because there are two potential problems:

1   Having to talk to the whole class is a very serious step and implies that the teacher has been unable to stem the tide of individual behaviour (Kyriacou 2007). An unfocused catalogue of wrongdoings delivered in an aggressive or exasperated tone may serve to reinforce this to pupils.
2   The sizeable minority who were behaving appropriately may be alienated if they feel they are being included in the blanket negative message.

The teacher can address both these problems by considering the language they use. The teacher might say, for example, 'Many of you were too noisy coming in today' because this allows those who came in appropriately to feel that they are not getting the blame. Other phrases might be, 'There are rather too many people . . . ' or 'I know it wasn't everybody but some people . . . ' Delivered calmly, these sorts of phrases also convey the message to the class as a whole that the teacher has weighed up the proportions and taken a decision as to how to act. In all cases, the statement of the problem should be followed by a statement of the required behaviour, or a reminder of the appropriate class rules or routines. Contrast this approach with sentences that start, 'This class is far too noisy . . . ' or 'How can anybody be expected to work with this noise . . . ' or 'I will not have this noise . . . ' These types of comment emphasise the global scale of the problem.

The use of sanctions

Sanctions come *after* strategies. At the end of the least to most intrusive hierarchy of strategies, the teacher reaches the point of imposing a sanction. This might be a class-based sanction such as working away from peers at a separate table, staying in at lunchtime to complete work not done in the lesson, a formal detention, exit to another class or area in the school, or referral to a senior colleague. As Chapter 5 explored, there are a number of types of sanctions used in schools. In this chapter, the focus is primarily on how these are issued by the classroom teacher.

Avoid unnecessary escalation

When a teacher positively corrects a pupil or imposes a sanction, this is not an emotion-free interaction, even though through the approaches described in this chapter we attempt to reduce the emotional component. The pupil may be upset, angry or resentful and it is very easy for the situation to escalate, particularly in schools that operate quite rigid tariff systems based on a sequence of steps the class teacher should follow. For example, the pupil, possibly annoyed after a first formal warning from the teacher, may continue to disrupt. The teacher could simply give one consequence after another until the pupil ends up being sent out of the classroom (Canter and Canter 1992). However, if employing the B4L approach, the teacher should be sensitive to how the first warning is experienced from the pupil's side of the relationship and be responsive to this. This might mean that, rather than rigidly adhering to policy and progressing to the next consequence, it is better to follow Canter and Canter's (1992) advice and either move in closer to the pupil to discuss the situation more privately or have a brief word with the pupil just outside the classroom door. We would suggest a conversation along these lines:

> 'Connor, you've received *<state the point in the sanctions hierarchy that has been reached>* and you have still carried on *<state the problem behaviour>*. If you choose to continue with this behaviour then I will need to *<state the next consequence in the sanctions hierarchy that has been reached>*. I need you to *<state the required behaviour>*'.

Depending on how receptive to this message the pupil appears, you might decide to offer the opportunity of some time to calm down. This can be an explicit suggestion to the pupil or you could direct them to do something that has the effect of giving them a few minutes to calm down, such as running an errand.

As with all behaviour management issues, professional judgement is crucial and this is why we have applied the subheading of 'Avoid unnecessary escalation'. Often it is entirely appropriate to move from one consequence to the next if the pupil continues with the behaviour. This, after all, is the point of the system. It is important to attempt to recognise the difference between the pupil who has locked themselves into a particular emotionally driven trajectory where intervening in a different way may be appropriate, and those who appear to be making more deliberate choices about whether or not they heed warnings and sanctions already imposed.

Make use of the full range of sanctions available

In suggesting that you should make use of the full range of the sanctions, we are not implying that you should progress to higher levels for behaviour that could be addressed without this. However, it is important not to create implicit ceilings on how far you will go in following the school's sequence of steps. Therefore, if your school's policy says, for example, that the next step after the point you have reached is referral to Head of Year, then this is what you should do. Otherwise, pupils will begin to see that you only ever get to a particular point in the class-based stages of your discipline plan and then stop.

An associated issue is those pupils who always seem to go through the class-based stages and get referred on beyond this but show no obvious behavioural change. Primary readers, typically encountering the pupil all day, every day, may have more responsibility and opportunity to develop individualised behaviour management plans, possibly in discussion with the SENCO or with advice from external agencies. Secondary subject teachers may only encounter the pupil once or twice a week. In this situation, unless notified of an alternative behaviour management plan that has been set up, the default position is to adhere to the school's policy. In other words, do not stop following the sequence of steps, just because the steps do not seem to work in changing behaviour. Secondary teachers will often say to us that they do not know what to do because every lesson the pupil is disruptive. The answer in the *immediate* situation when the behaviour is occurring is to follow the school's policy – unless to progress to this stage is predictably likely to lead to a more significant incident (see Chapter 9). A robust school policy will have systems (such as 'on call' staff) for such situations.

Of course, alongside following systems in the immediate situation, as part of being a professional you would:

- consider the purpose the behaviour is serving for the pupil and contextual variables open to your influence that may be having an impact on that behaviour
- reflect on whether there are things that you could do differently in the future to reduce the possibility of the behaviour occurring and escalating
- share your observations and concerns regarding the pupil's classroom behaviour with appropriate colleagues, such as the SENCO, pastoral staff and the senior leadership team.

Remember that the sanction is the sanction

Whatever the sanction, it should be imposed calmly and assertively as an inevitable consequence for the choices the pupil has made. It should not be seen as an opportunity to harangue or berate the pupil in an attempt to make the sanction matter more to them. In many cases it will not achieve this and it may also allow the pupil to shift the focus from their own behaviour towards resentment of the teacher. As we suggested in Chapter 5, the learning that we want the pupil to take from the sanction is that this is a consequence they could have averted by making different choices. This is important in learning about taking responsibility for their actions and recognising that it is within their power, through the choices they make, to affect what happens to them. A further practical consideration is that, if a pupil feels that the sanction is a personal attack, this is far more likely to create a confrontation.

The behaviour is the problem not the person

The principle that it is the behaviour that is the problem, not the individual, applies not just to the imposition of sanctions but to any interaction with the pupil about their behaviour. It is a principle that links with Roger's (1951) concept of unconditional positive regard. In school contexts, this can be interpreted as a relationship with the pupil that is based on accepting them as a worthwhile individual whatever they may do, say or feel, and believing them to be capable of changing their behaviour (Chaplain 2003; Cornwall and Walter 2006). However, it should be clear that unconditional positive regard does not mean that the teacher approves of the behaviour or allows it to go unchecked, (Chaplain 2003; Cornwall and Walter 2006). As Cornwall and Walter (2006: 81) stress, 'It is possible to have unconditional positive regard, while at the same time drawing clear boundaries about behaviour and expecting the young person to take the consequences for their behaviour, both positive or negative.'

When imposing the sanction or overseeing it (in the case of a detention, for example), make it clear in any interaction that may be necessary that it is the behaviour that is contrary to the school or class rules that has attracted the sanction. This reflects the broader behaviour management principle that we label the behaviour, not the individual. Therefore, it is the behaviour that is disruptive, unkind, unpleasant, naughty and so on, not the pupil. Maintaining this focus helps to convey the idea that it was the pupil's choice in behaving in this way that led to this sanction and different choices are possible in the future. To give a simple example, it is the difference between saying, 'You are a very unkind boy' and 'That was an unkind thing to do'.

What have I done to deserve this?

In Chapter 6, we suggested that it is important for the pupil to know why they have encountered a positive consequence. Therefore, we recommended that when a reward is given it is always accompanied by positive feedback that provides the pupil with this information. The same is true with regard to sanctions; the pupil needs to understand why they are receiving the sanction. This understanding needs to be more than just recognising, for example, that they received a certain number of ticks on the board. In the case of in-class sanctions, such as sitting away from the group, there is little opportunity to do more than just remind the pupil of the choices they have made. For example, the teacher might say, 'Kirsty, I gave you the choice of working quietly in your group. You have chosen to carry on disturbing the others. I need you to work by yourself now at the table by the door.' If the pupil is required to attend a formal detention or come back at break time or during lunch time, there is more of an opportunity to ensure they are clear about why they have received the sanction. There should be a clear distinction between ensuring the pupil understands why they have received the sanction and berating them for the behaviour that led them to this point. The discussion should be calm and matter-of-fact. In achieving this, it may be helpful to think about how you would check a pupil was clear about errors they had made in their academic work – it should be little different for behaviour.

Time out and thinking chairs

In a secondary classroom, a teacher might have some single desks available where pupils who have been through a least to most intrusive sequence can be directed to work away from the group. It would be rare for a secondary subject teacher to direct a pupil to go to a location within class for time away from the group without the expectation that they should continue with the required task. The temporary separation from peers is the sanction. Locating a pupil away from their group but with nothing to do potentially creates another discipline problem, particularly as the behaviour that has led them to this point has already indicated that they are unwilling or unable to comply with the teacher's expectations. If the pupil needs time out that is more than just continuing with their work away from the group in the classroom, this tends to be managed through a whole school system such as the use of a remove room or sending to another class.[2] For secondary teachers, it is important to understand how these systems operate, including expectations regarding the class-based stages to be followed first.

Some primary teachers operate forms of 'time out' within their classrooms that are more than simply requiring the pupils to continue with the task but away from their peers. This might simply be referred to as 'time out', although other terms might be employed such as the 'thinking chair'. The term 'time out' emphasises that this is a sanction by reinforcing the message that it is a period away from the group, whereas referring to a 'thinking chair' or 'reflection chair' places the emphasis on what the pupil needs to do there. We make this distinction not to imply a preference but just to highlight the difference. The choice teachers make regarding these terms is likely to be dependent on the age of pupil taught. Younger primary pupils may readily accept the term 'thinking chair' whereas older pupils might prefer the term 'time out'. Ultimately though, whatever the term, the aim is that the pupil should reflect on the behaviour that has led them to this point. The term 'thinking chair' may convey this through its name and remind pupils of the discussion the teacher will no doubt have had with the whole class about its purpose. 'Time out' does not convey the need for personal reflection through its title but, again, at the start of the year when talking about the rules and establishing expectations of behaviour the class teacher would have ideally explained its role. If the time-out area is a fixed location in the classroom, it is possible, as Rogers (2007) suggests, to have an illustrated chart on the wall explaining its purpose.

We have deliberately avoided the use of the term 'naughty chair' because this labels the pupil since presumably the kind of person who would need to sit on such a chair is a naughty one. This reflects the principle outlined earlier that we label the behaviour, not the pupil. We are, however, reminded of a research visit we made once to a particular school. The head teacher showed us around the infant department and we went into one class that had a chair set up with various labels, including arrows suspended from the ceiling indicating that this was the 'thinking chair'. The head teacher asked a nearby pupil what the chair was for. She duly replied 'It's the naughty chair.' Clearly, pupils will experience and interpret our disciplinary measures in their own way and it seems that, despite the school's best efforts, this pupil, and quite probably others, simply viewed this as the 'naughty chair'. The key point, however, is that if adults use this term it legitimises the interpretation. From the adults the pupils need to hear consistent messages that remind them of what is expected of them during the period of time out.

Inevitability, not immediacy

In Chapter 5, we stressed that the relationship between choices and consequences needs to be one of inevitability rather than severity. We should not, however, equate inevitability with immediacy. Although it is desirable, particularly with younger pupils, for the consequence to follow as soon as possible after the behaviour to which it relates, this principle should not override professional judgement. If, for example, you have directed a pupil to remain behind at break and they slip out either intentionally or because they have forgotten, you do not need to pursue them around the playground. You have a professional choice to make. If you feel that you want to go out to the playground and tell them to come back in, then you can, but if this requires your scouring a large site (as might be the case in a secondary school) or you suspect that with the heightened stimulus of the playground environment they will just run away, then adhere to the principle of inevitability. Watching a teacher giving chase to a pupil is potentially very entertaining for spectators and also contributes to the pupil's state of emotional arousal, meaning you have a potentially more significant incident to deal with than the initial behaviour that led to your wanting to keep them behind. Adhering to the principle of inevitability avoids this type of scenario. They may have slipped out at break time rather than staying behind but they know, and their peers know, that this will be followed up. In this particular example, you might see the pupil at lunch time instead, this time being more vigilant as the class leave the room to ensure that there is no opportunity for them to slip away. You then have the choice of whether you focus just on the original behaviour or, if you consider the earlier slipping away to be a deliberate act rather than forgetfulness, you may choose to comment on this as well. It is important that the pupil, and other pupils, recognise that there are consequences for actions and these do not go away.

Repair and rebuild

When a teacher positively corrects a behaviour or issues a sanction, this is underpinned by some adult assumptions already outlined in this chapter. The assumption is that the positive correction is experienced positively, addressing the behaviour but minimising risk to the pupil's relationship with self, with others and with the curriculum. The sanction is the consequence for a particular sequence of choices made, rather than a punishment. Despite the adult interpretation, the pupil may simply feel they have been told off or punished. Probably, however positively we frame the correction or imposition of a sanction, the relationship between the teacher and the pupil is placed under a degree of strain. How much strain comes back to the perennial issue of how the event is experienced and interpreted by the individual. Interpreting the teacher's positive correction as 'a fair cop' may cause minimal strain whereas, if the pupil interprets it as unfair or just another example of adults curtailing their enjoyment, the strain on the relationship may be greater.

After positively correcting behaviour or imposing a sanction, make a point of working to repair and rebuild the relationship. All we mean by this is taking action that attempts to put the relationship back on a positive footing. This might be very low key, such as a short time after a positive correction going back to the pupil and checking on how they are getting on with the task. Or you might remark on something positive you notice them doing. This does not require you to make any mention of the past behaviour. It is simply a way of showing that the positive correction happened but the relationship is intact – at least from your side. The same principle applies if you have issued a within-class sanction such as directing the pupil to sit by themselves. It is a little different if you have issued a deferred consequence such as a detention. In this case, the pupil has to complete the lesson with the sanction still hanging over them. Make low-key contact such as checking on how they are getting on with the task or remarking on something positive you notice them doing, but be receptive to the subtle behavioural cues; if they appear resentful, you may decide it is better to say nothing unless required routinely as part of the lesson or because of their behaviour. Make a point of speaking to them after the detention or other deferred consequence. Professional judgement based on knowledge of the individual should determine the nature of this conversation. For some pupils, the course of action might be simply to make a point of talking to them early on the next time that you see them about something that is unrelated to the behaviour, just to show them that the relationship is back on a positive footing. For others, a more direct approach may be better. The teacher might say something like:

> Last lesson I had to give you a detention because you chose to carry on talking after I had given you two warnings. Remember that you need to concentrate on your own work without disturbing others. I know you can do that, so let's see some really good learning today.

This interaction:

- makes reference to the past behaviour
- makes clear the required learning behaviour
- ends with an upbeat comment expressing high expectations.

Monitoring the distribution of sanctions

Activity 6.1 in the previous chapter encouraged you to evaluate your level of positivity within the classroom. The same exercise also allows the identification of the proportion of teacher comments made in a lesson that focused on correcting misbehaviour. It is also possible to see who those comments are directed towards. As we previously noted when considering positive feedback, it is probably not feasible to repeat such an exercise very often. However, it is important to informally self-monitor who you are directing behaviour-related corrective comments towards. As we suggested in the previous chapter, it is very easy to fall into a pattern where the same pupils only receive these types of comment. This has implications for the nature of the teacher–pupil relationship.

It is easier to keep a check on the distribution of sanctions. If some form of recording is not already built into the system, we would suggest that you find some means of keeping track of the pupils to whom you are giving sanctions. This data can then be reviewed. It is important to monitor in relation to, for example, ethnicity, gender, SEN and disability, and to take appropriate action when distribution implies there may be some bias (DCSF 2009a).

Conclusion

This chapter provides a starting point in developing a range of strategies and approaches to respond to more commonly occurring, predictable forms of classroom behaviour. The approaches detailed here are simply intended to increase the chances of a more positive outcome, with more pupils, more of the time.

It should be recognised that any quest for a definitive set of strategies that will work with all individuals in all circumstances is likely to prove futile. Rather the focus needs to be upon identifying which strategies work best with which individuals under which conditions. The reality is that the individual is not a passive recipient of the teacher's management techniques. They will experience and interpret any behaviour management technique as an individual. Therefore, the teacher's positively expressed correction can be textbook quality in its content and delivery, but be interpreted by a particular pupil as unreasonable, the oppressive hand of authority, victimising or embarrassing. Perhaps most importantly, it should be recognised that positive correction and use of sanctions are responses to a problem that has occurred. While we hope this chapter has encouraged a more reflective approach to responding based on how teacher actions are likely to be experienced by the pupil, there is no doubt that this represents a reactive activity. Focusing on the techniques to react more effectively should not be a substitute for engagement with more proactive approaches that establish the context and conditions where problematic behaviour is less likely to occur.

Notes

1 The term 'unwanted' here is used for brevity and refers to the teacher's perspective. It is acknowledged, however, that the behaviour has meaning and purpose for the individual and may be anything but unwanted from *their* perspective.

2 Under DCSF (2009b) guidance on such facilities, this term was recommended in preference to terms such as 'inclusion room' or 'seclusion room'. Current guidance from the Coalition Government (DfE 2014: 12) refers to 'isolation rooms'.

Chapter 8

Individual differences and special educational needs

Introduction

This chapter is concerned with individual pupils who exhibit significant behaviour problems and who do not respond as intended to the day-to-day behaviour management strategies used in the classroom. The rationale for referring to both individual differences and special educational needs (SEN) is to encompass all those whose behaviour gives considerable cause for concern. We have not sought to make a distinction between those pupils with significant behavioural problems who, based on criteria within the *Special Educational Needs and Disability Code of Practice* (DFE 2014a) may be classified as having SEN and those who are not. The 2014 SEN Code of Practice replaces the DfES (2001) *Special Educational Needs Code of Practice* from September 2014 and states that:

> Persistent disruptive or withdrawn behaviours do not necessarily mean that a child or young person has SEN. Where there are concerns, there should be an assessment to determine whether there are any causal factors such as undiagnosed learning difficulties, difficulties with communication or mental health issues.
>
> (DfE 2014a: 85)

Within this new national policy for SEN (DfE 2014a), the familiar SEN category of behaviour, emotional and social difficulties (BESD) is being replaced by social, emotional and mental health difficulties. As can be seen from the earlier quote, there is emphasis within the 2014 SEN Code of Practice on identifying and addressing the underlying factors that contribute to a pupil's behavioural difficulties.

As a class and/or subject teacher, you have responsibilities for teaching *all* pupils in your class, including those classified as having SEN. This is a well-established principle (e.g. DfEE/QCA 1999a, 1999b; DfES 2001, 2004b).

It is also a point emphasised again in the 2014 SEN Code of Practice through its statement that 'Teachers are responsible and accountable for the progress and development of the pupils in their class, including where pupils access support from teaching assistants or specialist staff' (DfE 2014a: 88).

The key messages to take from this are that:

- the responsibility is not always yours alone; other interventions and support may be provided by others
- although as class teacher you may not always be providing the support or intervention for the pupil, you are expected to understand what is being done and the intended outcomes of this, and to contribute to or lead on the monitoring of impact.

In light of these responsibilities, it is important that you develop an understanding of the changing perspectives (e.g. DfE 2014a) on identification and assessment in relation to behaviour as a special educational need. This is important because class and subject teachers can be crucial to the early identification of SEN and associated behavioural difficulties. It is also, of course, important that you develop an awareness of ways of problem solving in relation to the behaviour of any individual pupils exhibiting considerable behaviour problems.

Pupils with SEN or individual differences in behaviour will not be passive recipients of their classroom environment but will be required to relate positively to the curriculum on offer, and to their teachers and peers. Their own individual differences and experience will have an impact on how they feel about themselves, and this in turn will influence their behaviour.

Assessment of a pupil's individual educational need, SEN or otherwise, is largely informed by their behaviour in the context of their school and classroom. If, for example, a pupil experiences emotional problems that have a negative impact on their behaviour, this in turn will affect their schoolwork and classroom social interactions. Their behaviour in the classroom consequently reflects the interdependence of social, emotional and cognitive factors. This has implications for how the teacher makes decisions about the strategies and approaches that will best bring about change in the pupil's behaviour.

In this chapter, we have continued to apply the B4L approach as a tool for supporting teachers to both understand and improve pupil learning behaviour in the classroom. However, this chapter differs from others in the book because it applies the B4L approach in its 'extended' use form (see Chapter 1). This usage takes due account of the fact that some pupils exhibit 'clusters' of behaviour that reflect a combination of their emotional, social and cognitive differences and/or delays. If we succeed in eliminating or decreasing one aspect of their behaviour (e.g. running around the room), they are likely to replace this with another disruptive behaviour from the cluster, such as 'shouting out'. For such pupils, we need to explore further the learning and social *relationships* that underpin their behaviour in class. It is anticipated that improving these relationships will bring about changes to the cluster of behaviours that the pupil is exhibiting in class. This fits with a common sense view that, when we improve our own relationships with others, with our subject curriculum, or with ourselves, this has an impact on a range of our behaviours. Within the B4L approach, there is a focus on the behaviour we need to develop in order to improve the pupil's relationships for learning and participation in the classroom.

Such an approach differs from a more traditional SEN diagnostic or medical model where there is a focus on how an individual *differs from* a population average or norm in terms of their development and behaviour. The rationale for using the B4L approach is that, although a medically underpinned *diagnosis* of, for example, an autism spectrum disorder (ASD) will enable teachers to have some degree of understanding and preparedness for such pupils, it does not prescribe how any one *individual* will behave in a particular class, with a particular teacher, in a particular lesson or subject area. The next section discusses this further.

How useful are labels and categories?

When encountering individual differences in behaviour, one response may be to find 'labels' or 'categories' for such pupils so that we can differentiate them from the rest of the class. We may, for example, use labels to 'explain' pupil behaviour. For example:

- 'He's got ADHD so that's why he's always calling out.'
- 'She has dyslexia so that's why she is not getting on with her work.'
- 'He has BESD so that's why he keeps messing about.'

The perceived advantage of using labels is that the label carries with it information about what we can expect when we encounter a pupil who has been allocated that label and the best way to teach them. As you may have experienced, some labels are more useful than others in this respect. If a pupil's behavioural differences are such that they have been 'diagnosed' as having ASD or attention deficit hyperactivity disorder (ADHD), then there is a particular body of knowledge and research that could inform teaching and learning strategies and provide some understanding of how they are likely to be experiencing their world. However, it needs to be remembered that such knowledge relates to the heterogeneous group of individuals who share that label. It should not serve to deny individual differences in learning and behaviour that are evident within a particular category or grouping. More importantly, a label should never be used as a reason to restrict aspirations and expectations for the individual concerned.

A label of BESD, like its predecessor EBD (emotional and behavioural difficulties) and the replacement category of 'social, emotional and mental health difficulties' conveys very little. As we explore in more depth later, it represents an exceptionally broad category, stretching from withdrawn behaviours through to violence and aggression. All we might be able to say with any confidence is that pupils falling within this category do not relate to others in the manner generally expected, or required, in group settings (Ellis and Tod 2009). Consequently, the question 'What do I do with a pupil who has "behaviour, emotional and social difficulties"?' cannot be directly answered without gathering more information about:

- that pupil's particular behavioural characteristics
- the conditions under which they occur
- their response to tried and tested behaviour management strategies.

The issue with using any SEN labels for pupils who exhibit behavioural difficulties is that such labels are very broad. Some labels carry an inference of a biological difference, others a mixture of social and emotional factors, and some a complex interaction of all three. This point is illustrated by the categories of SEN within both the 2001 SEN Code of Practice (DfES 2001) and, more recently, the 2014 Code (DfE 2014a). Both versions have four broad core categories with three of them remaining the same across the 13 years between the publications. The 2001 Code referred to:

- communication and interaction
- cognition and learning
- sensory and/or physical needs
- behaviour, social and emotional development.

(DfES 2001)

As previously mentioned, in the 2014 Code (DfE 2014a) 'social, emotional and mental health difficulties' replaces the category 'behaviour, social and emotional development'.

Both versions of the SEN Code (DfES 2001, DfE 2014a) recognise the broadness of the SEN categories. For example the 2014 Code states:

> . . . individual children often have needs that cut across all these areas and their needs may change over time. For instance, speech, language and communication needs can also be a feature of a number of other areas of SEN, and children with an Autism Spectrum Disorder may have needs across all areas.
>
> (DfES 2014a: 74)

It should also be recognised that 'SEN' itself is essentially an administrative and socially constructed category. It tells teachers little about the pupil who will be sitting in front of them, except that they meet a set of largely subjective, interpretable criteria designed to identify SEN set out in the Code of Practice (DfES 2001) (Ellis and Tod 2012). The 2014 Code makes the point that 'The purpose of identification is to work out what action the school needs to take, not to fit a pupil into a category' (DfE 2014a: 86).

The next section considers when and why an individual's behavioural differences and/ or delays meet the criteria for classification as SEN. Although many teachers do not have direct or sole responsibility for the assessment and identification of SEN (Ellis *et al.* 2012), most work collaboratively with their Special Educational Needs Coordinator (SENCO) by supplying information about rates of progress, interactions with other pupils and response to provision.

Behaviour as a special educational need

Before considering behaviour as a special educational need, it is important to be clear about the definition of SEN. The 2014 Code of Practice states: 'A child or young person has SEN if they have a learning difficulty or disability which calls for special educational provision to be made for him or her' (DfE 2014: 4). A learning difficulty is defined as 'a significantly greater difficulty in learning than the majority of others of the same age' (DfE 2014: 9). Special educational provision is described as 'provision different from or additional to that normally available to pupils of the same age' (DfE 2014: 83).

The definition of SEN and these expanded definitions of a learning difficulty and special educational provision have, apart from some minor changes in the wording, remained the same since the 1981 Education Act.

It follows that in order for a pupil with behavioural difficulties to be classified as SEN, there is a need to provide evidence that they have a significant 'learning difficulty'. The 2014 Code uses rate of progress, or an attainment gap between the child and their peers, as a way of assessing a learning difficulty. While this assessment of a learning difficulty is largely illustrated in relation to academic attainment, the Code states that 'it can include progress in areas other than attainment – for instance where a pupil needs to make additional progress with wider development or social needs in order to make a successful transition to adult life' (DfE 2014a: 84).

A noticeable difference in the 2014 Code, most likely in response to Ofsted's (2010) concerns about the over-identification of SEN, is an emphasis on the underlying teaching quality: 'High quality teaching that is differentiated and personalised will meet the individual needs of the majority of children and young people. . . . Special educational provision is underpinned by high quality teaching and is compromised by anything less' (DfE 2014a:14).

Both the 2001 Code (DfES 2001) and the 2014 Code (DfE 2014a) are based on a graduated response to the pupil's SEN. The expectation is that the school will put in place the level of support needed to support the pupil 'in making good progress and securing good outcomes' (DfE 2014a: 89). This graduated approach is likely to work best for those whose needs are fairly stable across contexts and conditions. Pupils exhibiting behavioural difficulties may not fit well with a graduated response.

Their difficulties are often far from stable across contexts and conditions because they can suddenly surface via an unpredictable incident of harmful and/or dangerous behaviour but at other times be relatively settled. There may be times when the pupil needs intensive support and other times when they need very little. The school environment also exerts an influence. It has been noted that behavioural difficulties are 'often engendered or worsened by the environment, including schools' or teachers' responses (DfE 1994b: 4). A similar point was made in the 2001 Code of Practice (DfES 2001: 44) in relation to all pupils with SEN through the suggestion of the need to recognise that 'some difficulties in learning may be caused or exacerbated by the school's learning environment or adult/child relationships'. Consequently, it may be the case that with some adults, with some peers or in some subjects, the behaviour does not occur.

In considering individual differences in behaviour, a question we might reasonably ask is whether a pupil can be considered to have an SEN in the form of social, emotional and mental health difficulties if they are not currently exhibiting the level of behaviour we would associate with the label. Of course, the reality is that most schools base their identification on patterns of behaviour over time and pupils' proneness to exhibit problematic behaviour, even if in certain contexts or for periods of time this does not occur.

The assessment and identification of behaviour, social and emotional difficulties as an SEN has never been straightforward. The fluctuation in behaviour in response to context and conditions described earlier is one of the complicating factors. Another is the difficulty in defining who might fit within such a broad category. Guidance on emotional and behavioural difficulties produced in the mid 1990s suggested the following:

> The behaviour of these pupils may be evident at the personal level (for example through low self-image, anxiety, depression or withdrawal; or through resentment, vindictiveness or defiance); at the verbal level (for example the child may be silent or may threaten, or interrupt, argue or swear a great deal); at the non-verbal level (for example through clinginess, or truancy, failure to observe rules, disruptiveness, destructiveness, aggression or violence); or at the work skills level (for example through an ability or unwillingness to work without direct supervision, to concentrate, to complete tasks or to follow instructions.
>
> (DfE 1994b: 7)

In the face of such an extensive list, we may conclude that we might all be 'a bit EBD' from time to time. However, the guidance stresses that the judgement as to whether the pupil has EBD will be based on 'the nature, frequency, persistence, severity, abnormality or cumulative effect of the behaviour compared with normal expectations for child of the age concerned' (DfE 1994b: 4).

In describing BESD, the 2001 Code referred to pupils 'who demonstrate features of emotional and behavioural difficulties, who are withdrawn or isolated, disruptive and disturbing, hyperactive and lack concentration; those with immature social skills; and those presenting challenging behaviours arising from other complex special needs' (DfES 2001: 87).

The 2001 Code also viewed presenting 'persistent emotional or behavioural difficulties which are not ameliorated by the behaviour management techniques usually employed in the school' (DfES 2001: 53) as a trigger for 'interventions that are additional to or different from those provided as part of the school's usual differentiated curriculum offer and strategies' (DfES 2001: 52).

The adoption of the replacement term 'social, emotional and mental health difficulties' in the 2014 Code of Practice (DfE 2014a) indicates a change in thinking regarding the assessment and identification process. In seeking to define the range of pupils who might be considered to have social, emotional and mental health difficulties, the 2014 Code states:

> Children and young people may experience a wide range of social and emotional difficulties which manifest themselves in many ways. These may include becoming withdrawn or isolated, as well as displaying challenging, disruptive or disturbing behaviour. These behaviours may reflect underlying mental health difficulties such as anxiety or depression, self-harming, substance misuse, eating disorders or physical symptoms that are medically unexplained. Other children and young people may have disorders such as attention deficit disorder, attention deficit hyperactive disorder or attachment disorder.
>
> (DfE 2014a: 87)

The synthesis of emotional, social and mental health factors in this description is not entirely surprising. There had previously been recognition in the category descriptors of the 2001 Code (DfES 2001) that there is some overlap between the group of children with BESD and those who have mental health problems. The 2014 Code (DfE 2014a) has endorsed this view by emphasising the 'causal' role mental health problems have in relation to behaviour. This is consistent with a view that effective intervention might require locating a 'root cause' for an individual's behaviour (DfE 2011b).

Although not stated explicitly in the 2014 Code (DfE 2014a), it seems reasonable to conclude that a 'perceived' root cause of a pupil's behavioural difficulties is likely to play a part in whether they are classified as SEN. Clinical and medical 'causes' may become more influential than environmental factors in decision making under the guidance within the 2014 SEN Code (DfE 2014a). Such a stance would not take into account that long-term adverse *environmental* conditions can be just as valid as a stable pervasive 'root' cause such as a medical or clinical condition.

The implication for teachers and schools is that they should be responsive to advice within the revised Code (DfE 2013c) that assessment of pupils with behavioural difficulties should include rigorous assessment for any as yet unrecognised learning difficulties that allow for the pupil to meet criteria for membership of any of the existing four categories of SEN.

Applying the Behaviour for Learning conceptual framework to individual differences and special educational needs

Pupil behaviour in the classroom cannot be understood by just focusing on the pupil's individual differences or deficits. Each interaction with the curriculum, teacher and peers involves a dynamic reciprocal relationship, with each affecting the other. Within this context, the individual seeks to make sense of their own ongoing individual experience. Interestingly, in special school settings where pupils have a higher level of need, teachers often find it useful to conceptualise pupil behaviour as 'communication' (Ellis *et al.* 2012). This allows them to ask the important question: 'What is the pupil's behaviour telling us about how they are experiencing what is going on in the classroom?'

The B4L approach is based on the view that an individual pupil's behaviour can best be understood by considering how that pupil is responding cognitively, socially and emotionally to the group setting of the classroom environment. As such, it is suited to the task of problem solving around BESD and its replacement, social, emotional and mental health difficulties.

It would not suffice to try to explore these aspects of functioning by just 'testing' or 'assessing' a pupil *outside* the classroom. We need to understand how the pupil is actively adapting and responding to what is going on in their classroom so that we can understand why they are behaving in the way that they are. More importantly, we can hope to identify under what conditions they behave at their best so that we can try to create these in order to facilitate development of the most appropriate learning behaviour.

In using the B4L approach, it is important to recognise that the three core relationships (with self, with others and with the curriculum) are:

- reciprocal
- interdependent.

Reciprocity within a relationship

If we consider a pupil who has been identified as having speech, language and communication needs (SLCN) and appropriate action is taken to address their barriers to learning and participation, then there may be no behavioural issues. If this does not happen and the pupil experiences frustration and failure in learning, then they may respond by exhibiting behavioural problems and develop a negative relationship with the subject area being taught.

Interdependence between relationships

If a pupil experiences a lack of self-belief and confidence (i.e. a relationship with self issue), this can have an impact on their relationship with others and/or their relationship with the curriculum. Although how we feel about ourselves can have a pervasive effect on our learning and social behaviour, the interdependence between emotional, social and cognitive functioning allows us to use the curriculum and social groupings to improve a pupil's perception of self.

The pupils we are referring to in this chapter exhibit significant behavioural difficulties that are unlikely to be addressed by reliance on any one set of strategies or changes to rewards and sanctions ratios. For this reason, we draw on the principles of reciprocity and interdependence and use the Behaviour for Learning conceptual framework to try to understand:

- how the *quality* of each one of the three relationships has an impact on a pupil's behaviour
- if there is a significant imbalance *between* the three relationships that is having an impact on the pupil's behaviour.

Pertinent to this chapter is the consideration that, for some pupils with significant behaviour, emotional and social difficulties, their relationships with the curriculum and with others are compromised and their emotional state drives their behaviour. Although we refer to cognitive, social and emotional aspects of functioning separately for the purpose of understanding and/or explaining a pupil's behaviour, we fully acknowledge that individuals do not experience that separation. This helps us to be vigilant if there is a significant imbalance – as is the case when a highly emotional individual does not respond to our trying to reason with them (see Chapter 9).

In order to support children with significant individual differences and/or SEN, teachers need to be aware of any potential limiting factors associated with the individual's difference and/or disability. They then need to use this knowledge to adopt flexible approaches to learning, teaching and assessment in order to maximise learning and participation.

Why do pupils misbehave?

Although it is important to have an understanding of why children misbehave and why some children demonstrate more challenging behaviour' (DfE 2011a: 3), it is unlikely to be feasible, or necessary, to explore the reasons for the behaviour of most of the individuals in your class. However, for the few individuals with persistent problems, 'going beyond the surface' in order to better understand why they are misbehaving will enable you to refine your strategy use.

Why are some pupils not responding to my behaviour management strategies?

Most teachers use behaviour management strategies that reward positive behaviour. In addition, they often give pupils choices about behaviour along with an explanation of the consequences of their choice. Implicit in the use of these strategies is the assumption that pupils are making a decision to behave in a particular way. This is not always the case. For example, pupils on the autism spectrum often take language very literally and struggle to understand figurative language. Some therefore may respond to the teacher's comment 'You are going to have to pull your socks up' by literally carrying out that action, not recognising that by this statement the teacher meant they needed to get on with the task. In this example, the pupil has experienced the instruction differently from the way that the teacher intended. The pupil has in fact been compliant based on their interpretation and, as such, is not misbehaving. Such a pupil would not of course be sanctioned for this behaviour. Most teachers know that their schools have to take account of SEN and disability within their behaviour policies and practices.

This example brings out an important point when dealing with individual differences in behaviour in the classroom. In this case of the pupil on the autism spectrum, it is reasonable to conclude that they did not have the skill to comply with the teacher's intended instruction. In such a case, the teacher might need to find out more about the pupil's individual differences with regard to language and communication and make necessary changes – such as avoiding the use of idioms or teaching the pupil some common ones. The behaviour that is expected of such pupils needs to be made explicit and not open to interpretation (Law and Plunkett 2009).

The reason teachers need to distinguish between those pupils who 'cannot' 'and 'will not' behave is that it informs strategy choice. Recognising these pupil differences also allows them to understand why some individual pupils are not responding as expected to their classroom behaviour management strategies. *School Discipline and Pupil-Behaviour Policies* identified three broad reasons 'why some pupils may behave inappropriately' (DCSF 2009a: 53). Each reason has implications for the teacher's response:

1 Pupils who do not have the necessary understanding or skills.
   Any ongoing sanctions for non-compliance are likely to be ineffective in cases where the pupil is simply unable to produce the desired behaviours or complete the set learning task.

2 Pupils who can behave but choose not to.
   Sometimes it is difficult to understand why a pupil keeps risking punishment for persistent behaviour misdemeanours when the teacher knows that they can behave if they want to. The notion of choice needs some elaboration in this context. It is perhaps more helpful to think of the current behaviour as serving a *purpose* for the pupil.

3 Pupils who have the necessary skills but are experiencing trauma.
   Pupils included in this category are those who have the necessary understanding and competences to follow school rules but who, because of particular life experiences, act in ways that are often irrational and unhelpful to themselves or others. As noted earlier, 'irrational' behaviour may be entirely rational if it serves a purpose for the individual. It is clearly important to understand pupil behaviour from *their* perspective and not just the logic behind schools' behavioural policies. But 'irrational' can also be sudden, unpredictable behaviour, without any clear purpose, even from the individual's perspective. Most schools and teachers would agree with the DSCF (2009a) guidance that noted this group of pupils as presenting the greatest challenges to schools in relation to the application of behaviour policies. Normally such policies require teachers to look at the antecedents of behaviour in order that they can employ preventative strategies or de-escalate the situation more effectively when the behaviour starts to occur. Such tactics, although intrinsic to effective behaviour management policies, will not suffice for this group of pupils. Trying to establish what 'purpose' the behaviour is serving for the pupil is helpful in that it encourages teachers to try to understand behaviour from the pupil's perspective.

Exploring the reasons behind the behaviour

The individual pupil

Each pupil exhibiting behavioural difficulties will differ in the kind of behaviour they present. As a consequence, it is often difficult for policy makers, researchers and teachers to describe what a pupil with behavioural, emotional and social difficulties is like. There is consistency between researchers and policy makers (DfE 1994c, DfES 2001, Evans *et al.* 2004) that such pupils exhibit a *cluster* of behaviours. These include:

- age-inappropriate behaviour or that which seems otherwise socially inappropriate or strange
- behaviour that interferes with the learning of the pupil or their peers (e.g. persistent calling out in class, refusal to work, persistent annoyance of peers)
- signs of emotional turbulence (e.g. unusual tearfulness, withdrawal from social situations)
- difficulties in forming and maintaining positive relationships (e.g. isolation from peers, aggressiveness to peers and adults).

Given this cluster of behaviours, it is clearly difficult for teachers to tackle the issue by systematically seeking to eliminate or reduce the problematic behaviours one by one. Likewise, it can be difficult to explain why a pupil's behaviour can change quickly from being vulnerable and tearful to being aggressive and resilient to discipline.

The situation for the teacher is that, if an individual is experiencing anxiety or a heightened emotional state, they cannot predict their behaviour because this will, to some extent, be driven by context. In the company of an empathetic adult, the individual may be tearful, with peers they may be aggressive, with their work they may be disengaged and withdrawn.

For this reason, we are seeking to understand the interplay between the individual's emotional, cognitive and social functioning as a route to addressing their myriad of behavioural problems.

Activity 8.1

In Table 8.1, the first column sets out a range of behaviours exhibited by individual pupils when they go off task. The adjoining columns pose a possible explanation for the pupil's behaviour and, based on this, suggest a possible action.

Table 8.1 Different explanations for the behaviour of pupils who are not getting on with their work (adapted from Powell and Tod 2004)

Frequently observed behaviour	Possible explanation for pupil behaviour	Desired learning behaviour	Possible action
Shouting out and distracting others	The pupil is getting more attention by being off task		Consistently reward on-task behaviour
Keeps looking around and asking questions	Pupil thinks they are unable to do the task.		Work with the pupil to reappraise task, identify what parts of the task they can do/ need help to do
Does not start the task – uses strategies to avoid starting	Pupil fears failure		Offer increased adult or peer support so that success is assured to start with – work to increase success but also work with class to 'make positive use of mistakes/ errors'
Makes noises, does not stay in seat, does not respond to or comply to requests	The pupil's behaviour is consistent with that allowed in their home environment. Other children in the family may run around a lot at home and are unsupervised in the street		Build on the positives, emphasise existing behaviour management strategies, model/teach skills, possibly involve in a nurture group or social skills group. Work with parents and pastoral colleagues

Frequently observed behaviour	Possible explanation for pupil behaviour	Desired learning behaviour	Possible action
Does not direct attention to the task given to them, short attention span, keeps asking questions, fidgeting	Perhaps the pupil has a learning difficulty e.g. attention deficit hyperactivity disorder (ADHD) and/or a language difficulty		Seek advice from the SENCO, personalise and emphasise existing class behaviour management e.g. rule reminders, pace of work, instructions, distractions, external rewards
Not listening, wandering about, playing aimlessly with pen/pencil	This may be due to overall developmental delay – the pupil may not be ready to work independently. There may be an underlying sensory difficulty and/or language difficulty		Seek advice from the SENCO. Consider a possible need for allocation of additional adult support; set more suitable learning challenges

Consider these questions:

- Based on the information provided in columns 1 and 2, can you identify a learning behaviour you would seek to develop?
- Based on the information provided in columns 1 and 2 *and* the learning behaviour you identified, how effective do think the suggested actions are likely to be?
- Can you think of any additional and/or different actions to those listed?

For pupils who exhibit a wide range of behaviours when they are off task, there may be a combination of explanations for their behaviour. A pupil may experience a chaotic home environment, fear failure *and* have a learning difficulty. The key point to be taken from Table 8.1 is that there is a need to consider which strategy or combination of strategies is likely to be the most effective in dealing with which behaviours.

The individual pupil and the effect of their classroom relationships

The B4L approach seeks to explore the nature of, and balance between, the pupil's cognitive, emotional and social behaviour as a route to addressing their behavioural difficulties. This involves looking closely at the types of relationship they are experiencing in the classroom – namely, with the curriculum, themselves and others. The following four case studies seek to illustrate this approach through a teacher's analysis of real-life incidents of disruptive behaviour.[1] Each case study is followed by a behaviour for learning commentary exploring key points and the issues arising.

Case study 1: Incessant whispering and talking in class

Table 8.2 Case study 1: Incessant whispering and talking in class

Behaviour in class	Impact on teacher/class	Reason?	Action
The pupil is mouthing things silently across the classroom and giggling without giving a reason. When the teacher asks 'What are you talking about?' the reply is 'Nothing, Miss.'	This behaviour has the effect of isolating the teacher (and the learning) as if the teacher is part of the friendship group. This could distract the teacher from teaching, isolate them and reduce their confidence.	To make whatever is being discussed seem more important than the learning?	Make the learning the 'social group' so that pupils want to be part of it. Ignore the behaviour. Up the pace of the lesson so that cognitive demands are increased – with the aim of giving the pupil more direction as to what learning is required and less time for interacting with peers.

Behaviour for learning commentary

Such behaviour is probably well known to many secondary teachers. In this instance, the teacher knows that the pupil's relationship with the subject curriculum, which should be fuelled by subject interest and their need to achieve, has been marginalised by their pursuit of their relationship with others. The pupil's social relationship with peers is driving their behaviour. The teacher could coax them, use sanctions, change the grouping or seek to use their interest in peers to enable them to engage cognitively with the subject material. If such pupils continue to behave in this way, they risk underachieving as well as receiving sanctions. Their view of themselves becomes increasingly influenced by the response of their peer group, not by their own achievement. They are vulnerable in that peer friendships in school can sometimes be fragile. They are resilient within their little group because they do not act alone. The teacher's suggested action aims to rebalance the pupil's relationship with others with their relationships with self and the curriculum.

Case study 2: Arguing and seeking peer attention

Behaviour for learning commentary

Arguing with the teacher in the public view of the classroom gives the impression that the pupil is confident of their own viewpoint, has the support of his peers, and does not 'fear' the annoyance of the teacher. However, blaming others signifies that the individual is attributing their own behaviour to external causes. This suggests that the pupil's emotional development is such that he does not accept that he has at least some control over what happens to him – he sees himself as a victim of circumstance. If this view is maintained, he is unlikely to change. His behaviour is serving the short-term purpose of either avoiding doing work and/or getting some positive social interaction with peers. He has developed some effective arguing skills in that he is hinting that the teacher is being unfair to him. The teacher may seek to defend themselves and this in turn would take the focus away from subject learning. Emotional feelings and peer social behaviour are driving the pupil's behaviour at the expense of learning and relating to the teacher. The short-term rewards that are sustaining this behavioural pattern will in time have an adverse effect on the pupil's achievement. The teacher needs to work on redressing the balance between the pupil's relationships with self and others and their relationship with the curriculum as a route to building the pupil's self-esteem.

Table 8.3 Case study 2: Arguing and seeking peer attention

Behaviour	Impact on teacher/class	Reason	Action
The pupil is angry and upset and questions the teacher: 'What? I didn't say anything. Connor was talking to me. I can't help it if people talk to me. It's always me isn't it? Why does no one else get told off?'	The class may respond by giggling and chatting, leading to general low-level disruption. By a complete denial that anything has occurred the pupil has pushed the focus onto others. There is a suggestion of victimisation by the teacher and adults in general.	Poor experiences with education leading to constant telling off, a lack of success and a bickering relationship with adults?	Do not get involved in a 'I saw your mouth moving' whole class debate that you will not win. If the pupil displays poor behaviour, choose someone (maybe a 'better behaved' pupil) first: 'Lower your voice, Ryan. It's not fair that Lewis has to be silent and you don't.' In group work/cooperative learning, remind all pupils of the behaviour expected from them. In self-evaluation, question what it was about the planning or the execution of the task that meant the pupil had trouble engaging with it.

Case study 3: Using SEN as a limiting factor on learning

Table 8.4 Case study 3: Using special educational needs as a limiting factor on learning

Behaviour	Impact on teacher/ class	Reason	Action
The pupil says 'I don't understand it.' When asked 'Which part?' the typical responses are 'None of it. I can't read' or 'I'm dyslexic so I can't spell.'	The pupil is self-deprecating in their comments and displays an open lack of confidence with a particular area or subject leading to refusal to participate. In not being specific it makes it difficult for the teacher to give appropriate, timely support.	Serves the purpose of implying that the pupil and others with a learning difficulty do not have to tackle certain things because they 'cannot do it'. Parents can inadvertently reinforce this view by saying such things as 'I was always rubbish at Maths.' Does the parent convey low expectations at home in how they talk about their child's learning difficulty?	Plan a situation in which this pupil can succeed. If it cannot happen easily in your subject then observe them somewhere else. Use this information in the more problematic lesson, e.g. 'I saw how excellent you were at leading in Dance so I've put you in charge of the group today.' Be careful to praise either publicly or personally based on your knowledge of the pupil. During self-evaluation, question why you didn't know exactly what they didn't understand; is work needed on assessment strategies? Look at the seating plan to see if there is a peer who can support. Speak to the parent without the pupil present and provide positive feedback on what they have done in class so the parent can reinforce progress at home.

Behaviour for learning commentary

The pupil's relationship with the curriculum has been adversely affected over time by their learning difficulty. They seek to cope with this by being openly self deprecating. There is a need to build a more positive relationship with the curriculum in order that the pupil can achieve and be able to sustain some appropriate independent learning behaviour in class.

We can see from both Table 8.1 and the case studies in Tables 8.2–8.4 that seeking an explanation for a pupil's behaviour – in particular, the purpose it is serving for them – allows us to make a more informed, and it is hoped more effective, strategy choice.

The case studies reflected that a pupil's complex pattern of changing behaviour is influenced by the dynamic interaction of their classroom relationships. Teachers need a way of dealing with this complexity if they are to secure a level of understanding of individual differences in behaviour that will enable them to employ the most effective strategies.

As noted earlier in this chapter, when a pupil exhibits a *cluster* of behaviours that are causing considerable concern, we focus on the *relationships* that underpin those behaviours. In such cases, the B4L approach in its extended use form offers a way to systematically address not just the development of learning behaviours but the actual relationships themselves. The rationale behind this approach is that, by improving the social, emotional and cognitive relationships that are being experienced by the pupil in the classroom, there will be a greater impact on their overall behaviour. We now describe this approach in more detail.

Problem solving and strategy selection based on extended use of the Behaviour for Learning conceptual framework

What shall we do with Jamie?

In this section, we use a case study to illustrate the application of the B4L approach in its extended use form. The case study depicts a pupil who exhibits a cluster of behaviours that are of considerable concern in his classroom. Although the case study refers to a primary age pupil, it is still likely to be relevant in the secondary school setting for pupils who exhibit clusters of behaviours that typify individuals identified under the umbrella term of behaviour, emotional and social difficulties.

It is often the case that such pupils have all manner of strategies and interventions directed at them to the point where it is not clear what is working, to what degree and why. The rationale for using the B4L approach in its extended use form is that this offers both a route for systematic problem solving and an opportunity to evaluate the efficacy of intervention.

Illustrative case study

Jamie, Year 2, has posed difficulties for his class teachers since he started school. The main problem for his class teacher is that getting and keeping Jamie's attention is an ongoing challenge. He seems incapable of working independently and so the teacher feels that she is not teaching him anything unless she is able to give him individual attention. This is difficult given the demands of the rest of the class. He demonstrates aggression and unresponsiveness to direction, and he doesn't care about or follow rules. He doesn't appear to have any friends, cannot work in a group situation, disrupts others and gets into fights. He blames others for his misbehaviour, and does not respect other pupils' belongings.

We can see from the case study that Jamie is likely to need a personalised approach to behaviour management that may require working collaboratively with other colleagues, professionals and parents both within and beyond the school setting. However, the initial question that is likely to be asked by his teacher is 'What do I do with Jamie?'

In seeking to address this question, we apply extended use of the B4L approach to achieve the following:

1   Improve the *quality* of Jamie's learning relationships. This involves working on developing the learning behaviours that underpin each of the three B4L relationships. As an example, in Jamie's case, we would seek to improve his relationship with the curriculum by using strategies that promote the development of the learning behaviours that relate to him 'directing and sustaining attention'.

2   Redress any *imbalance* between the three relationships. In the case of pupils who are described as having behaviour, emotional and social difficulties, it can often be observed that their emotional state is driving their curricular learning and social behaviour. In such cases, the aim of intervention would be to use the curriculum and the social setting of the classroom as a route to reducing the characteristic fluctuations and lack of control that are evident in the pupil's emotional behaviour.

The process for achieving these two aims involves the following stages:

- Stage 1: Identifying the target relationship
- Stage 2: Prioritising areas for improvement
- Stage 3: Selecting routes to improvement
- Stage 4: Identifying learning behaviours
- Stage 5: Selecting appropriate strategies
- Stage 6: Developing evaluation criteria.

We now set out a worked example of these stages based on the case study. This can be used as a guide for your own practice in problem solving in relation to the needs of a pupil who exhibits behaviour, emotional and social difficulties.

Stage 1: Identifying the target relationship

Table 8.5 outlines the data collection process involved in getting more information about the social, emotional and cognitive learning behaviours exhibited by Jamie within the context of his classroom.

In order to plan provision for Jamie we need to find out the following:

- What personal characteristics or dispositions have remained stable over time and may be considered to be either constitutional in origin or deeply rooted adaptive and/or habit behaviours emanating from his past and ongoing experiences?
- Which behaviours have been observed to be responsive to situational changes?

The reason for answering these questions is that we need to ascertain what limiting factors there may be in bringing about change to Jamie's behaviour. We also need to know how we can use the contextual features of the class room (i.e. structure, peers, rules, routines, rewards and sanctions) to bring about improvements to Jamie's emotional, social and cognitive behaviours.

Table 8.5 Suggested questions and answers that provide information about the pupil's social, emotional and cognitive behaviours in the classroom (questions from Watkins and Wagner 2000)

Question	Possible answers?
What behaviour is causing concern? (specify clearly, do not merely re-label)	Inability to pay attention to what the teacher wants him to attend to; running around; aggressive outbursts have potential to hurt others.
In what situations does the behaviour occur? (in what settings/context, with which adults and peers?)	When the teacher is talking to the class, and when he is required to get on with his work on his own in class, when out of routine.
In what situations does the behaviour NOT occur? (in what settings/context, with which adults and peers?)	When he is with LSA/TA, when he is playing on his computer, when he is playing football, doing 'easy' work with younger children, when in the head teacher's room.
What happens before the behaviour? (a precipitating pattern? A build up? A trigger?	Nothing seems to trigger his difficulty with sustaining attention; a trigger for running around is often when he is told off.
What follows the behaviour causing the concern? (something that maintains/reinforces the behaviour?)	He is usually told to 'get on with his work', 'stop messing about', 'don't run around, get back in your seat' and sometimes 'I have had just about enough of your behaviour'.
What skills and positive dispositions does the pupil demonstrate? (social/communication skills? learning/classroom skills?)	If enabled to attend to his work he is able to make progress. He is adept at making excuses, getting attention. He uses overlearned automatic modelled utterances. His social behaviour, although often that of a younger child, does manage to cause maximum irritation. He can be helpful if given a job, knows quite a lot about football. Likes watching videos.
What skills and positive dispositions does the pupil apparently NOT demonstrate?	He does not seem to understand how his behaviour affects others, he seems to enjoy others getting in trouble, he does not seem to be able to control his emotions, he accepts sanctions as part of his life. Nothing seems to 'touch' him; he is behind academically probably because he is so rarely on task.
What view does the person have of their behaviour? (What does it mean to them? What purpose might it serve?)	Difficult to say; when asked for reasons he says 'don't know' or 'cos I want to'.
What view does the person have of themselves? (And may their behaviour enhance that view?)	Difficult to say; he seems confident and outgoing but often prefaces tasks by saying 'I can't do that'.
What view do others have of the person? (how has this developed? Is it self-fulfilling? Can it change?)	The class on the whole find him irritating and are pleased when he is absent from school. Most teachers have trouble with him except the one male teacher in the school that also teaches football.

What we essentially need to find out is under what conditions Jamie's behaviour is at its best for learning in the group setting of the classroom. Table 8.5 provides some questions that may be helpful in exploring this issue along with some example answers.

Once we have identified the problematic behaviours Jamie exhibits, they can be used to define the nature of the emotional, social and cognitive relationships he experiences in the classroom. Figure 8.1 illustrates this process using the Behaviour for Learning conceptual framework.

Relationship with Self
Predominantly **EMOTIONAL**

- Difficulty in directing and sustaining attention (to what teacher requires)
- Unwilling to attempt other than 'easy' tasks
- Does not accept responsibility for actions, blames others
- Aggressive at times
- Resistant to failure and/or sanctions
- Seeks attention

Jamie's Negative Behaviours

Relationship with Others
Predominantly **SOCIAL**

- Finds it difficult to share attention during group work
- Will distract and is easily distracted by others
- Social behaviour not age appropriate
- Difficulty in controlling his own social behaviour
- Unresponsive to demands and feelings of others

Relationship with the Curriculum
Predominantly **COGNITIVE**

- Displays little interest in tasks given to him
- Unresponsive to task instructions
- Very low persistence
- Low-effort behaviour
- Acts before thinking
- Immature language usage
- Avoidance of failure

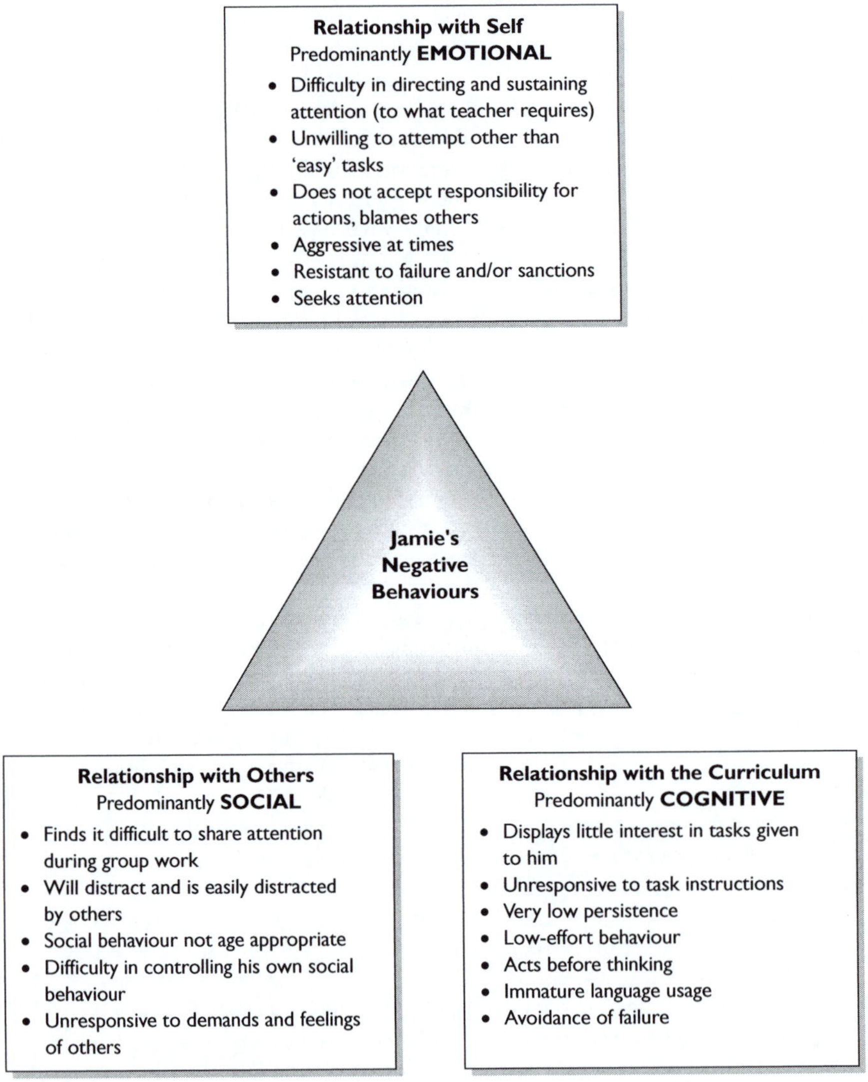

Figure 8.1 Using the Behaviour for Learning conceptual framework to support identification of the target relationship

Looking at the nature of the three relationships in Figure 8.1, it suggests that his emotional behaviour (i.e. relationship with self) is having a negative impact on his relationship with others and his relationship with the curriculum. Jamie's relationship with self therefore becomes the target relationship.

Stages 2 and 3: Prioritising areas and selecting routes for improvement

Having decided which relationship to target, a decision needs to be made about whether it is best to *directly* work on that relationship or to *indirectly* address Jamie's emotional behaviours by improving his social and cognitive learning behaviours. For example, if Jamie gets upset or angry, it may be possible to calm him down by using the curriculum to redirect his energies towards an activity that allows him to experience success. Table 8.6 seeks to synthesise the information needed for stages 2 and 3 of the problem–solving process.

Stage 4: Identifying learning behaviours

This stage involves deciding which cluster of behaviours needs to be tackled in order to have a positive impact on the target relationship. In Jamie's case, the target relationship is his emotionally driven relationship with self. Table 8.7 demonstrates the process of

Table 8.6 Guidance for decision making regarding the target relationship and possible routes for improvements

Question	Sample answer
1 What is the relationship I need to promote for learning in a group setting?	Relationship with self, i.e. emotional
2 Is it better for the individual pupil if I focus directly on the target relationship or seek to develop it via one or both of the other two relationships?	Develop this through relationship with the curriculum, i.e. cognitive, and relationship with others, i.e. social
3 Is there a relationship that I feel more confident/competent to work on initially?	Relationship with the curriculum
4 What knowledge, skills and understanding does the pupil bring to the relationship?	He has been in school long enough to know what behaviour is expected of him. He has experience of school routines, he knows the staff and pupils, he knows how to get attention
5 What knowledge, skills and understanding can I contribute to this relationship?	My subject knowledge and enthusiasm, good interpersonal relationships with colleagues, experience in promoting learning in group settings, differentiation techniques, forming positive relationships, knowledge of core behaviour management approaches, a strong desire to help Jamie.
6 Do I need any additional advice, guidance and support from within my school or from multi-agency partners?	Discuss Jamie with the SENCO

Table 8.7 Examples of desired learning behaviours as alternatives for emotionally driven negative behaviours

Observed negative behaviours	Examples of desired learning behaviours
Inability directing and maintaining attention	Demonstrates some interest in subject /school work/ other areas of school curriculum; has some idea of what he is able to do and what he cannot do, is willing to manage distractions.
Inability to work independently	Is willing and able to work independently as appropriate; knows how, and is willing to get help; willing to take appropriate responsibility for own learning; willing to make mistakes and 'move on'.
Unresponsive to school rules	Can identify behaviour of others that breaks class rules; knows the behaviours expected of him; can identify which behaviours he is able to produce; can identify which rewards he will respond to; knows the consequences of some of his behaviour.
Aggressive to others	Can recognise his own and others' emotions; can identify and use strategies to cope when he gets angry.
Disrupts others	Can use appropriate communication skills to interact with others; is willing and able to manage and resolve conflicts.
Blames others	Recognises feelings and perspectives of others; recognises that he has some control over his own behaviour.
He messes about with other people belongings	Can recognise others' property; is able to stop himself meddling with others' property, has some understanding of why he should respect others' property.

changing the problematic behaviours into desired learning behaviours. If these can be developed, then Jamie's relationship with self will be strengthened and this will have a positive impact on his overall behaviour.

Stage 5: Selecting appropriate strategies

Having identified which desirable learning behaviours are needed in order for Jamie's relationship with self to be improved, the appropriate strategies for their development can be selected. Table 8.8 provides an example of that process, taking into account the purpose Jamie's behaviour may be serving.

Stage 6: Developing evaluation criteria

Having decided at Stage 4 which cluster of learning behaviours you are seeking to develop, you have also decided upon your evaluation criteria. In asking '*How effective have my strategies been?*', you can look at information you have recorded concerning development of, or increase in, these desired learning behaviours. You are then able to judge the following from your evidence:

Table 8.8 Strategy selection designed to reduce a cluster of problematic behaviours exhibited by the pupil

Behaviour	Purpose it serves for the pupil (Jamie)	Possible strategy
Reluctance to try new things	Protection from failure. Jamie feels more in control with the familiar, does not trust and fears change.	Build on what Jamie can do, reward effort rather than final outcome, do not introduce too many new task requirements at once e.g. topic, difficulty, type of response needed.
Easily frustrated by lack of immediate success	Cannot cope with delayed gratification. Current emotional state not conducive to mental concentration.	Break task down into achievable steps, maybe allow Jamie to work with a peer to facilitate persistence.
Non-compliance with authority	Gives Jamie control over his situation.	Provide Jamie with choices and consequences so that he has some control.
Detaching himself from active curricular learning	Provides 'time out' from work and peer pressures.	Provide Jamie with 'active learning' tasks and those that require working with others.
Dependency on others	Avoids making the effort and can blame others for lack of success.	Take care not to overuse adult support, employ 'scaffolding' techniques (Wood *et al.* 1976; Vygotsky 1978), reward independence and self-review of work.
Is negative, critical, sarcastic, cynical to others	This may serve to make Jamie feel better about himself (a habit response) or he may just want to join in with other peers who are behaving in this way.	This could be tackled at whole class level (e.g. considering the effect on others, reinforcing that the school does not tolerate negative interactions with others and questioning with the group 'Does hurting others make us feel better about ourselves?')
Blames his behaviour on others	Protects self and delays any adverse consequences – this can become a habit and involves lying.	Reward truthfulness; don't get into long discussion in class; speak one to one with Jamie in a safe setting to look at what he could have done differently; avoid delayed sanctions. Clearly outline consequences of Jamie's behaviour to him and take action – examine serious consequence of not telling the truth through non-personal examples (e.g. literature, films and the media that demonstrate importance of trust, etc.)

• Which strategies have been effective for bringing about what particular changes to the target relationship and its associated learning behaviours?
• Have those behavioural changes resulted in improved learning as measured by achievement and attainment data?

Using the B4L approach in its extended use form set out in Stages 1–6 reflects a systematic approach to problem solving and addressing the behaviour of those individual pupils whose changeable and disruptive behaviour has a negative impact on their own and others' learning in the classroom. These stages may need to be repeated as the class and/or subject teacher, along with any other colleagues, seek to systematically address the range of behaviours exhibited by pupils with individual differences and/or SEN.

Adding the detail to broad strategy selection for Jamie

In the next sections, we have provided some more detailed illustrative strategies that might be useful both in Jamie's case and for others like him. The expectation is not that teachers implement all the strategies but, using their knowledge of the pupil, choose those that are most likely to have an impact on the cluster of behaviours that are causing concern.

Strategies to improve Jamie's relationship with the curriculum as a route to improving his emotional behaviour

In the case of Jamie, our overall aim is to *improve his relationship with the curriculum as a route to improving his emotionally driven behaviour*. A priority for action in this endeavour is to address his difficulty with directing and sustaining attention. To do this, we have to be fully aware of the limits of Jamie's attention span and to 'clear the space in his head' from emotional distractions. This is a priority because he needs to increase the time he spends on curriculum learning and reduce the time he spends messing around. Some specific strategies are now outlined:

- Place Jamie's desk near to his teacher's – engineered as a privilege not a punishment.
- Make sure Jamie is seated away from distractions (doors, windows, pencil sharpeners, etc.). Remove any clutter from his desk and surrounding area (e.g. bags and lunch box out of sight).
- At the start of each task, ask Jamie what equipment he needs for that task; then let him get it and put away at the end of the task.
- Plan work so that Jamie is given short achievable tasks initially.
- Try to plan these short tasks so that they require Jamie to be active with his learning (e.g. 'listen for' activities at story time and recognition tasks rather than generating his own response).
- Keep your attention on his curricular learning – do not be distracted by talking about his behaviour or responding to non-work related interruptions.
- Give Jamie frequent and immediate feedback on his learning behaviour.
- If feasible, allow Jamie some physical breaks to move around by asking him to hand out or collect materials, put equipment away – anything that gives him permission to come off task for brief periods. Do not use loss of break time as a sanction – he needs permissible opportunities to be physically active.
- Change the rewards frequently to help prevent Jamie from adapting and becoming bored with them; tangible token rewards that he can see increasing may work well.
- Jamie needs to experience the stability of routines and rules, but he may also respond to some variation in the position in which he works (e.g. at his work station or

an area that has been pre-defined in discussion with him as his 'listening place' or 'thinking place').

- Identify a safe place or person who Jamie can go to as an alternative to him being removed from class and peers. The latter could have a negative impact on his view of self and/or others – it is important that this is not a sanction but a permissible alternative.

- Implement agreed (with the teacher) non-verbal systems for conveying current emotional state and action (e.g. green card – 'I'm ok', amber – 'I need support', red – 'I'm going to my safe place').

- Give Jamie an index card or a computer screen with core rules that he has personalised by illustrating them – you can then just use eye contact or other non-verbal strategies to remind or reward him.

- Jamie could have a schedule on his desk so that if he keeps asking 'What do we do next?' you can ask him to check – you may also want to give him the responsibility to remind the class of the sequence of events.

- Make full use of multisensory approaches (visual, auditory, use of concrete equipment, etc.) when trying to get Jamie to access and process information.

- Keep instructions short. Avoid instructions with multiple elements such as 'Draw a picture of three things we saw when we visited the church yesterday. Colour them in and label them neatly – if you do not know how to spell them, ask someone at your table to help you or put your hand up and I will help you.' Jamie (and probably others in the class) may not have automated such skills as listening, thinking and writing, and this is likely to lead to an 'overload' that may result in him exhibiting problematic behaviour.

- Allow him use of a timer to show how much time he has remaining for an activity.

- If it proves helpful, allow him to have a soft malleable ball or equivalent to fiddle with during times when he has to listen.

- Try pairing him at times with a study buddy who can help give reminders or refocus him when he gets off track.

Strategies to improve Jamie's relationship with others in the classroom as a route to improving his emotional behaviour

The overall aim is to use the peer group as models for appropriate social behaviour. It is hoped that explicitly teaching the class about social behaviour will have some impact on Jamie. Tackling indirectly in this way means he is less likely to feel personally criticised. By discussing with the class, via the curriculum and their own experiences, such issues as 'What do you do when you get angry, stuck, fail, fall out with friends, get told off?', it is hoped that Jamie will acquire some acceptable strategies for the classroom as an alternative to those he currently relies upon. He can choose to accept or reject other pupils' strategies without emotional involvement because these strategies do not belong to him. Some specific strategies are now outlined:

- Give Jamie frequent and immediate feedback on his social behaviour, making it clear what specific behaviour you are rewarding (e.g. 'Thanks for waiting your turn').

- Keep reminding the class and Jamie of the consequences of behaviour – in particular, what behaviour will be rewarded.

- Aim to give Jamie immediate attention for positive behaviours and provide immediate positive feedback. Ignore any problematic behaviours that are minimal and not disruptive.
- Try to ensure that you use a biased and favourable reward to sanctions ratio, such as 5:1 (DfES 2005a; Dix 2007). We know that Jamie does not react in an age-appropriate manner to being reprimanded or corrected, and we want to keep his emotional levels down while he is required to engage with curricular learning.
- Have core rules and a visual class timetable displayed with regular reminders for all pupils.
- Give concise one- or two-step directions regarding behavioural expectations. Avoid 'overloading' with too much information, such as 'You know what I told you yesterday and you said that you would be good today – it's not fair on the others.' Just state the behaviour you want to see and repeat if necessary.
- Have a flow chart for all pupils for 'What to do when stuck' so that they are cued into getting on independently. This will help Jamie to develop strategies as an alternative to constantly and noisily seeking help from a teacher. If Jamie does interrupt, it is then possible to non-verbally direct him towards the flow chart.
- If appropriate and feasible, give the class a plan of how to stage their work and encourage them to use this to keep 'on track'.
- Help the class and Jamie specifically to develop social skills (e.g. knowing how to join in, how to ask for things, how to express their point of view (ATL 2002; DfES 2005c)).
- Teach and rehearse useful strategies that pupils, specifically Jamie, can use to either deal with or extricate themselves from social situations that they currently find difficult. This could include the sometimes vacuous, but socially useful, language and behaviour of apology. It might also include developing socially acceptable responses to criticism.
- Get the class to analyse an incident (either real or from literature, etc.) in order to identify the key triggers, the choice points, the efficacy of the responses and the outcomes for all. Provide opportunities for the pupils to identify their existing effective self-regulation strategies and to explore socially acceptable strategies used by peers and others involved. Write about, discuss or role play alternatives.
- Identify with Jamie a particular role (e.g. leader, participant, reporter) within a collaborative group work activity that seeks to address his particular behavioural and/ or learning difficulty.
- Work with Jamie one to one or in a small group to identify the difference between designating a choice as 'good' because of its impact on the individual pupil (e.g. immediate sense of fun and excitement) and 'good' in relation to its effect on others.

As has been stressed throughout this chapter, there is no easy answer to 'What should we do with a pupil who exhibits significant and often complex behavioural problems in the classroom?' All such pupils have different learning needs and the contexts and conditions of school classrooms vary between and within schools. What we have offered through extended use of the B4L approach is a model for systematic problem solving. This seeks to acknowledge the interdependence of the pupil's emotional, social and cognitive functioning in contributing to their complex and pervasive behavioural patterns.

Conclusion

The combination of individual differences and special educational needs in the title of this chapter reflects the view that individual behavioural differences lie on a continuum. Some individuals on that continuum may meet the criteria required for SEN classification (DfES 2001; DfE 2014a). Classification of behaviour as a special educational need is not straightforward. Given that class teachers contribute to the identification of SEN, and are responsible for teaching *all* pupils in their class, this chapter has included information to support increased understanding of identification criteria for pupils with considerable behavioural differences.

There is a need to dispense with a view that somewhere out there is a definitive list of strategies that suffice to address the learning needs of pupils identified as having behaviour, emotional and social difficulties (DfES 2001) – or even social, emotional and mental health difficulties (DfE 2014a).

The plethora of books and resources available on pupil behaviour would seem to support a view that, while there are principles and theoretical underpinnings that can support the development of effective practices, there is no neat link between 'label' and 'treatment' as might be the case with, for example, some physical illnesses.

Identification of SEN does not, in itself, prescribe what will be the most effective strategies for any one *individual* pupil who has been allocated to a particular SEN category. Each pupil, whether they are classified as SEN or not, will adapt differently to the *group* setting of the classroom. Their behaviour will communicate to us information about their ongoing experiences of, and response to, their class and teacher.

The additional Government guidance (TA 2012) intended to improve teacher training in relation to behaviour prescribes that teachers gain an understanding of why some pupils misbehave. This is a useful pursuit in terms of exploring what purpose the behaviour serves for that individual. However, it is unlikely that finding a *root* cause for individual behavioural differences will prescribe an effective 'treatment' or set of strategies. Each individual, irrespective of whether their behavioural difficulties are classified as SEN, will experience and interpret the specific context and conditions of the classroom differently. Their behaviour will be subject to situational changes, both real and perceived, and strategies used by the class teacher will also have to be responsive and flexible.

The Behaviour for Learning conceptual framework is a model for helping teachers to explore what individual pupils are 'thinking, feeling and doing' as they adapt to the complexities of the dynamic relationship that influence their behaviour in the classroom. The model places a focus on the pupil's experience of these classroom relationships. It seeks to identify what positive learning behaviours, personal attributes and traits can be harnessed to support the pupil in taking up the learning opportunities on offer in the classroom.

Schools and their teachers are in a unique situation to provide a safe environment where changes in behaviour can be supported through the consistency of routines and discipline, opportunities for individuals to succeed and appropriate models of peer and adult behaviour. These contextual features may not be available to some children and young people outside their school setting. A systematic exploration of the pupil's misbehaviour through the B4L approach can give insight into how teaching and learning can be improved, not just for the target pupil but for the whole class.

Note

1 Supplied by secondary English teacher, Kate Tod Forbes, July 2013.

Chapter 9

Dealing with more challenging behaviour

Introduction

As we suggested in earlier chapters, a lot of behaviour is predictable to a degree and can be planned for. Although, as this book has stressed throughout, it needs to be recognised that individuals experience and interpret events *individually*, it is possible to develop a repertoire of teacher strategies, approaches and responses at a whole school policy level that is likely to be effective with most pupils most of the time. This chapter is concerned with behaviours that may be experienced as more challenging.

Although 'challenging behaviour' is a widely used term, there is not necessarily a shared understanding of its meaning. Part of the difficulty is that, when we refer to 'challenging behaviour', we are not only conveying a sense that in some way the behaviour is significantly beyond what might typically be expected, but also indicating something about how we, as the adults, experience this behaviour. Challenging behaviour is essentially any behaviour that the observer finds challenging. What one person experiences as challenging may be experienced as difficult, unwelcome, but not particularly challenging by another. For example, no teacher is likely to enjoy being sworn at or find it acceptable, but they may feel confident in dealing with it. In this sense it is not challenging. Equally, a teacher who subscribes to the view that all pupils must be passive and compliant at all times could perceive quite a minor behaviour as challenging.

Many forms of behaviour that may be deemed challenging can be dealt with effectively at the level of *managing* the situation through adherence to the school's policy. For example, for the pupil who settles in response to teacher intervention but soon resumes the behaviour, there is a next step in the teacher's least to most intrusive hierarchy, leading on to other stages of the school's behaviour policy. Similarly, for the pupil who persists with behaviour during a lesson despite positive correction and the warning and issuing of a sanction, there is typically a next step such as a senior member of staff who is 'on call' for such situations. It is hoped that progression through these steps is monitored and more proactive measures put in place to support the pupil in developing the learning behaviours required to learn more effectively in the classroom, but, at the level of managing the behaviour at the time it occurs, the classroom discipline plan and the school's behaviour policy help the teacher to know how to respond.

In this chapter, we are not using the term 'challenging behaviour' in relation to these types of behaviours. Instead we are focused on those incidents that involve anger and aggression. Physical and verbal aggression towards staff and peers and significant damage to property are perhaps the more obvious examples, but this category would also include the pupil who metaphorically, and perhaps physically, has backed themselves into a corner and refuses to comply with adult directions. A defining characteristic is that the individual concerned does not operate within what the observer, and possibly the person themselves on other occasions, views as normal parameters. They may not be amenable to reason or influenced by the range of internal and external inhibitors (Davies and Frude 2000) that usually serve to regulate behaviour. The individual may therefore not act in a predictable manner. This chapter is premised on the view that, by developing an understanding of the emotion behind the anger and the likely trajectory of the incident, it is possible to plan responses.

Challenging behaviour in the context of the behaviour for learning approach

The behaviour for learning approach emphasises the importance of understanding how a pupil is experiencing and interpreting events. When considering incidents that involve anger and aggression, it is this understanding that can guide us in the steps that we take – and help us to recognise those actions that we should avoid. There is a need to recognise that at some level the behaviour is likely to make sense and have some purpose for the individual. This is not to suggest that the pupil is taking considered actions or is consciously goal orientated; as this chapter explains, the purpose may simply be rooted in a perceived need for protection that is served by a flight or fight response.

The nature of the adult's relationship with self is critical in dealing with these incidents. As the adult involved, we may experience a degree of threat to our feelings of professional competence when confronted by behaviour that we cannot control and that may be beyond our normal range of experience. A concern for teachers early in their careers in particular may be how it will look to others if this behaviour is happening in their classroom. Certainly the behaviour is likely to provoke a degree of anxiety in us. This may be rooted in a concern for our professional identity as outlined earlier or, depending on the nature of the incident, for the individual concerned and the rest of the class. As our anxiety levels rise, we respond physiologically; essentially our brains are telling us there is a threat and that something needs to be done to reduce the anxiety that is causing this discomfort (Canter and Canter 1992). If we are trying to understand how the pupil is experiencing and interpreting events, there is a need to recognise and manage our own thoughts and feelings; otherwise the risk is that we approach incidents of this nature as though they are all about us.

Understanding the emotion behind the behaviour

The emotion typically associated with the type of behaviour discussed within this chapter is anger. However, it should be recognised that the display of anger and the surface emotionality associated with it will often cover up very different eliciting emotional states (Bowers 2005), including feelings of frustration, anxiety, loss or affront. It is also important to recognise that feelings such as anger, frustration and anxiety are normal human emotions. The concern for teachers is usually the behaviour that results. Davies and Frude (2000) provide a useful model that helps us understand why some people may be more likely to display their anger in the form of violence and aggression. They put forward a five-stage process shown in Figure 9.1.

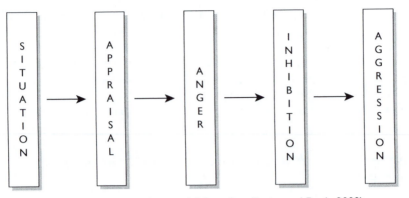

Figure 9.1 The aggressive incident model (based on Davies and Frude 2000)

The *situation* is the triggering event. Davies and Frude (2000) suggest that there are typically three elements that may lead to anger. These are as follows:

1   Irritants: these might be aspects in the physical environment (e.g. loud or repetitive noise, smells) or the irritating actions of others.
2   Costs: personal loss (e.g. of money or goods), loss of status or 'face', and other forms of detriment.
3   Transgressions: these involve a person breaking a rule (or doing something 'out of order').

However, it is not the situation in itself that produces the emotional responses but the *appraisal* an individual makes. For example, if two pupils happen to collide in the corridor, one may view this as an unfortunate accident while the other may interpret it as deliberate. The interpretation made by the individual will determine whether the resulting predominant emotion is anger. There are a number of influencing factors on the appraisal an individual makes, including the following:

•   The way the individual usually views things – do they usually put a negative slant on events?
•   The individual's mood at the time. People who are already angry or pressured tend to view things in a more negative way.
•   What other people are saying about the situation. Peers or others significant in the pupil's life may encourage a particular appraisal by, for example, suggesting that a particular act was underpinned by malicious intent or that to not interpret it as hostile is a sign of weakness.

Anger is an emotional state which can lead to aggression, although it does not necessarily do so in all individuals or on all occasions. It does, however, need some form of outlet because, while suppressing anger can be a useful and necessary strategy for all of us in certain circumstances, too much suppression can be problematic and lead to repressed anger that seeps out and influences our behaviour in ways we may not even be aware of (Faupel *et al.* 1998).

It is conceivable that two individuals may have been exposed to the same situation, made the same appraisal and experienced the same feeling of anger, yet only one reacts

Table 9.1 Internal and external inhibitors

Internal inhibitors may include:	External inhibitors may include:

• strong self-control
• anticipated feelings of guilt
• moral inhibitions
	• fear of:
	  ○ physical retaliation
	  ○ social consequences
	  ○ legal consequences
	  ○ material losses
	  ○ embarrassment

(Davies and Frude 2000)

aggressively or violently. This difference can be explained in terms of an individual's *inhibitions*. Within Davies and Frude's (2000) model, *inhibition* is used as a neutral phrase; it is not intended necessarily to imply a degree of suppression or repression. Inhibitions may be *internal* or *external* as shown in Table 9.1.

Inhibitions may be high towards the actual source of anger. The result may be displaced anger, where the pupil directs their anger at a target where their inhibitions are lower.

Aggression is the final stage of Davies and Frude's (2000) model. This term covers behaviours ranging from the verbal through to the physical. Physical aggression covers a wide range of behaviours from aggressive or intimidating posturing through to pushing, pulling, hair grabbing, biting, punching, kicking and, at the most extreme end, use of weapons.

It should be evident from Davies and Frude's (2000) model where there is scope for intervention. For example, it might be possible to work with pupils on their *appraisal* of situations or develop their awareness of likely consequences to strengthen their external *inhibitions*. Although the focus of this chapter is not on proactive approaches to working with pupils for whom anger is a problem, it is important to recognise that incidents involving aggression should signal the need for longer term work with a pupil with regard to managing emotions and self-regulation of behaviour. As the class teacher, this may not be your responsibility; it may be, for example, that the pupil would benefit from inclusion in an anger management group or access to some individualised work. Even if not directly involved in the intervention, you may find that you are required to provide feedback on the pupil's performance in class or support particular strategies that have been put in place by, for example, the SENCO or a member of the pastoral team working with the pupil.

Dealing with incidents

Breakwell (1997) presented the assault cycle (Figure 9.1) as a way of understanding the process that occurs during a typical episode of physically aggressive behaviour. This understanding helps to identify the priorities at each stage. The model has been presented in a more generic form as the 'anger mountain' (Long 1999; Long and Fogell 1999), relating the process to other incidents in addition to those that involve physical aggression. It is a way of understanding the process when an assault or some other form

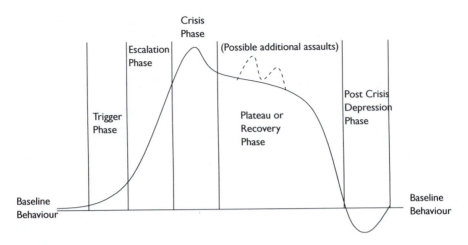

Figure 9.2 The assault cycle (Breakwell 1997: 43)

of physical aggression is likely, but equally it is relevant when considering events such as verbal aggression, panic attacks or any loss of control such as a pupil storming out of the room or off site. Within this section of the chapter, it is this broader perspective that is applied to the assault cycle.

The assault cycle links to the instinctive survival response of fight or flight. The fight or flight response has its origins long ago in human history, when our ancestors were faced with dangerous but not especially complex threats. It is important, therefore, that we recognise the fight or flight response as both primitive and instinctive. It involves physiological changes as the body alters its priorities from long-term survival to emergency short-term survival.

Trigger phase

People have a normal baseline set of behaviours, and for almost everybody this normal behaviour is non-aggressive most of the time (Breakwell 1997). In the trigger phase, something occurs that is *perceived* as a threat. The key point to recognise is that it does not matter whether the teacher, another person or peers would perceive this as a threat – the important factor is that the individual concerned views it as such. The threat may be to physical or emotional well-being. Although the anger may have multiple causes, the individual is likely only to be cognitively aware of one (Beadle and Murphy 2013). To use Davies and Frude's (2000) terminology, there is likely to be an irritant, cost or transgression to which the individual is reacting.

It may be possible to remove the trigger or distract the pupil from it. Distractions would include asking the pupil to run an errand, directing them to another activity or even simply asking them a question about an unrelated matter to engage them in dialogue. If the pupil has been taught any 'calm down' strategies, they could be reminded of these and also of times in the past when they have used them successfully. It can be helpful to remind the pupil of the consequences of reacting to the trigger. This strategy should be used with caution and should not be conveyed as a threat. It is a way of drawing the pupil's attention to a factor that may act, in Davies and Frude's (2000) terms, as an inhibitor.

Escalation phase

During the escalation phase, the body is preparing itself physiologically for the fight or flight response. The release of hormones, such as adrenaline, cause blood pressure to increase and breathing to become more rapid as the body prepares itself for the muscular effort involved in making a fight or flight response (Faupel *et al.* 1998). The person may start to pace up and down and the speed and volume of their speech may increase (Breakwell 1997). There may also be more subtle physical movements signifying increased agitation, such as drumming fingers on the table. Although distraction techniques referred to previously remain relevant, as the escalation phase moves towards crisis, it should be recognised that the individual will be less amenable to reason and less able to make rational judgements.

If it is clear that the escalation phase is developing, assistance should be summoned. Most schools will have an on-call system for these purposes. In some cases, the teacher's own presence may be acting as an ongoing trigger at this point, particularly if the incident started as a result of an interaction between them and the pupil. In such a situation, it may be better that the supporting colleague takes over the management of the incident. This action is not an indication of failure (Beadle and Murphy 2013): it is a strategy that is focused on the needs of the pupil with the intention of securing the most positive outcome possible in the situation.

When the incident is developing in a classroom, consideration should be given to removing the rest of the class. In such a situation, the seriousness of the incident that the teacher is attempting to prevent takes precedence over the disruption to teaching and learning. Remember that at the point such an action becomes a consideration, teaching and learning are already likely to be significantly affected.

Crisis phase

During the crisis phase, the individual will be unable to think clearly, make rational judgements or respond to requests and instructions. They may, however, pick up on tone of voice or body language, so it is important that the teacher does not signal additional threat by invading personal space, moving quickly, becoming highly animated or raising their voice. It is of little use, and potentially aggravating to the situation, to threaten with sanctions or the displeasure of senior staff who may need to be summoned.

The priority for the teacher at this stage is keeping the individual, others and themselves safe. Clearing any remaining audience is important because it keeps them safe and also removes additional stimulus for the individual who is in crisis. If it is safe to do so, remove any objects nearby that may endanger the individual, could be thrown or may lead to the individual being in more trouble if broken.

Recovery phase

During the *recovery phase*, the anger begins to subside but the individual is at a heightened level of susceptibility to triggers. Relatively minor events that they would not normally react to may be sufficient to re-ignite their anger during this phase. It is not the time to start analysing the incident with the pupil or demanding explanations (Breakwell 1997). Breakwell suggests that this phase could last 30–90 minutes, while Faupel *et al.* (1998) suggest leaving at least 45 minutes but ideally an hour before discussing a major incident with a pupil. There will be differences between individuals and also age and the severity of the incident are likely to be factors, but the key message is that time needs to be allowed for the physiological and psychological arousal to subside. The implication, therefore, is that the facility needs to be available for the pupil to calm down away from obvious triggers, including inquisitive passers-by who may ask questions.

Post-crisis depression phase

The *post-crisis* phase is one of resting and recovering from the high state of arousal that the body has just experienced. The ability to think clearly and to listen begins to return at this stage. The pupil may become tearful, remorseful, guilty, ashamed, distraught or despairing. They are vulnerable at this stage and so it is important that the teacher or adult managing this part of the process supports them in distinguishing between guilty feelings about themselves and remorse about the behaviour. Guilt directed at oneself may reduce self-esteem and have a negative impact on the pupil's relationship with self. In contrast, remorse about the behaviour could lead to effective responses such as apologising and making amends, which may help to rebuild their relationships with others, or the generation of alternatives to this behaviour in the future (Faupel *et al.* 1998).

Managing yourself: the defusing style

Hewett (1998) refers to the defusing style (Figure 9.3) to capture the idea that the adult needs to give consideration to both their outward presentation in an incident and their internal thought processes.

Voice

The teacher should adopt a calm but firm tone of voice (Long and Fogell 1999). Remaining unnaturally calm, or assuming what might be termed almost a clichéd calm tone, is not likely to help matters.

It is important for the teacher to listen more than talk. Usually if the pupil is talking, even if this is a rant and/or contains language that on other occasions the teacher would attempt to limit, there is a greater chance that the situation will end without physical aggression. The adult needs to monitor the pace and pitch of their own speech. Increases in the pace of speech or a raising of the pitch are associated with emotional arousal and so do not convey calming signals to the pupil. Unless monitored, these changes in speech can inadvertently happen because the adult's state of emotional arousal increases when faced with a difficult situation.

Although a considerable percentage of the meaning communicated is conveyed not by the actual words we say but by tone of voice and body language, it is important to pay attention to the words used:

- Avoid phrases like 'I know how you feel . . . ', 'I understand how you feel . . . ' The pupil may react angrily to this presumption on the part of the teacher. Instead name

Voice

- Calm, even, not loud
- Monitor pace and pitch of own speech
- Listen more than talk

Face

- Careful use of facial expression, not changing frequently
- Avoid smiling unless sure it will defuse
- Give good, attentive eye contact but monitor intensity – don't stare; lower eyes if necessary

Body Language

- Stay sensitive to personal space
- Avoid square-on positions
- Adopt a relaxed stance
- Move slowly and predictably
- Don't stand on the other person's centre line

Hands

- In view
- Open, with palms visible
- In a low, relaxed position

Thoughts

- Stay calm
- Draw on mental structures
- Focus on effective outcomes rather than 'winning' or 'losing'
- Positive self talk
- Keep a sense of perspective

Other issues

- Tune in to the other person for signals
- Be prepared to hand over to a colleague

Figure 9.3 The defusing style (based on Hewett 1998)

the feeling that the outward display of behaviour conveys by saying for example, 'I can see that you're angry/upset/frustrated . . . ' A degree of judgement applies as to whether to use the term 'upset' because, for some older pupils, the fact that they have lost control and perhaps are tearful may be a source of embarrassment. To reinforce this with the word 'upset' may therefore be unhelpful, and 'angry' may be the better generic phrase. However, this is not an exact science and there is a counterargument that 'upset' conveys sympathy, which is a good way of building a caring relationship (Long 1999). If applicable, the teacher could also name the source of the anger – for example, 'I can see that you are upset because you think I was unfair . . . '

- Avoid phrases like 'Don't be silly . . . ', 'It's not worth getting upset/angry over it . . . ', 'Come on, it can't be that bad . . . ' and 'There's no need to get upset about it . . . ' Whatever has triggered the incident *is* of significance to the individual and isn't silly, so clearly at some level for them it was worth getting upset or angry over. Phrases like 'It sounds really awful . . . ', 'That must have been really difficult for you . . . ', 'I can see that this has made you angry . . . ' or 'I can see this is really important to you . . . ' help to demonstrate an understanding on the part of the teacher of the significance to the pupil.

- Phrases like 'I hear what you're saying . . . ' and 'I can see where you're coming from . . . ' should be used in moderation. They can be useful but they have become somewhat clichéd to the point where they can appear as simply a form of jargon with little personal engagement. It would be far better to use phrases such as 'It sounds awful . . . ' or 'Yes, I see' (Braithwaite 2001).

- Prohibitions such as 'can't . . . ', 'mustn't . . . ' and 'shouldn't . . . ' should be avoided. Negative words such as these only add to the negative state of aggression being expressed (Braithwaite 2001). Phrases such as 'I can help you if you can stop shouting . . . ' or 'We can work this out if you come and sit down . . . ' that suggest possibilities of what can be done are generally better than prohibitions.
- Avoid phrases like 'Come on, let's see a smile . . . ', 'Cheer up' and 'Pull yourself together'. The individual is showing strong emotions and, as the assault cycle indicates, is likely to take a while to recover. To assume the individual can switch emotions is trivialising, patronising and ultimately unrealistic.
- Avoid phrases such as 'Well, this isn't going to achieve anything...' and 'You won't get anywhere like that . . . ' The implication of these phrases is that there is rationality behind the behaviour. The incident is a loss of control on the part of the individual so they are unlikely to be able to contemplate the pros and cons of this behaviour as an attempt to achieve anything.
- The teacher can ask questions to check their own understanding of the situation by using a phrase such as 'Let me see if I've got this right, you're angry because . . . ' or inviting more information by asking, 'I'm not sure I understand . . . Could you tell me a little more?' (Long 1999). Checking for understanding serves to slow the pace down and encourages the pupil to articulate the difficulty. It is a useful de-escalation technique and also shows that the teacher is not just listening but is also keen to fully understand (Long 1999).
- Affirmations such as 'Yes', 'Right' and non-specific utterances (e.g. uh-huh, mm-hmm) help demonstrate that the teacher is listening and also encourage the speaker to continue. These affirmations can be coupled with the use of occasional nods and appropriate subtle changes in expression to show surprise, disbelief, concern and so on.
- Use 'Sorry' sparingly but effectively. The teacher can be sorry even if they are not at fault through phrases such as 'David, I'm sorry this has happened' (Braithwaite 2001) or 'I'm sorry you're feeling like this'. If there is an element of fault on the part of the teacher, this can be acknowledged by, for example, saying 'I'm sorry I shouted at you.' It is also possible to use a token concession (Long 1999) such as 'Yes, I admit I could have handled it better' as a strategy for diffusing current negativity within the relationship. Braithwaite (2001) advises that overuse of 'sorry' can cause it to lose its impact and risks misinterpretation as a manipulative tool.

Body language

Movements should be smooth and predictable. Rapid or big arm and hand movements may well be perceived as threatening gestures. Hewett (1998) refers to the avoidance of the other person's central line. This is an important consideration when both approaching the pupil and talking to them. The central line is an imaginary line extending directly out in front of the pupil. The teacher should approach the pupil at an angle, keeping to one side or the other of the central line (see Figure 9.4). This is less threatening than walking directly at someone. This is especially true if the teacher is physically bigger than the pupil.

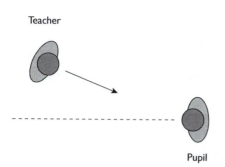

Teacher

Pupil

Figure 9.4 Approaching a pupil (Ellis and Tod 2009)

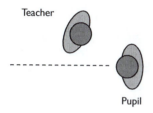

Teacher

Pupil

Figure 9.5 Talking to a pupil (Ellis and Tod 2009)

When talking to the pupil, the same principle applies: the teacher should keep off the central line (see Figure 9.5). Standing square on to the pupil would be far more confrontational; it also means there's no 'flight' response available to the pupil to the front, which risks increasing the possibility of a 'fight' response.

A relaxed posture should be adopted – Hewett (1998) suggests relaxed neck, shoulders and arms, hands open and visible and weight distributed to one side, giving a relaxed, slightly leaning posture. However, it is important that in adopting a relaxed posture a balance is struck in order to appear calm while still conveying an appropriate level of interest, involvement and appreciation of the significance the source of upset has to the pupil. Braithwaite (2001) suggests hands in pockets can convey a lack of interest and thumbs stuck in belt loops or the top of a pocket can indicate arrogance or intransigence. Arms folded or hands on hips may convey similar messages.

Throughout the interaction, the teacher should have regard for the pupil's personal space. It is considered that a distance of 15–46 cm is the intimate zone into which people only allow those who are emotionally close, such as lovers, parents, spouses, children, close friends, relatives and pets (Pease and Pease 2004). The teacher should avoid straying into this zone because it is provocative and likely to be perceived as a threat. Outside the intimate zone is the personal zone, which extends from 46 cm to 1.22 m. People tend to stand this distance from others at social functions and friendly gatherings (Pease and Pease 2004). As an approximate guide, the teacher should stand at the outer end of this range. Braithwaite (2001) makes the suggestion that the average space requirement is about two arm lengths if standing and perhaps one-and-a-half arm lengths if sitting.

Hands

Hands should ideally be in view, open, with palms visible and held in a relaxed position by the sides. They can also be used either singly or together in a gentle palms down motion to accompany a 'Let's calm down' message (Long 1999). Pointing or wagging the index finger at the individual is provocative and in close proximity is likely to encroach too far into the pupil's personal space.

Face

Eye contact should be established if possible but without staring because this may be perceived as a challenge (Braithwaite 2001). Eye contact should not be demanded (e.g. 'Look at me when I'm talking to you') because this is likely to escalate matters (Long and Fogell 1999). In a confrontation, the aggressor may stare, retaining eye contact for an unusually long period. The teacher needs to avoid matching this, lowering their eyes if necessary, because this would be conveying an aggressive signal back.

In the right circumstances, a smile may help to defuse but as a general principle smiling should be avoided because it may be interpreted as a smirk (Braithwaite 2001) or an indication that the situation, which is a cause of obvious distress to the individual, is not being taken seriously.

Thoughts

The type of incidents referred to in this chapter are likely to be unwelcome and difficult. Feelings may run from a frustration that this is an interruption to the normal course of events through to fear of the harm the individual might do to themselves or others. Thoughts will determine the adult's behaviour during the incident and, of course, how any individual responds cognitively under pressure is, to a large extent, personal. However, there are a few considerations that may help:

- Stay calm: this is easier said than done when confronted with a significant incident. If the teacher takes a moment to assess and take in all the contextual information, it is likely to help in better informing their response and in slowing the pace. The other points listed may further contribute to calmness.
- Draw on mental structures: Hewett (1998) uses the term 'mental structures' to refer to frameworks that help us understand what is happening and/or inform decision making. Breakwell's (1997) assault cycle is one such structure. It is a way of conceptualising an incident as a sequence of stages in order to understand the priorities associated with each stage. A specific behaviour management plan for the particular pupil could also be considered a mental structure.
- Focus on effective outcomes rather than 'winning' or 'losing': if the teacher assumes that, as the adult, they have to 'win' or somehow 'come out on top' having stamped their authority on the situation, it limits the options available to them and is likely to engender a behaviour based on achieving control and dominance. The focus needs to be on effective outcomes, which may be that the pupil calms down and nobody gets hurt.
- Positive self-talk: some people may find it helpful to have a phrase they repeat to themselves when confronted with a difficult incident. This might be something like 'This is difficult but I've seen it before: I've got good technique and can handle it' or 'This is difficult but we have a sound policy so I know what to do next'.

- Keep a sense of perspective: like 'Stay calm', this may appear as little more than a platitude rather than a practical consideration. In reality, an accurate understanding of what is at stake will exert a significant influence over the adult's actions. Most incidents in school are not likely to be life threatening. Once this is established, some perspective is introduced. The next consideration may be whether there is any real risk of physical harm. By going through this process it will often become clear that, although the situation is difficult, is impeding what the adult, the pupil and their peers should be doing and needs to be addressed, instant action is not necessary. This is not to diminish the significance of the situations teachers and others may face but to convey the message that they can take a few moments to appraise and determine their response.

Other issues

As well as monitoring their own actions, it is important that the teacher monitors all possible communications from the pupil. This, of course, means listening to what they say and how they say it, but also looking at their face and body language for information about what they are thinking or feeling at that moment. This information should be used to inform the teacher's next action based on whether the pupil is, for example, becoming more aroused or giving signs of calming down. There are certain signs to look out for that indicate physical conflict may occur. These are:

- direct prolonged eye contact
- pale, patchy or blushed skin
- rapid speech
- unusually loud or quiet speech
- standing up if sitting, pulling themselves up to full height or other actions that have the effect of making them appear physically bigger
- fists clenching and unclenching
- feet spread for balance
- forward movement, closing the space between you and them.

An important aspect of the defusing style is the acceptance by the adult that they may be contributing to the developing situation and that possibly their previous actions and demands of the pupil, however justified, acted as the trigger. As already suggested earlier in this chapter, the person who is present when the incident occurs is not necessarily the best person to work to resolve it. In any incident, an honest appraisal should be made by the teacher of whether their presence is contributing negatively to the situation.

Physical intervention

When dealing with more challenging forms of behaviour, there may be occasions where physical intervention is a consideration. 'Physical intervention' is used here as a generic term to cover those occasions when a teacher may consider it necessary to make physical contact with a pupil in response to the behaviour exhibited. Other terms applied include 'positive handling', 'use of reasonable force' and 'physical restraint'. The latter is heard less often because it has connotations of a higher level of physical intervention than is typically employed. There is nationally produced guidance on physical intervention and this has been updated numerous times since Circular 10/98 (DfEE 1998) first attempted to clarify teachers' powers in the wake of the Children Act 1989 where confusion had been introduced through a range of non-statutory guidance explaining how the Act should be interpreted (Allen 1998). There is no requirement for schools to have a policy on the use of force but current guidance advises that it is good practice to set out, in the behaviour policy, the circumstances in which force might be used (DfE 2013a). The guidance also encourages the governing body to notify the head teacher that it expects the school behaviour policy to include the power to use reasonable force.

The purpose of this section of the chapter is not to cover specific techniques or to replace national and local guidance on this subject but to highlight some key issues to consider.

Who can physically intervene?

The 2013 guidance states that 'all members of school staff have a legal power to use reasonable force' (DfE 2013a: 5) and specifies that:

> This power applies to any member of staff at the school. It can also apply to people whom the headteacher has temporarily put in charge of pupils such as unpaid volunteers or parents accompanying students on a school organised visit.
>
> (DfE 2013a: 5)

The situations in which school staff can physically intervene

The current guidance (DfE 2013a: 4) states that 'Reasonable force can be used to prevent pupils from hurting themselves or others, from damaging property, or from causing disorder'. It then provides the following list of examples of situations where reasonable force could be used:

- Removing disruptive children from the classroom where they have refused to follow an instruction to do so.
- Preventing a pupil behaving in a way that disrupts a school event or a school trip or visit.
- Preventing a pupil leaving the classroom where allowing the pupil to leave would risk their safety or lead to behaviour that disrupts the behaviour of others.
- Restraining a pupil from attacking a member of staff or another pupil, or to stop a fight in the playground.
- Restraining a pupil at risk of harming themselves through physical outbursts.

(DfE 2013a)

The list of examples reflects a perennial problem with all guidance produced from Circular 10/98 (DfEE 1998) onwards. Coverage of physical intervention to address issues of discipline is always included alongside coverage of physical intervention to prevent harm or serious injury. It is unfortunate in the list of examples provided by the guidance (DfE 2013a) that so many refer to disruption. While there may be a relatively high degree of consistency in judgements to physically intervene when a pupil is at serious risk of harming themselves or others, judgements over whether a pupil is 'causing disorder' (DfE 2013a: 4) at a level to warrant physical intervention are likely to be highly subjective.

The decision is likely to be influenced by a range of factors including the school's ethos and expectations, the context in which the behaviour occurs, and the individual teacher's awareness of, and willingness to use, a range of alternative non-physical strategies. The guidance is non-statutory and an interpretation of the 2006 Education and Inspections Act.[1] It states:

> A person to whom this section applies may use such force as is reasonable in the circumstances for the purpose of preventing a pupil from doing (or continuing to do) any of the following, namely—
>
> (a) committing any offence,
> (b) causing personal injury to, or damage to the property of, any person (including the pupil himself), or
> (c) prejudicing the maintenance of good order and discipline at the school or among any pupils receiving education at the school, whether during a teaching session or otherwise.
>
> (p. 74)

Previous guidance (e.g. DfEE 1998; DCSF 2007, 2010b) has quoted these categories and it has served as an important reminder that 'prejudicing the maintenance of good order and discipline' is only one of three. The repeated reference to disruption in the current guidance (DfE 2013a) arguably gives this category undue prominence. It is the one where we would suggest teachers need to consider extremely carefully whether a physical intervention is appropriate or whether there are other better ways of managing the situation.

The reference to committing an offence within the Act is talking about criminal offences. It includes pupils under the age of criminal responsibility, whose actions would be an offence if committed by an older pupil. The current DfE (2013a: 5) guidance also includes reference to the power of head teachers and authorised staff to 'use such force as is reasonable given the circumstances to conduct a search' without a pupil's consent for the following list of prohibited items:

- knives and weapons
- alcohol
- illegal drugs
- stolen items
- tobacco and cigarette papers
- fireworks
- pornographic images
- any article that has been or is likely to be used to commit an offence, cause personal injury or damage to property.

It should be noted that 'Force cannot be used to search for items banned under the school rules' (DfE 2013a: 5). It would therefore be inappropriate, for example, to search a pupil for a mobile phone or chewing gum because to possess these was against the school rules.

It is important that schools ensure that staff interpret possession of one of the prohibited items as a situation in which they *may* consider intervening physically; specifying these does not mean that staff *should* physically intervene. Factors influencing the decision to physically intervene are discussed later.

The concept of reasonable force

Despite successive claims by Government that guidance will be clarified, since Circular 10/98 (DfEE 1998) there has never been any real lack of clarity over the power to physically intervene or the situations in which this might be appropriate. The source of anxiety for many schools and teachers relates to the concept of reasonable force. By its nature this is an unclear concept. The last guidance on physical intervention produced by the Labour Government stated:

> There is no statutory definition of 'reasonable force'. Whether the force used is reasonable will always depend on the circumstances of individual cases. Deciding on whether the use of force is justified will depend in part upon the context in which the misbehaviour takes place. The test is whether the force used is proportionate to the consequences it is intended to prevent. The degree of force used should be the minimum needed to achieve the desired result. Use of force could not be justified to prevent trivial misbehaviour.
>
> (DCSF 2010b: 9)

It is interesting to note that this paragraph refers specifically to 'misbehaviour', which may imply a view that many of the challenges over the reasonableness of the force used are likely to concern physical intervention in relation to behaviour considered to be 'prejudicing the maintenance of good order and discipline' (DCSF 2010b: 8).

The current guidance (DfE 2013a) leaves any real attempt at a definition of reasonableness to an answer within a set of 'Frequently Asked Questions' where it states:

> The decision on whether to physically intervene is down to the professional judgement of the teacher concerned. Whether the force used is reasonable will always depend on the particular circumstances of the case. The use of force is reasonable if it is proportionate to the consequences it is intended to prevent. This means the degree of force used should be no more than is needed to achieve the desired result.
>
> (DfE 2013a: 9)

The decision to physically intervene

Circular 10/98 (DfEE 1998) was only a 10-page document. It increased to 19 pages in the 2007 guidance (DCSF 2007) and 234 pages in the 2010 guidance (DCSF 2010b). Reflecting a general trend in Coalition Government guidance, the current document (DfE 2013a) is only 11 pages long. Whether 234 pages was too unwieldy for schools to practically use, particularly in light of numerous other lengthy guidance documents produced by central Government related to many other aspects of school policy, is an area for debate. However, in reducing the size of the document so substantially, there is a risk that useful material on the complex area of physical intervention is lost and a perception is created that the issue is really not that complex.

The 2010 guidance (DCSF 2010b) contained some useful general advice that is still helpful in outlining the considerations before taking the decision to physically intervene. It states that staff need to make the clearest possible judgement about the following:

- The chances of achieving the desired result by other means. The lower the probability of achieving the desired result by other means, the more likely it is that using force may be justified.
- The seriousness of the incident, assessed by the effect of the injury, damage or disorder which is likely to result if force is not used. The greater the potential for injury, damage or serious disorder, the more likely it is that using force may be justified.
- The relative risks associated with physical intervention compared with using other strategies. The smaller the risks associated with physical intervention compared with other strategies, the more likely it is that using force may be justified.

(DCSF 2010b: 14)

Is a 'no touch' policy an acceptable option?

The 2013 guidance is clear that schools should not have a 'no contact' policy, suggesting 'There is a real risk that such a policy might place a member of staff in breach of their duty of care towards a pupil, or prevent them taking action needed to prevent a pupil causing harm' (DfE 2013a: 6).

This should not be interpreted as meaning that staff *must* physically intervene to exercise their duty of care. Their duty of care requires that they do *something* but this does not necessarily need to be physical. The previous guidance (DCSF 2010b) had confronted the same issue and, despite somewhat ominously referring to 'the potential consequences of not using this power' (DCSF 2010b: 5), actually provided a more reassuring message:

> Some members of staff may be concerned about the repercussions of failure on their part to use force; for example, if a complaint is brought against them on the grounds that they could have avoided a child suffering injury if they had used force to break up a fight. In a situation such as this, it is extremely unlikely that a teacher would be found to be negligent by a court, provided they had taken all reasonable steps to ensure the safety of pupils short of using force.

(DCSF 2010b: 5)

How to physically intervene

In a departure from previous versions, the 2013 guidance (DfE 2013a) does not attempt to provide any guidance on how to physically intervene beyond identifying four specific techniques that are considered to present an unacceptable risk when used on children and young people. Schools are simply advised to take their own decisions about staff training. In many ways, this brevity is a positive move because an issue associated with previous guidance was that some of the general techniques suggested, such as 'leading a pupil by the hand or arm' or 'ushering a pupil away by placing a hand in the centre of the back' (DCSF 2007, 2010b), posed risks to the pupil if they forcibly resisted these attempts to move them. Inevitably within a guidance document, there was not sufficient scope to give the detailed consideration to escorting and guiding methods that there is within training. A further suggestion was that the adult might intervene by 'standing between pupils or blocking a pupil's path'. Clearly physically standing between two tall 16–year-old pupils engaged in a fight places the adult at considerable personal risk.

Training providers are likely to be able to offer specific techniques for escorting a pupil or breaking up fights that are considerably safer than those described in the Government guidance.

Training has never been mandatory for teachers in any of the guidance (e.g. DfEE 1998; DCSF 2007, 2010b). While this issue is not given the same prominence as it is within the 2010 guidance (DCSF 2010b), the current guidance states that 'The head-teacher should consider whether members of staff require any additional training to enable them to carry out their responsibilities and should consider the needs of the pupils when doing so' (DfE 2013a: 6). Despite the brevity of this statement, there is a clear implication that schools should be considering the training needs of their staff in relation to physical intervention. If you have not had any training in this area, it would be reasonable to raise this issue with the appropriate person in your school.

Training in physical intervention is typically delivered in the broader context of a whole school approach to behaviour management and coverage of preventative strategies and de-escalation techniques. Trainers usually provide some coverage of these areas as well as teaching the physical techniques and providing time in the session to practise these in a controlled, supervised environment with colleagues.

Although most physical intervention providers rightly stress the importance of the non-physical elements and provide some coverage, it would be naïve as a school to accept the extent of this training as sufficient. Other services such as local authority behaviour support teams and educational psychologists may be able to provide valuable additional training in these areas.

Recording

The current guidance (DfE 2013a: 7) merely states:

> It is good practice for schools to speak to parents about serious incidents involving the use of force and to consider how best to record such serious incidents. It is up to schools to decide whether it is appropriate to report the use of force to parents.

Clearly records of any incidents of physical intervention, completed as soon as possible after the event, are important in responding to any query, complaint or allegation. Your school will be able to advise on its expectations in these situations. Once again, it is the more detailed 2010 guidance that provides the better general guide to the principles for recording physical interventions. Schools were advised to keep records of significant incidents. 'Significant' is of course an interpretable term. In deciding whether or not an incident must be reported, the guidance suggested schools needed to be aware that:

- An incident where unreasonable use of force is used on a pupil would always be a significant incident.
- Any incident where substantial force has been used (e.g. physically pushing a pupil out of a room) would be significant.
- The use of a restraint technique is significant.
- An incident where a child was very distressed (though clearly not over reacting) would be significant.

(DCSF 2010b: 19)

It was recommended that schools took into account:

- the pupil's behaviour and the level of risk presented at the time
- the degree of force used and whether it was proportionate in relation to the behaviour
- the effect on the pupil or member of staff.

(DCSF 2010b: 19)

The example incident form provided within the guidance asks for the following:

- details of the pupil on whom force was used – name, class, and any SEN, disability or other vulnerability
- the date, time and location of the incident
- details of other pupils involved (directly or as witnesses), including whether any of the pupils involved were vulnerable for SEN, disability, medical or social reasons
- a description of the incident by the staff involved, including any attempts to de-escalate and warnings given that force might be used
- the reason for using force and a description of the force used
- information on any injury suffered by staff or pupils and any first aid and/or medical attention required
- the reasons for making a record of this incident
- information on the follow-up, including post-incident support and any disciplinary action against pupils
- any information about the incident shared with staff not involved in it and external agencies
- details of when and how those with parental responsibility were informed about the incident and any views they expressed
- a note of whether any complaint had been lodged (but details of it should not be recorded on the incident form).

(DCSF 2010b)

Follow-up

When an incident results in injuries to a pupil or to staff, immediate action should be taken to provide first aid and to access medical help for any injuries that go beyond this.

Serious incidents that involve the use of physical intervention can also be upsetting and unsettling to all concerned – the pupil, the adult(s) and observers. Consideration needs to be given to the support needed by all involved. In following up the incident with the pupil, it is important to be mindful of the recovery and post-crisis depression phases of Breakwell's (1997) assault cycle described earlier in this chapter. The adult's emotional state may have followed a similar cycle and schools should recognise that after a significant incident it may be very difficult for a member of staff to simply turn their attention to their teaching duties.

The priority at the time of the incident is resolving it as safely as possible. However this does not exempt the pupil from consequences. This may involve the use of sanctions which need to be considered in accordance with the school's behaviour policy. Consideration should also be given to the provision of an opportunity for the pupil to repair the relationships with staff and pupils involved in the incident (DCSF 2010b). If a pupil's last contact with, for example, their History teacher, was being held, it is very difficult for both them and their teacher to meet perhaps 4 or 5 days later in a lesson and resume the normal teacher-pupil relationship as though nothing had happened.

At a preventative level, the pupil needs to be supported to develop strategies to avoid repeating crisis points in future. The incident should trigger a consideration by the school of specific interventions the pupil may require. It might, for example, be appropriate to incorporate them in an anger management or social skills group or provide access to a school counsellor.

It is also necessary for the teacher to review their own part in the incident in order to develop strategies to avoid repeating crisis points in the future. This will involve reviewing antecedents, including any actions they took, and a consideration of things that could have been handled differently. Some schools will have clear systems to support staff in this process. It is important that any such process is supportive rather than about blame and provides a genuine opportunity to analyse, reflect and learn from the incident.

The ethics of physical intervention

We can probably all conceive of situations in schools when physical intervention may be necessary. Scenarios about which there is likely to be a higher degree of consensus are most likely to fall in the category of pupils causing personal injury to themselves or others. We would not wish to suggest physical intervention can always be avoided but we would encourage readers to reflect critically on this issue, particularly in relation to the disruptive behaviour referred to in current guidance (DfE 2013a).

Activity 9.1

Read the following quote from Hewett and Arnett (1996):

'If a pupil is generally unco-operative, the educational imperative should be the development of participation, not subjugation of her/his will especially with the youngest of children. The early years are the time to work on the fundamentals of participation, and the temptation to pick up a tiny child and to dominate him or her physically (just because he or she is tiny) must be resisted. Unfortunately schools are often subject to pressures demanding instant results and consequently their intention to work through co-operation and participation may be undermined.'

(Hewett and Arnett 1996: 132)

- To what extent do you agree with or disagree with their argument?
- What questions does it raise for teachers of young children in particular when considering whether to physically intervene?

Now consider these three points from Cornwall (2000):

1   'Physical restraint practices give out a very strong "enforcement" message to young people. Should we accept that it is the teachers' role to coerce and control young people to remain in the classroom against their will?' (Cornwall 2000: 22).

2   'Using physical control whilst at the same time motivating and socialising troubled children does not seem compatible' (Cornwall 2000: 22).

3   'If challenging and physically aggressive behaviour is seen as a form of communication – then what is communicated to pupils when they are physically restrained by a group of adults? Might is right?' (Cornwall 2000: 20).

- What is your response to the points raised in quotes 1 and 2 regarding the teacher's role?
- What is your response to the point raised in quote 3 regarding what the pupil and others who witness it may learn from a physical intervention?
- To what extent are there parallels between Cornwall's (2000) points and the concerns expressed by Hewett and Arnett (1996)?

Conclusion

Serious behavioural incidents are fortunately relatively rare (DfES 2005a). This chapter has sought to provide information to guide practice when such incidents do occur. The nature of such incidents means that that they are always likely to be unpredictable but awareness of the emotions behind the behaviour contributes to a better understanding of how the pupil is experiencing the situation and models such as Breakwell's (1997) assault cycle can inform priorities at any given stage of a developing incident.

Physical intervention remains a complex and contentious issue. Despite the need for clarification implied by repeated Government promises, schools' powers in this area have arguably been clear since Circular 10/98 (DfEE 1998). There are no easy answers; the types of situation where physical intervention is a consideration are likely to involve high stakes decisions that necessarily take into account many variables. More nationally produced guidance is unlikely to provide any greater clarity. Rather, the way forward would seem to be professional dialogue within staff teams that ensures teachers and others are clear about the content of existing national and local guidance and the expectations regarding the interpretation of this within their own school.

Note

1 Available online at www.legislation.gov.uk/ukpga/2006/40/pdfs/ukpga_20060040_en.pdf (accessed 21 July 2014).

Chapter 10

Professional development, reflection and theory

Introduction

The 2012 Teachers' Standards differed from preceding sets because they set out a single set of standards that applied 'to the vast majority of teachers regardless of their career stage' (DfE 2011a: 1). This was a significant difference to the model that had developed under the Labour administration (1997–2010). The 2007 set of professional standards defined the characteristics of teachers at particular career stages:

- The award of qualified teacher status (QTS)
- Teachers on the main scale (core)
- Teachers on the upper pay scale (post-threshold teachers)
- Excellent Teachers
- Advanced Skills Teachers (ASTs).

The five sets of standards were intended to 'provide the framework for a teacher's career and clarify what progression looks like' (TDA 2007: 2). The existence of five distinct sets of standards reinforced the message that there was recognition and an expectation of progression from trainee, to early career teacher and beyond. The current standards are described as representing 'the minimum level of practice expected of trainees and teachers from the point of being awarded QTS' (DfE 2011a: 2). Providers of initial teacher training (ITT) are advised to 'assess trainees against the standards in a way that is consistent with what could reasonably be expected of a trainee teacher prior to the award of QTS' (DfE 2011a: 3). Head teachers (or appraisers) are required to:

> assess teachers' performance against the standards to a level that is consistent with what should reasonably be expected of a teacher in the relevant role and at the relevant stage of their career (whether they are a newly qualified teacher (NQT), a mid-career teacher, or a more experienced practitioner).
>
> (DfE 2011a: 3)

Although at a structural level the adoption of a single set of standards could be seen as conveying less of an expectation of professional progression than the five distinct sets, the 2012 standards clearly state that:

> Appropriate self-evaluation, reflection and professional development activity is critical to improving teachers' practice at all career stages . . . As their careers progress,

teachers will be expected to extend the depth and breadth of knowledge, skill and understanding that they demonstrate in meeting the standards, as is judged to be appropriate to the role they are fulfilling and the context in which they are working.

(DfE 2011a: 4)

This chapter focuses on how, in relation to pupil behaviour, teachers can seek to develop their practice through the use of theory and reflection.

Changing priorities

In an article reporting on research carried out with a small group of trainee teachers, McNally *et al.* (2005) made the point that behaviour management was at best a temporary conceptualisation of use to trainees. Powell and Tod (2004: 2) acknowledged that 'skills in delivering a range of strategies are clearly a *necessary* part of an NQT's survival toolkit'. From both authors, the implication is that a focus on a discrete set of teacher skills known as *behaviour management*, typically construed as an awareness of strategies to use in response to misbehaviour, might have some utility in the early stages of a teacher's career. In many ways, this links to how we often learn to tackle other complex tasks that ultimately involve multiple skills being used in an integrated and sometimes simultaneous manner. The notion of a progression from unconscious incompetence to unconscious competence is a relevant consideration:

- Unconscious incompetence: the individual does not understand or know how to do something, but they do not necessarily recognise their own deficits in this area or the skills it will be necessary to acquire.
- Conscious incompetence: although the individual does not understand or know how to do something, they recognise their current limitations and have some understanding of how much there is to learn.
- Conscious competence: the individual understands or knows how to do something. However, performing the skill or applying the knowledge requires a lot of conscious effort because little has become automated or second nature.
- Unconscious competence: the individual is so familiar with performing the skill or applying the knowledge that it has become second nature. As a result, considerably less conscious effort needs to be devoted to it and the individual can give more attention to other tasks.

(based on O'Connor and Seymour 2003)

Within this model, the word 'incompetence' may be a little distracting because of its more common association with failure to meet a standard and inadequacy in a role. However, the important message is that, at the early stage of learning, an individual has to devote a lot of conscious effort to being competent. A beginning teacher is likely to need to devote a lot of conscious attention to individual aspects of their role and one of these is likely to be behaviour management. With experience, it is hoped that strategies related to behaviour management will become seamlessly integrated into the teacher's practice and require less conscious attention, particularly in relation to the more commonly occurring, predictable behaviours.

A challenge sometimes in providing observation opportunities for new teachers is that the teacher who is regularly and overtly using strategies to manage incidents of misbehaviour is probably not the 'good' behaviour manager. The teacher who provides the example of good practice may be doing a lot of very subtle, barely noticeable things that serve to maintain 'a good and safe learning environment' (DfE 2011a: 8). This teacher may be operating at the unconscious competence level and struggling themselves to actually specify what all these subtle elements are.

Research has suggested that teachers progress through a number of stages as they move from being a trainee into their early careers. Fuller and Brown (1975) referred to three discrete stages of student teachers' development. The first two stages were defined as 'survival' and 'mastery'. At the third stage, Fuller and Brown (1975) argued, the student either settles into routines and becomes resistant to change or becomes 'consequence orientated'. The teacher who is 'consequence orientated' effectively shifts their attention to a concern for their impact on their pupils and is responsive to feedback about their teaching. This progression can be summarised as moving from 'survival concerns' to 'task concerns' to 'impact concerns' (Furlong and Maynard 1995). The suggestion that behaviour management is either a temporary conceptualisation (McNally *et al.* 2005) or a necessary part of an NQT's survival toolkit (Powell and Tod 2004) reflects the idea that an explicit and discrete focus on this area of activity may be necessary, understandable and justified. In many ways, the behaviour for learning approach is about moving from the survival concern of 'How will I cope with behaviour?' and the task concerns of 'Do I know enough strategies to manage behaviour?' to a concern regarding impact, expressed in terms of the development of learning behaviour.

Central to this chapter is the belief that, although there may be different priorities early on related to coping with and managing behaviour, professional development and growth in relation to behaviour occurs through reflective practice and engagement with theory.

Reflective practice

The concept of 'reflective practice' can be traced back to Dewey (1910, 1933). He was among the first to identify reflection as a distinct form of thinking, defining reflective thinking as 'active, persistent and careful consideration of any belief or supposed form of knowledge in the light of the grounds that support it and further conclusions to which it tends' (Dewey 1933: 9).

Dewey considered that the process of reflective thinking consisted of two elements:

> Reflective thinking, in distinction from other operations to which we apply the name of thought, involves (1) a state of doubt, hesitation, perplexity, mental difficulty, in which thinking originates, and (2) an act of searching, hunting, inquiring to find material that will resolve the doubt, settle and dispose of perplexity.'
>
> (Dewey 1933: 12)

Schön (1983) built on Dewey's work in his seminal text *The Reflective Practitioner: How Professionals Think in Action*. He distinguished between reflection-in-action and reflection-on-action. Reflection-in-action reflected Schön's view that in order to cope with the complex, unpredictable and messy nature of practice, professionals have to be able to do more than follow set procedures. They need to act both intuitively and creatively, drawing on both practical experience and theory as they think on their feet and improvise (Finlay 2008).

Reflection-on-action occurs after an activity has taken place and involves the teacher in thinking about their own actions and how pupils responded, making judgements about effectiveness and considering whether any changes to their actions could have resulted in different outcomes.

Summarising the reflective practitioner discourse, Moore (2004) suggests that the emphasis is not on 'discrete practical skills, techniques and areas of knowledge but, rather, the particular skills needed to reflect constructively upon continuing experience as a way of improving the quality and effectiveness of one's work' (Moore 2004: 100). Based on research conducted with student teachers, Moore (2004) identified five 'sites' of reflective practice. These were:

1   Thinking about practice 'on your feet'.
2   Solitary 'in-the-head', retrospective reflections on lessons or events carried out some time after the lesson or event has occurred.
3   Evaluations (usually written, carried out after individual lessons, confined to individual lessons and focusing on pupil and teacher performance).
4   Intra-professional verbalised reflections carried out in the company of others in the same community of practice (for example, other teachers or beginning teachers, not necessarily working at the same school).
5   Extra-professional verbalised reflections carried out in the company of selected support networks (for example, family or friends working in other occupations).

The criticism that could be levelled at the reflective practitioner discourse is that a new teacher in particular, by virtue of their limited experiences, may bring very few reference points upon which to base their professional reflection. Dewey (1910) himself noted that reflection depended on 'a certain fund or store of experiences or facts from which suggestions proceed' (Dewey 1910: 30). Viewed from this perspective, some of Moore's (2004) sites of reflection may raise some issues:

•   Thinking about practice 'on your feet' and solitary 'in-the-head' reflection are bounded by what the individual knows, understands and believes about behaviour. This will vary in each individual, based on experiences up to this point.
•   When written evaluations are completed, this is likely to be to fulfil a school or training provider requirement and may limit reflection to a consideration of practice only in relation to a list of standards or competences the teacher is required to meet. This may be at the expense of the teacher 'reflecting on the systems, histories and conditions within which they are practising' (Moore 2004: 108).
•   Intra-professional verbalised reflections carried out in the company of others in the same community of practice introduces a broader perspective, particularly when involving teachers from other schools. However, the quality and breadth of reflection is constrained by the range and nature of teachers to which an individual has access.
•   Extra-professional verbalised reflections carried out within selected support networks may fulfil a human need to offload. However, pupil behaviour is one topic that tends to engender strong opinions in the general public in terms of cause, the perceived scale of the problem and possible solutions. The teacher needs to be professionally discerning in what they take from the contribution of others in this situation.

The central tenet of this book is that the Behaviour for Learning conceptual framework provides the reference point for professional reflection-on-action and reflection-in-action

(Schön 1983). Additionally, it is a framework that allows for professional reflection before action in the sense of providing the means by which to judge the appropriateness of any strategy, approach, intervention or course of action the teacher considers incorporating into their practice. To reiterate, any strategy, approach, intervention or course of action should:

- contribute to the development of positive learning behaviours
- protect, enhance but never compromise relationship with self
- protect, enhance but never compromise relationship with others
- protect, enhance but never compromise relationship with the curriculum.

The framework allows a general level of reflection whereby the teacher considers how any strategy, approach, intervention or course of action is likely to be experienced by a typical pupil, and the more specific level whereby the reflection is based on how a particular pupil might have experienced it.

As Moore (2004) notes, reflection draws on the range of strategies and techniques the teacher has at their disposal but may also necessitate the development of new ones. There is an implication too that the teacher has:

> a sound understanding . . . of relevant educational theory and research – including theories of cognitive, linguistic and affective development – in order to address issues not restricted to the 'what' and 'when' of education but embracing also questions of 'how' and even 'why'.
>
> (Moore 2004: 101)

Moore's (2004) observations highlight the point that reflection may result in an awareness of the need for more learning on the part of the teacher in order to develop new strategies and techniques and extend their understanding of educational theory and research.

What do you need to know more about?

A defining feature of the behaviour for learning approach is that it emerged from a literature review. Theories found in the literature consulted gave rise to the three relationships (with self, with others and with the curriculum). This foundation can be used as the basis for targeting the development of your knowledge, skills and understanding related to behaviour based on need or simply curiosity (see Figure 10.1).

Do you need theory?

On the back cover of her popular book *Getting the Buggers to Behave*, Cowley asks, 'How many of us, snowed under with reports to write and lessons to plan, have time to wade through endless theory?' (Cowley 2003: back cover).

Whether this represents the relationship teachers generally have with theory is unclear. However, sales of Cowley's book would suggest that it is a message that resonates to some degree. The implication is that theory is at best a luxury or an optional extra that could be engaged with if there were fewer day-to-day pressures. There is no suggestion that theory could play an important role in informing practice.

Cowley's (2003) reference to 'endless theory' may conjure up images of very thick, rather dusty, difficult to read textbooks that are detached from the realities of the

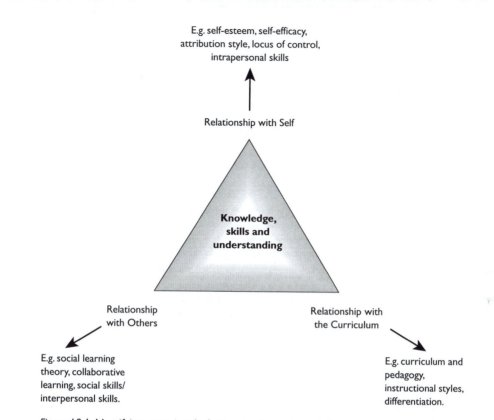

Figure 10.1 Identifying areas in which to extend your knowledge

classroom. When people talk about theory in the social sciences, there is no one mean-ing (Thomas 2009) and at this point it is perhaps helpful to stop and consider what we mean by theory in the context of this chapter. We are essentially using a definition that we believe many teachers implicitly apply; this is that theory simply refers to anything that is not practice. Practice encompasses learning from doing the job of teaching, formal and informal opportunities to observe colleagues, and informal and formal advice given by colleagues. Theory would include, for example, research reports, well-referenced academic texts, books aimed at practitioners, national Ofsted reports, specialist and other websites, and nationally or locally produced guidance materials. The common theme is that these represent perspectives from outside the teacher's own immediate school envi-ronment. There is a risk, particularly with the increase in school-based routes to QTS, that a teacher's experience can be insular with their professional development constrained by the quality and range of practice in a particular school.

Reading critically

There is a plethora of material available related to behaviour. It is important to recognise the nature and quality of what you are accessing. Table 7.1 suggests some questions you could ask yourself.

Table 10.1 Judging the nature and quality of material you access

Question	Consideration
Who is the author?	Is it an individual, an organisation, etc.?
Do the author's credentials give you confidence that they have a good knowledge of the topic?	Remember this does not necessarily have to be experience as a teacher.
Have they published other work?	Are they well known in this field or does this appear to be their first foray into this area?
What is the purpose of the text?	For example, is it research intended to provide enhanced understanding of an issue, a practitioners' guide or a Government guidance document?
Is it a report on research carried out by the authors?	Based on their sample size and method, is it reasonable to generalise findings to your own setting?
Is it funded research or produced by or on behalf of a particular organisation?	Look out for indicators that it might be presenting a one-sided view or be underpinned by a particular agenda.
If it is an article, is it from a peer-reviewed journal?	If peer reviewed it provides the reassurance that others in the field consider it suitable for publication.
Does it contain a list of references at the back or other citation information indicating other sources that have informed the content?	Without references you may simply be reading the idiosyncratic ideas of an individual.

A number of points in Table 10.1 can usefully be applied to websites. The internet is a valuable and readily accessible source of information but it is unregulated. As Thomas (2009) notes, a website is just a medium for carrying information and so has no inherent strengths or weaknesses. It is up to the individual to make judgements regarding the quality of any site they access. Table 10.2 sets out some additional considerations to bear in mind when accessing web-based material.

An important point to make in relation to Tables 10.1 and 10.2 is that an issue identified through the 'considerations' column only becomes a problem if you do not notice it and rely unquestioningly on one source to guide your practice that, for example, happens to present a biased, insufficiently considered or misguided view. Engaging with multiple perspectives from different sources and deciding where you locate yourself professionally within a debate, or clarifying your own stance in response to views expressed in a specific source, can be valuable.

Evidence-based and evidence-informed practice

A question that teachers 'snowed under with reports to write and lessons to plan' (Cowley 2003: back cover) may not ask themselves often enough is whether there is any evidence to indicate that the practices and approaches they use in relation to behaviour, or are contemplating implementing, are supported by any evidence.

Following the movement towards evidence-based practice in the field of medicine (Sackett *et al.* 1996, 2000), this approach has gained prominence in other areas of

Table 10.2 Additional considerations when accessing web-based material

Question	Consideration
Does the website belong to an organisation or individual?	If it is an organisation: • Is it one you have heard of and believe to be reputable? • Even if reputable, is it an organisation that you know to have a particular stance or agenda? If it is an individual: • Is it someone you know as an expert in the field? • If not known to you, try doing a search using their name to see what else they have written or whether they are referenced by others. • What are their credentials?
How is the website funded?	If funding comes from advertising or sponsorship, it is important to consider whether this could influence the views expressed and range of material presented.
Who is the intended audience?	Is the intended audience academics, professionals, parents or just other like-minded people?
Quality of presentation	Does the website generally look amateurish? Does it look inappropriately informal for the type of professional issues it refers? Are there numerous spelling and grammatical errors or other signs of general sloppiness?
Does the material display signs of bias?	Does the material overtly or implicitly promote a particular viewpoint? If presenting a particular view, is there any engagement with alternative perspectives? If so, does this take the form of critical debate or is any counter-perspective simply denigrated? If the website reports the views of other writers, pursue these original sources and see if their views are represented reasonably accurately.
Is the material current?	When was it written? Is there any indication of when it was last updated?
How do the views presented compare with other sources?	Check the information against recognised other sources in which you have confidence. If the website contains specific facts, check these for accuracy against other sources that report them

healthcare as well as education, public administration and, to a limited extent, business more generally (Lester 2007; Nevo and Slonim-Nevo 2011). Sackett *et al.* (1996: 71) defined evidence-based practice as 'the conscientious, explicit and judicious use of current evidence in making decisions about care of individual patients'.

Nevo and Slonim-Nevo (2011: 1177) cite Webb's generic definition of evidence based practice as ' . . . the conscientious, explicit and judicious use of current best evidence in making decisions regarding the welfare of service-users and carers' (Webb 2001: 61). The terminology used within this definition makes it more applicable to a wider range of professions than Sackett *et al.*'s (1996) version.

In a conference presentation, Hammersley observed that it is difficult to argue with the notion of evidence-based practice because the name itself represents 'a slogan whose rhetorical effect is to discredit opposition' (Hammersley 2001). The implication built into the phrase 'evidence-based practice' is that opposition to it can only be irrational, based on a view that practice without evidence might somehow be a desirable alternative. Criticism of evidence-based practice tends to focus on the issue that it may privilege particular forms of quantitative data and encourage methodological approaches that value what is measurable rather than necessarily measuring what is valuable.

As a complex social endeavour, teaching inevitably involves a range of interacting variables related to the pupils, the teacher and the school context, and it does not lend itself to an interpretation of evidence-based practice as reviewing empirical evidence and choosing effective strategies, approaches and interventions. Nevo and Slonim-Nevo (2011) argue in favour of the term 'evidence-informed practice' (EIP). While excluding entirely baseless strategies, approaches and interventions and those based simply on personal hunches and preferences, tradition or ideology, evidence-informed practice leaves ample room for 'the constructive and imaginative judgement and knowledge of practitioners and clients who must be in constant interaction and dialogue with one another for most interventions to succeed' (Nevo and Slonim-Nevo 2011: 3).

For teachers, we would suggest that evidence-informed practice takes the form shown in Figure 10.2.

There are external evidence bases that will range from research studies through to recommendations from a variety of sources where it is necessary to place a degree of trust in the provider's professionalism. For example, if an educational psychologist recommends a particular intervention, the assumption would reasonably be that this was informed by some form of evidence. It is also reasonable for a teacher to ask about the evidence base in response to such a recommendation. With the emphasis on schools working together to improve practice, either formally through federations or informally, there is a need to recognise a distinction between recommendations based simply on the principle of 'what worked for me' and those that are underpinned by a broader evidence base. While the former may be helpful and in some cases benefit from the recommender's

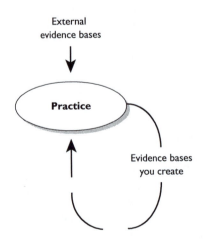

Figure 10.2 Developing evidence-informed practice

direct knowledge of the pupil or school, there is still a need to consider whether the approach, intervention or strategy is based on evaluated effectiveness or reflects a recognised approach that features in literature related to behaviour.

It should be recognised that in relation to behaviour the evidence base that informs practice will typically take the form of literature related to behaviour (or the specific intervention, approach or intervention you are interested in) and broad theoretical perspectives on behaviour, such as behavioural, cognitive-behavioural, eco-systemic, humanistic, psychodynamic and social learning models. In their literature review investigating teaching strategies and approaches for pupils with SEN, Davis and Florian (2004) found that in relation to behaviour, emotional and social development there were three main theoretical perspectives that underpinned the research literature:

- *behavioural* models, which use principles of reinforcement and punishment to reduce maladaptive or inappropriate behaviours and increase adaptive behaviours
- *cognitive-behavioural* models, which are an elaboration of learning theory to take account of the capacity of individuals to understand and reflect on their behaviour (in particular focusing on the way internalised speech serves to regulate behaviour)
- *systemic* models, (incorporating eco-systemic) which take account of the organisational context within which inappropriate behaviour occurs and attempt to change behaviour by modifying the context (e.g. arranging the classroom environment to minimise distractions).

(Davis and Florian 2004: 23)

The other form of evidence base is that which the school or individual teachers create as a result of practice. The value of such evidence should not be neglected. It is the type of evidence that emerges through the routine monitoring of interventions. For example, if a school puts in place a particular intervention for literacy for a group of pupils, it is hoped that attainment data before and after the intervention will show the rate of progress pupils have made. Conclusions can be drawn, particularly when an intervention is used regularly, as to whether it does lead to progress, how much progress it generally leads to, and the profile of pupils who will typically gain most and least from this. This can then inform future planning. However, the challenge in relation to behaviour is the type of data that is available. Ofsted (2004: 12) noted that:

While schools were able to point to improvements in behaviour, for example, in the reduction of referrals and in the use of sanctions, few schools analysed the progress such pupils made in their learning and were therefore unable to evaluate the impact of their provision for them.

Some schools may have found this judgement a little harsh. Their provision may have brought about attitudinal and behavioural changes that were conducive to improvements in learning but these improvements may not necessarily have registered yet in terms of academic progress. The behaviour for learning approach offers a way of measuring change through its focus on the development of learning behaviours. While we have deliberately avoided the production of checklists because this would imply that there is a fixed range of learning behaviours to be developed, we do advocate that time is spent defining the target learning behaviours for individuals or groups. Monitoring and evaluation then takes the form of looking for the emergence of the learning behaviours. This provides the evidence base in relation to the individual but it can also be used collectively as the evidence base for particular interventions. For example, it would be possible to define a set of learning behaviours to be developed in individuals through an anger management group and to judge the efficacy of this intervention by the extent to which individuals display these learning behaviours.

The teacher as researcher

Consideration of the evidence base developed by the school or individual teacher naturally leads on to consideration of the teacher taking on a more structured role as a researcher of their own or their school's practice. Sometimes this move will be the result of Master's level study through a higher education institution. The value of such study is that it develops enduring and transferable skills in critical thinking that the teacher can apply within their practice. However an enquiry-based approach could also be adopted:

- by an individual teacher seeking to develop their own practice in relation to pupil behaviour
- when a department, year group or key stage team is working towards improving practice
- as the framework for a working party's activity to address an identified behaviour issue within the school.

Although it is conceivable that a well-motivated individual teacher might decide to engage in an enquiry investigating their own practice, it is perhaps more likely that this will occur in a school where a research culture already exists. Handscomb and MacBeath (2003: 4) proposed that schools could become research engaged by placing research and enquiry 'at the heart of the school, its outlook, systems and activity'. Sharp et al. (2006) suggested that a research-engaged school displayed eight key characteristics:

1   The school leadership is committed to using evidence for school improvement.
2   The school's culture encourages challenge and learning.
3   Commitment of resources to enable staff to spend time on research.
4   A collaborative ethos among members of staff (the research team).
5   Access to sources of research expertise to advise the planning, conduct, analysis and interpretation of research.
6   Access to mentoring support (e.g. from colleagues within the school).
7   Commitment to share research within the school.
8   Commitment to forging research communities within and beyond the school.

Whether you in are such an environment or are unilaterally adopting an enquiry-based approach, the following general points may be helpful.

Finding a focus

The focus for the enquiry should be based on genuine need. As a starting point in developing your focus, you could consider the following:

- An established or newly introduced aspect of your own or your school's practice where there might be some doubt (or simply a lack of existing evidence) about whether it is leading to the outcomes anticipated. An example might be use of a 6-session anger management group for pupils who exhibit difficulties in this area.
- A strategy, approach or intervention that is being introduced where it is necessary to gather data on how this is experienced and interpreted by pupils and others (e.g. colleagues and parents) and its overall impact. An example might be the introduction of a nurture group for new Year 7 pupils identified as vulnerable by their primary schools.
- An issue or phenomenon in your classroom or school about which there is currently insufficient understanding (i.e. something is happening but you don't really know why). An example might be a disproportionately high number of pupils sent to the time-out room by the department you work in.

Once a broad area has been identified, it should then be developed into one clear research question, probably broken down into a series of secondary or sub-questions. To take an example, a teacher might decide that their overarching question is: 'How effective is our use of lunch time detentions in promoting positive learning behaviours?' The sub questions might then be:

- When do teachers issue lunch time detentions?
- How many pupils regularly and repeatedly receive lunchtime detentions?
- What are pupils' and teachers' perceptions of the effectiveness of the lunchtime detentions in promoting positive learning behaviours?'

Good sub-questions are likely to begin to stimulate initial thoughts on where data are located and even hint at the method for gathering the information needed. For example, in exploring when teachers issue lunchtimes detentions, we might ask colleagues via interviews or questionnaires about the behaviours that typically result in the issuing of lunchtime detentions.

Although we have given examples that relate to broader school issues, investigating issues concerning individual classroom management is equally relevant. You might, for example, simply want to know 'How is my use of positive feedback and positive correction and sanctions experienced by pupils?' One sub-question might relate to the balance between these, and the activity in Chapter 6 would be one way of gathering data on this.

Locating your enquiry within a broader perspective

If you were undertaking your enquiry as part of an academic course, there would typically be an expectation that you would include a critical review of literature related to your focus area. Even if you are not engaged in an enquiry for this reason, it is still important to explore what others are saying about your area of interest. This is a way of locating your enquiry within a broader perspective. It could be, for example, that your experiences in your classroom reflect known issues, or the intervention you are investigating has been the subject of a substantial evaluation. Consulting the literature will reveal the areas of consensus, areas of difference, the controversies and the contentious areas related to your chosen topic. Just as with theory, the term 'literature' can be interpreted broadly.

It is not just limited to academic texts and research reports; it can extend to sources such as books aimed at practitioners, national Ofsted reports, specialist and other websites, and nationally or locally produced guidance materials. In selecting and using sources, we would refer you back to Tables 10.1 and 10.2.

A brief word on paradigms

Any investigation you undertake in your school is likely to be framed within a qualitative, interpretative paradigm, although in linking these terms ('qualitative' and 'interpretative') to summarise a broad perspective we would note that strictly they are not equivalent and interchangeable (Klein and Myers 1999; Neuman 1997). Sample sizes will typically be small and there may be many interacting variables that could be affecting the outcomes that you cannot realistically control, meaning the potential to generalise to a wider population is inevitably limited. Instead, you are prioritising the development of specific, in-depth findings that allow you to generate some implications for future practice. You are likely to be concerned with participants' perceptions, feelings, ideas, thoughts and actions (Thomas 2009). Rather than attempting to stand outside the research as an independent researcher, you will be capitalising on the additional contextual understanding you have as an insider.

None of the above means that you cannot collect data that are quantitative. For your area of research you might, for example, draw on pupil progress data or develop a method of data gathering that yields results that can be represented in numerical form. Our point is simply that it is important to recognise that, by the type of small-scale enquiry you undertake and your role as a practitioner researcher, you are almost inevitably located within a qualitative, interpretative paradigm. Awareness of this can help to avoid under-lying assumptions about what represents research, often based on the influence of the positivist tradition, leading to thinking, approaches and priorities being applied that are neither relevant to, nor fit comfortably with, the type of research being undertaken.

Selecting your methods of enquiry

A mind-mapping exercise is a useful way of moving from the questions to methods. For each of the sub-questions, try to identify the key stakeholders or other sources of infor-mation. These should be identified first. Once this is done it is then possible to insert the method of accessing this information. Figure 10.3 provides an example of how this approach could be applied to one of the sub-questions.

The example presented in Figure 10.3 adopts a traditional approach based on inter-views and questionnaires. In this case, group interviews are used for pupils because these are likely to be a less daunting experience than a one-to-one interview. Group interviews also provide the opportunity for comments from individual participants to stimulate the thinking of others in the group and so generate responses that might not have occurred in a one-to-one interview. Additionally, the interviewer can often get an indication of whether there are shared views or varying opinions in a group. The disadvantages include the possibility that some individuals may dominate and others may not want to voice views that they anticipate will be out of step with the general view within the group. The following list, developed from Durrant and Holden (2006), illustrates that, in addition to the more traditional research methods of interviews, questionnaires and observations, there are a number of other options:

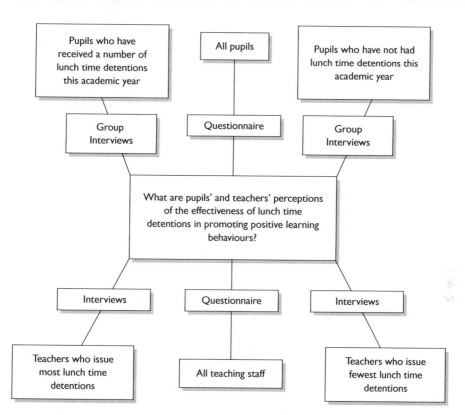

Figure 10.3 Selecting your methods of enquiry

- questionnaires, audits and surveys
- interviews – parents, pupils, teachers
- pupils interviewing each other in pairs and taking notes
- observations in the class, in the playground and so on
- observations and conversations in other schools
- whole class or focus group discussion, notes on a flipchart
- small group discussion summarised on posters
- notes taken by teaching assistant during normal lessons in relation to the focus topic
- teacher's own reflective journal of the lesson
- pupils use digital cameras and camcorders to present their own perspectives
- pupils keep a journal or blog, participate in online discussion or email the teacher
- email and discussion board correspondence between colleagues in relation to the focus topic
- people's (staff's or pupils') reflections expressed verbally, in writing (poetry, story, analogy and factual) and in pictures or diagrams
- critical incidents (analysis based on incident log)
- colleagues use a diamond ranking or other card-based activity to identify issues and priorities

- issue 'sticky notes' and ask for comments related to the focus topic to be stuck onto posters in the staffroom
- time allocated on the agenda of an existing meeting for a discussion related to the focus topic that can be minuted.

Analysis of data

There are many different techniques that can be used in the analysis of data, which are well documented in methodological literature (e.g. Silverman 2011; Miles *et al.* 2013; Bazeley 2013). As Thomas (2009) notes, some texts may be useful but others may make the analysis process appear more complicated than it actually needs to be. It is also necessary to recognise that different forms and quantities of data may require different approaches to analysis. For example, for a set of questionnaires with primarily tick-box response options, you would be able to add up the number of people giving different answers. From this you might see patterns such as most of the teaching assistants holding one view while most of the teachers hold another. If you had notes or transcripts from half a dozen interviews, you might be able to compare and contrast them to identify the emerging themes and issues. If you had notes or transcripts from 20 interviews, you would probably need to employ some form of coding method to identify the emerging themes.

In illustrating some generic steps that can be applied when approaching the task of analysis, it is helpful to return to the earlier example of an investigation into use of lunch time detentions (see Table 10.3).

Having analysed the data in relation to each of the sub-questions, the next stage would be to consider what the data might be indicating collectively about the effectiveness of the system of lunchtime detentions. You might, for example, find out that generally teachers are using this sanction as part of a least to most intrusive approach in line with the school's behaviour policy, and that it is generally well understood by pupils and staff when a lunchtime detention would be issued. There might be pockets of inconsistency in certain departments. There might be a concern that the lunchtime detention system is not especially good at *changing* behaviour because it is generally the same pupils who repeatedly receive the sanction.

Generating implications for practice

The richer understanding developed through the gathering and analysis of data can then generate some implications for practice. Sometimes the implication will be that there is a need to look more closely at an issue that has emerged. It is important not to move too quickly to make changes if there is more that needs to be found out. In the example of lunchtime detentions, it is possible that one implication might be that it is necessary to raise awareness among staff of the sequence of steps that they are expected to go through before issuing a lunch time detention. The issue that the same pupils repeatedly receive lunchtime detentions might lead to consideration of whether reaching a certain number in a set period needs to trigger involvement of the pastoral team.

Table 10.3 An example of an approach to analysing data

Research question: 'How effective is our use of lunch time detentions in promoting positive learning behaviours?'

Sub-question: 'When do teachers issue lunch time detentions?'

You could analyse from the perspective of:	This might reveal:
• What individual teachers have told you about when they would issue a lunch time detention	Some teachers moving quickly to lunch time detentions whereas others follow a number of steps first
• Whether there is any consistency between teachers	Variations across the staff team in the level or persistence of behaviour that triggers the issuing of lunch time detention
	The degree to which practice reflects what is stated in the school behaviour policy

Sub question: How many pupils regularly and repeatedly receive lunchtime detentions?

You could analyse from the perspective of:	This might reveal:
• Pupils whose names appear frequently in records of lunch time detentions	It is predominantly the same core group of pupils who regularly receive lunch time detentions
• The number of lunch time detentions received by pupils in different year groups	There are more lunch time detentions issued for certain year groups or by particular departments or teachers
• The number of lunch time detentions issued by different departments	
• The number of lunch time detentions issued by individual teachers	

Sub question: 'What are pupils' and teachers' perceptions of the effectiveness of the lunch time detentions in promoting positive learning behaviours?'

You could analyse from the perspective of:	This might reveal:
• Positive views expressed by teachers	The extent to which key stakeholders believe this element of the school's behaviour policy is effective
• Positive views expressed by pupils	
• Negative views expressed by teachers	Differences in perspective between pupils and teachers on the effectiveness
• Negative views expressed by pupils	
	Whether among teachers there is a common view on effectiveness
	Whether among pupils there is a common view on effectiveness

Conclusion

Although there is recognition that 'appropriate self-evaluation, reflection and professional development activity is critical to improving teachers' practice at all career stages' (DfE 2011a: 14), there is no particular specification of how much or the form this should take. If we accept McNally *et al.*'s (2005) suggestion that behaviour management is at best a temporary conceptualisation useful to those in the earliest stages of their careers, then there is a need to consider how progression from this point is supported and assured.

The reflective practitioner discourse has a certain appeal in positioning the teacher as continually learning from their own experiences and adapting their practice accordingly. The question we would ask is whether a teacher, especially in the early stage of their career, has a sufficiently broad range of reference points against which to reflect. Without these, reflection may be little more than feelings and reactions based on all manner of conscious and subconscious assumptions informed by all manner of sources about what matters, including what constitutes a good teacher, what constitutes being a good behaviour manager, how teachers and pupils should relate, how pupils learn to behave and what good behaviour is. We hope the Behaviour for Learning conceptual framework that underpins this book provides a reference point for reflection. As this chapter has illustrated, however, it is a starting point that may trigger the need to develop knowledge, skills and understanding in relation to one or more of the three relationship areas in order to better be able to foster the development of learning behaviour in groups and individuals. Such a need may be in response to specific groups or individuals where the teacher's existing knowledge, skills and understanding are not sufficient or the teacher simply recognising that there is an area where professional development is desirable.

Although there is no shortage of material related to behaviour available, the individual experience and interpretation made by pupils of any strategies employed by a teacher may lead to a feeling that strategy selection can only ever be based on trial and error. If teachers engage with literature and research, the range of options within the 'trial' element are at least likely to be evidence informed. The original systematic literature review (Powell and Tod 2004), upon which the behaviour for learning approach is based, stressed the importance of applying theory and conceptual frameworks to the task of selecting and evaluating the use of strategies for behaviour management. In the face of sometimes unpredictable responses from pupils, awareness that the strategy or approach is recognised good practice underpinned by an evidence base is potentially reassuring.

The natural extension of a consideration of evidence-informed practice and the teacher as reflective practitioner is that the teacher themselves could engage more formally in research activities, adopting a more structured and systematic approach to their reflection, and contributing to the evidence base for practice. Employing an investigative approach enables teachers to understand the often complex factors influencing behaviour within their school context and, using the evidence they have gathered, to identify action points to develop their own or their school's practice. It is an approach that places teachers at the heart of the school improvement process.

Appendix

Resource list of learning behaviours for the classroom

This list of learning behaviours should not be viewed as exhaustive or definitive. It is intended to provide a stimulus for thinking about the learning behaviours you want to promote in your classroom or develop in particular pupils. Some schools and teachers may like to develop their own preferred learning behaviours that may be specific to their subject curriculum or their pupils' social behaviour in school. Some of the broader learning behaviours may need to be promoted through smaller steps. Learning behaviours concerned with Relationship with Self are mainly dispositional in nature but some may necessitate some underlying skill development if they are to be enacted in the classroom.

Learning behaviours associated with *relationship with the curriculum*

Learning behaviour related to motivation

Skills

- Can self-direct attention in order to locate any personal interest in task or subject
- Pursues coherence, relevance and meaning
- Responsive to teacher's motivational strategies, e.g. asks questions, volunteers information
- Is able to get started on tasks without delay
- Can plan steps in task needed for successful completion
- Is able to persist and tolerate the discomfort of effort
- Has strategies for sustaining attention and effort
- Can sustain a focus on positive outcomes

Will/disposition

- Is willing to search for interest in task or subject
- is willing to direct attention to the task in hand
- Is responsive and will ask questions and volunteer information
- Is willing to get started without complaining or moaning about having to get on with learning
- Gets started without using delaying tactics
- Is willing to imagine what it feels like to succeed

Learning behaviours related to learning organisation

Skills

- Brings correct materials to class
- Can select necessary equipment for the task
- Is able to share equipment
- Looks after own/others' property
- Keeps desk tidy, checks computer ready for use, etc.

Will/disposition

- Is willing to bring correct materials to class
- Is willing to share equipment with others
- Takes responsibility for looking after own/others' property
- Responds to requests and/or independently keeps desk organised and tidy

- Has a sense of time, punctual, is able to get started on tasks promptly, work at a reasonable pace, knows when to move on to the next activity or stage
- Sets appropriate goals
- Monitors own progress

- Is willing to apply effort in such a way that tasks are started promptly, work is carried out at a reasonable pace and completed in allocated time frame
- Takes responsibility, when needed, to set own targets and goals
- Is willing to monitor own progress

Learning behaviours related to learning in group settings

Skills
- Can focus and sustain attention on learning
- Is able to work when others around them are talking at a reasonable level
- Can recognise interruptions and has a range of strategies to reduce or deal with these
- Is able to wait for teacher/adult attention when necessary
- Knows when it is appropriate to speak and follows group/class conventions for asking for help or expressing view
- Is able to work productively with others
- Is able to work independently when required
- Is able to respond to and use advice from peers

Will/disposition
- Is willing to self-direct attention towards what is required for curriculum learning – responds to request to redirect attention towards learning
- Makes effort to concentrate, and is willing to respond appropriately to instructions that are required for successful task completion.
- Is willing to make an effort to work when others around are talking at a reasonable level
- Is willing to use a range of strategies to reduce or deal with interruptions
- Will wait quietly for teacher/adult attention when necessary
- Is willing to follow group/class rules for asking for help, answering questions and expressing own views
- Is willing to work productively with others
- Is willing to learn alone and with others
- Is willing to have work fairly compared with that of others

Learning behaviours related to dealing with difficulties when learning

Skills
- Works independently unless a problem arises that cannot be solved without adult intervention
- Tells the teacher/other adult when they do not understand
- Uses a range of strategies to solve problems for themselves before asking for help
- Makes appropriate use of peer support
- Has the necessary language skills to ask teacher/other adult why/where they went wrong
- Knows how to refer to previous work before asking the teacher for help
- Persistent and tolerates the sometimes 'difficult' feelings associated with learning new things
- Knows own strengths and weaknesses in relation to curriculum learning

Will/disposition
- Is willing to work independently unless a problem arises that cannot be solved without adult intervention
- Is willing to ask for help from the teacher/other adult when they do not understand what they are required to do
- Is willing to try to solve problems for themselves before asking for help
- Is willing to make appropriate use of peer support
- Is interested enough in their own learning to ask teacher/other adult why/where they went wrong
- Is willing to self-help by referring to previous work before asking the teacher for help
- Will persist and tolerate the sometimes 'difficult' feelings associated with learning new things

- Uses feedback to improve performance

- Will tolerate aspects of lesson/subject perceived as 'boring'
- Is willing, and can cope with, making mistakes and learning from them
- Is willing to respond to feedback on their learning and progress

Learning behaviours associated with processing of information

Skills
- Has the language and working memory skills needed to process information in pursuit of coherence, relevance and meaning
- Understands how, and is able, to think rigorously and methodologically
- Looks for link with other subjects
- Is able to learn in different ways
- Can organise learning tasks so that they can be successfully completed

Will/disposition
- Is willing to get involved in learning and actively seek coherence, relevance and meaning
- Makes an effort to actively process information
- Is willing to put the required effort into thinking rigorously and methodologically
- Actively and independently seeks links within and between tasks and subjects
- Is willing to learn by using different approaches and strategies
- Is willing to put effort into planning so that learning tasks can be successfully completed

Learning behaviours linked to communication within group settings

Skills
- Is able to talk about learning to adults and peers
- Is able to convey information clearly and knows when it is appropriate to speak
- Is able to alter voice pitch and tone appropriately and uses non-verbal signals effectively, e.g. eye contact, stance, distance
- Is able to organise communication in both individual and group situations
- Thinks through before offering an opinion
- Is able to justify what they have said
- Is able to act in a manner appropriate to the classroom situation and with due regard to teacher's expectations and 'class rules'
- Is able to work without seeking the attention of others
- Is able to control unauthorised talking to other pupils
- Is able to communicate with others without physical actions such as nudging or poking

Will/disposition
- Is willing to discuss own learning with adults and peers
- Is willing to turn take and speak when it is appropriate
- Is willing to alter voice pitch and tone appropriately and uses non-verbal signals effectively, e.g. eye contact, stance, distance
- Wants to communicate effectively and appropriately in both individual and group situations
- Is willing to monitor communication in a group and think through before offering an opinion
- Is willing to justify opinions and actions without undue resentment when asked
- Responsive to rules and instructions about appropriate communication in the classroom
- Is willing to control unauthorised talking to other pupils
- Is willing to communicate with others without physical actions such as nudging or poking

Learning behaviours associated with *relationship with others*

Skills
- Is able to seek attention appropriately and control need for peer attention in class
- Can show concern and understanding
- Is able to wait for his/her turn to speak

Will/disposition
- Resists the impulse to interrupt and seek attention inappropriately
- Is willing to think about how own behaviour has an impact on others

- Is able to listen to, understand and respond to the ideas of others without negative comment
- Has developed appropriate strategies for resolving arguments and conflict
- Gives and defends own view without using 'put downs', verbal aggression or other coercive tactics
- Is able to be responsive to school rules and conventions for communication with teachers and peers

- Is willing to respond to teaching aimed at improving social skills
- Will show concern and understanding
- Will respond to requests to wait his/her turn to speak
- Will listen to the ideas of others and actively make an effort to control responding with negative comments
- Is willing to work on strategies for resolving conflict
- Is willing to give and defend own viewpoint without using 'put downs', verbal aggression or other coercive tactics
- Is willing to be responsive to school rules and conventions for communication with teachers and peers.

Learning behaviours associated with *relationship with self*

Skills

- Is able to set realistic aspirations for self
- Can identify own positive attributes and achievements
- Makes positive self-reference statements
- Can respond appropriately to criticism and praise
- Is able to recognise and control mood changes
- Can identify and apply different ways of doing things
- Can work independently when necessary
- Is able to ask for help
- Can self-direct attention to task
- Can tolerate making mistakes
- Can make favourable comparisons with self and others
- Works to achieve success rather than to avoid failure
- Is able to make and sustain effort in order to successfully complete work
- Is responsive to school rules and routines
- Can make decisions and weigh up options
- Is responsive to but not overly influenced by peers
- Has realistic belief in own ability
- Is able to take responsibility for own actions
- Is able to predict and accept consequences of own actions
- Is able to postpone immediate reward for longer term goals
- Can adjust self-perceptions when appropriate

Will/disposition

- Is willing to reconsider own perceptions
- Is willing to accept praise and positive comments
- Is willing to postpone immediate gratification for long-term achievements
- Is willing to listen to, and try, alternative ways of doing things
- Accepts some responsibility for own actions
- Is willing to try and make an effort
- Is willing to risk making mistakes
- Is willing to compare self with others
- Is willing to recognise the positive attributes of others
- Is willing to share attention with others
- Will risk making decisions
- Will respond appropriately to school rules and discipline
- Will admit wrongdoings and is willing to learn from mistakes
- Is willing to accept that others can hold differing views from those held by self
- Is willing to use strategies to control anger
- Is willing to attempt things that may be difficult
- Is willing to self-assess own work against given criteria
- Has appropriate self-belief about what they can do in relation to the work that has been set
- Is willing to accept and follow advice from others about ways in which own learning can be improved

References

Albert, L. (1996) *Cooperative Discipline*. Circle Pines: American Guidance Service.

Allen, B. (1998) 'New guidance on the use of reasonable force in schools 1998'. *British Journal of Special Education*, 25(4), 184–8.

ATL (Association of Teachers and Lecturers) (2002) *Achievement for All: Working with Children with Special Educational Needs in Mainstream Schools and Colleges*. London: ATL.

Bandura, A. (1977) *Social Learning Theory*. Englewood Cliffs, NJ: Prentice Hall.

Bandura, A. (1997) *Self-efficacy: The Exercise of Control*. New York: WH Freeman and Company.

Bandura, A. (2002) *Social Foundations of Thought and Action: A Social Cognitive Theory*. Englewood Cliffs, NJ: Prentice Hall.

Barnes, R. (2006) *The Practical Guide to Primary Classroom Management*. London: Paul Chapman.

Bazeley, P. (2013) *Qualitative Data Analysis: Practical Strategies*. London: Sage.

Beadle, P. and Murphy, J. (2013) *Why Are You Shouting At Us? The Dos and Don'ts of Behaviour Management*. London: Bloomsbury.

Black, P. and Wiliam, D. (1999) *Assessment for Learning: Beyond the Black Box*. Cambridge: University of Cambridge School of Education.

Bowers, T. (2005) 'The forgotten "E" in EBD', in Clough, P., Garner, P., Pardeck, J. and Yuen, F. (eds) (2005) *Handbook of Emotional and Behavioural Difficulties*. London: Sage.

Boyle, S., Fahey, E., Loughran, J. and Mitchell, I. (2001) 'Classroom research into good learning behaviours', *Educational Action Research*, 9(2), 199–224.

Braithwaite, R. (2001) *Managing Aggression*. London: Routledge.

Breakwell, G. (1997) *Coping with Aggressive Behaviour*. Leicester: British Psychological Society.

Brophy, J. (1981) 'Teacher praise: a functional analysis' *Review of Educational Research*, 51(1), 5–32.

Brophy, J. (1996) *Teaching Problem Students*. New York: Guilford.

Butler, R.J. and Gasson S.L. (2005) 'Self esteem/self concept scales for children and adolescents: a review'. *Child and Adolescent Mental Health*, (10)4, 190–201.

Canter, L. and Canter, M. (1992) *Assertive Discipline: Positive Behavior Management for Today's Classroom*. Santa Monica, CA: Canter and Associates, Inc.

Capel, S. and Gervis, M. (2005) 'Motivating pupils', in Capel, S., Leask, M. and Turner, T. (eds) (2005) *Learning to Teach in the Secondary School* (4th edition). Abingdon: Routledge.

Chaplain, R. (2003) *Teaching without Disruption in the Secondary School*. London: RoutledgeFalmer.

Chowdry, H., Crawford, C. and Goodman, A. (2009), *Drivers and Barriers to Educational Success: Evidence from the Longitudinal Study of Young People in England* (Research Report RR102). Nottingham: DCSF.

Claxton, G. (2002) *Building Learning Power*. Bristol: TLO.

Claxton, G. (2006) 'Expanding the capacity to learn: a new end for education?' Opening keynote address, British Educational Research Association annual conference, 6 September, Warwick University. Available online from www.tloltd.co.uk/downloads/BERA-Keynote-Update-Feb10.pdf (accessed 9 January 2014).

Coles, M. and Werquin, P. (2005) *The Growing Importance of NQS as a Resource for Lifelong Learning Policy*. Paris: OECD.

Coopersmith, S. (1967) *The Antecedents of Self-Esteem*. San Francisco: W H Freeman.

Cornwall, J. (2000) 'Might is right? A discussion of the ethics and practicalities of control and restraint in education'. *Emotional and Behavioural Difficulties*, 5(4), 19–25.

Cornwall, J. and Walter, C. (2006) *Therapeutic Education: Working with Troubled and Troublesome Young People*. London: Routledge.

Cowley, S. (2003) *Getting the Buggers to Behave* (2nd edition). London: Continuum.

Croll, P. and Moses, D. (1985) *One-in-Five: The Assessment and Incidence of Special Educational Needs*. London: Routledge and Kegan Paul.

Curwin, R. and Mendler, A. (1989) 'We repeat, let the buyer beware: a response to Canter'. *Educational Leadership*, 46(6), 68–71.

Damon, W. (1984) 'Peer education: the untapped potential.' *Journal of Applied Developmental Psychology*, 5, 331–43.

Davies, W. and Frude, N. (2000) *Preventing Face-To-Face Violence* (4th edition). Leicester: Association of Psychological Therapies.

Davis, P. and Florian, L. 2004) *Teaching Strategies and Approaches for Pupils with Special Educational Needs: A Scoping Study*. Nottingham: Department for Education and Skills.

DCSF (Department for Children, Schools and Families) (2007) *The Use of Force to Control or Restrain Pupils*. Nottingham: DCSF.

DCSF (2008) *Practice Guidance for the Early Years Foundation Stage*. Nottingham: DCSF.

DCSF (2009a) *School Discipline and Pupil-Behaviour Policies – Guidance for Schools*. Nottingham: DCSF.

DCSF (2009b) *Internal Exclusion Guidance*. Nottingham: DCSF.

DCSF (2010a) *The National Strategies Personalised Learning*. Available from www.standards.dcsf.gov.uk/ NationalStrategies (accessed 8 February 2010).

DCSF (2010b) *The Use of Force to Control or Restrain Pupils*. Nottingham: DCSF.

DES (Department of Education and Science) (1989) *Discipline in Schools* (the 'Elton Report'). London: HMSO.

Dewey, J. (1910) *How We Think*. Boston, MA: DC Heath & Co.

Dewey, J. (1933) *How We Think: A Restatement of the Relation of Reflective Thinking to the Educative Process*. Chicago, IL: Henry Regnery Co.

DfE (Department for Education) (1994a) *Circular 8/94: Pupil Behaviour and Discipline*. London: DfE.

DfE (1994b) *The Education of Children with Emotional and Beahvioural Difficulties*. London: DfE.

DfE (1994c) *Code of Practice on the Identification and Assessment of Special Educational Needs*. London: DfE.

DfE (2010) *The Importance of Teaching* (white paper). Nottingham: DfE.

DfE (2011a) *Teachers' Standards*. Available from www.gov.uk/government/publications/teachers-standards (accessed 17 December 2013).

DfE (2011b) *Support and Aspiration: A New Approach to Special Educational Needs and Disability* (green paper). Nottingham: DfE.

DfE (2012) 'Trainee teachers to get a better grip on managing behaviour' (press release). Available online from www.education.gov.uk/inthenews/inthenews/a00210970/trainee-teachers-to-get-a-better-grip-on-managing-behaviour (accessed 17 December 2013).

DfE (2013a) *Use of Reasonable force: Advice for Headteachers, Staff and Governing Bodies*. Available online from www.education.gov.uk/aboutdfe/advice/f0077153/use-of-reasonable-force (accessed 29 November 2013).

DfE (2013b) *Equality Act 2010: Advice for School Leaders, School Staff, Governing Bodies and Local Authorities*. Available online from http://media.education.gov.uk/assets/files/pdf/e/equality%20act%20guidance %20february%202013.pdf (accessed 22 March 2013).

DfE (2014a) *Special Educational Needs and Disability Code of Practice: 0 to 25 Years*. Available online from www.gov.uk/government/uploads/system/uploads/attachment_data/file/319639/Code_of_ Practice-Final-10June2014.pdf (accessed 13 June 2014).

DfE (2014b) *Behaviour and Discipline in Schools: Advice for Headteachers and School Staff.* Available online from www.gov.uk/government/uploads/system/uploads/attachment_data/file/277662/Behaviour_and_Discipline_in_Schools_-_A_guide_for_headteachers_and_school_staff.pdf (accessed 6 February 2014).

DfEE (Department for Education and Employment) (1998) *Circular 10/98: Section 550A of the Education Act 1996: The Use of Force to Control or Restrain Pupils.* London: DfEE.

DfEE/QCA (Qualifications and Curriculum Authority) (1999a) *The National Curriculum Handbook for Primary Teachers in England.* London: DfEE/QCA.

DfEE/QCA (1999b) *The National Curriculum Handbook for Secondary Teachers in England.* London: DfEE/QCA.

DfES (Department for Education and Skills) (2001) *Special Educational Needs Code of Practice.* Nottingham: DfES.

DfES (2002) *Including All Children in the Literacy Hour and Daily Mathematics Lesson.* Nottingham: DfES.

DfES (2003) *Key Stage 3 National Strategy Behaviour and Attendance Training Materials: Core Day 1.* Nottingham: DfES.

DfES (2004a) *Key Stage 3 National Strategy Behaviour and Attendance. Core Day 2: Developing Effective Practice Across the School.* Nottingham: DfES.

DfES (2004b) *Removing Barriers to Achievement: The Government's Strategy for SEN.* Nottingham: DfES.

DfES (2005a) *Learning Behaviour: The Report of the Practitioners' Group on School Behaviour and Discipline* (the 'Steer Report'). Nottingham: DfES.

DfES (2005b) *Leading on Inclusion.* Nottingham: DfES.

DfES (2005c) *Excellence and Enjoyment: Social and Emotional Aspects of Learning: Guidance.* Nottingham, DfES.

DfES (2006) *Effective Leadership: Ensuring the Progress of Pupils with SEN and/or Disabilities.* Nottingham: DfES.

DfES (2007) *Social and Emotional Aspects of Learning (SEAL): Guidance Booklet.* Nottingham: DfES.

Disability Rights Commission (2002) *Code of Practice for Schools.* London: The Stationery Office.

Dix, P. (2007) *Taking Care of Behaviour: Practical Skills for Teachers.* Harlow: Pearson.

Docking, J. (1987) *Control and Discipline in Schools.* London: Harper & Row.

Dreikurs, R. and Grey, L. (1968) *A New Approach to Discipline: Logical Consequences.* New York: Hawthorn Books.

Dreikurs, R., Grunwald, B. and Pepper, F. (1998) *Maintaining Sanity in the Classroom.* London: Accelerated Development.

Dunne, M., Humphreys, S., Sebba, J., Dyson, A., Gallannaugh, F. and Muijs, D. (2007) *Effective Teaching and Learning for Pupils in Low Attaining Groups.* Research Report No. DCSF-RR011. Nottingham: DCSF.

Durrant, J. and Holden, G. (2006) *Teachers Leading Change.* London: Paul Chapman.

Ellis, S. and Tod, J. (2009) *Behaviour for Learning: Proactive Approaches to Behaviour Management.* Abingdon: Routledge.

Ellis S. and Tod, J.(2012) 'Identification of SEN: Is consistency a realistic or worthy aim?' *Support for Learning,* 27(2), 59–66.

Ellis, S., Tod, J. and Graham-Matheson, L. (2012) *Special Educational Needs and Inclusion: Reflection, Renewal and Reality.* Birmingham: NASUWT.

Emmer, E. and Hickman, J. (1991) 'Teacher efficacy in classroom management and discipline'. *Educational and Psychological Measurement,* 51, 755–65.

Evans J., Harden A. and Thomas J. (2004) 'What are effective strategies to support pupils with emotional and behavioural difficulties (EBD) in mainstream primary schools? Findings from a systematic review of research'. *Journal of Research in Special Educational Needs,* 4(1), 2–16.

Faupel, A., Herrick, E. and Sharp, P. (1998) *Anger Management: A Practical Guide.* London: David Fulton.

Finlay, L. (2008) 'Reflecting on reflective practice' (commissioned discussion paper). Available online from www.open.ac.uk/cetl-workspace/cetlcontent/documents/4bf2b48887459.pdf (accessed 3 December 2013).

French, J. and Raven, B. (1960) 'The bases of social power', in Cartwright, D. and Zander, A. (eds) *Group Dynamics: Research and Theory*. New York: Harper Row.

Fuller, F. and Brown, O. (1975) 'Becoming a teacher', in Ryan, K. (ed.) *Teacher Education: The Seventy-fourth Yearbook of the National Society for the Study of Education* (Vol. 11, 25–52). Chicago, IL: National Society for the Study of Education.

Furlong, J. and Maynard, T. (1995) *Mentoring Student Teachers: The Growth of Professional Knowledge*. London: Routledge.

Galloway, D., Ball, T., Blomfield, D. and Seyd, R. (1982). *Schools and Disruptive Pupils*. London: Longman.

Galvin, P. (1999) *Behaviour and Discipline in Schools* (2nd edition). London: David Fulton.

Giallo, R. and Little, E. (2003) 'Classroom behaviour problems: The relationship between preparedness, classroom experiences, self efficacy in graduate and student teachers'. *Australian Journal of Educational and Developmental Psychology*, 3, 21–34.

Gibson, S. and Dembo, M. (1984) 'Teacher efficacy: A construct validation'. *Journal of Educational Psychology*, 76(4), 569–82.

Goleman, D. (1995) *Emotional Intelligence: Why it can Matter More than IQ*. London: Bloomsbury.

The Guardian (2014) 'Michael Gove urges "traditional" punishments for school misbehaviour', 2 February. Available online from www.theguardian.com/education/2014/feb/02/michael-gove-traditional-punishments-school-misbehaviour (accessed 16 March 2014).

Hallam, S. and Rogers, L. (2008) *Improving Behaviour and Attendance at School*. Maidenhead: Open University Press.

Hammersley, M. (2001) 'Some questions about evidence-based practice in education'. Paper presented at the Annual Conference of the British Educational Research Association, University of Leeds, 13–15 September, 2001.

Handscomb, G. and MacBeath, J. (2003) *The Research Engaged School*. Chelmsford: Forum for Learning and Research Enquiry (FLARE), Essex County Council.

Hardin, C. (2008) *Effective Classroom Management*. Upper Saddle River, NJ: Pearson.

Hattie J.C. (2009) *Visible Learning: A Synthesis of Over 800 Meta-Analyses Relating to Achievement*. London and New York: Routledge.

Hewett, D. (1998) 'Managing incidents of challenging behaviour – practices', in Hewett, D. (ed.) (1998) *Challenging Behaviour: Principles and Practices*. London: David Fulton.

Hewett, D. and Arnett, A. (1996) 'Guidance on the use of physical force'. *British Journal of Special Education*, 23(3), 130–3.

Higgins S., Kokotsaki, D. and Coe, R. (2011) *Toolkit of Strategies to Improve Learning – Summary for Schools, Spending the Pupil Premium*. Sutton Trust. Available online from www.cem.org/research/toolkit-of-strategies-to-improve-learning-summary-for-schools-spending-the-pupil-premium (accessed 21 July 2014).

Hook, P. and Vass, A. (2002) *Teaching with Influence*. London: David Fulton.

House of Commons Education Committee (2011) *Behaviour and Discipline in Schools First Report of Session 2010–11* (Vol. I). Available online from www.publications.parliament.uk/pa/cm201011/cmselect/cmeduc/516/516i.pdf (accessed 8 March 2014).

Klein, H.K. and Myers, M.D. (1999) 'A set of principles for conducting and evaluating interpretive field studies in information systems'. *Management Information Systems Quarterly*, 23(1), 67–88.

Kohn, A. (1996) *Beyond Discipline*. Upper Saddle River, NJ: Prentice Hall.

Kohn, A. (1999) *Punished By Rewards*. New York: Houghton Mifflin.

Kounin, J. (1970) *Discipline and Group Management in Classrooms*. London: Holt, Rinehart and Winston.

Kyriacou, C. (2007) *Essential Teaching Skills* (3rd edition). Cheltenham: Nelson Thornes.

Kyriacou, C. and Goulding, M. (2006) *A Systematic Review of Strategies to Raise Pupils' Motivational Effort in Key Stage 4 Mathematics* (technical report). London: EPPI-Centre, Social Science Research Unit, Institute of Education, University of London.

LaVigna, G.W. and Donnellan, A.M. (1986) *Alternatives to Punishment: Solving Behaviour Problems with Non-Aversive Strategies*. New York: Irvington Publishers.

Law, J. and Plunkett, C. (2009) *The Interaction between Behaviour and Speech and Language Difficulties: Does Intervention for one Affect Outcomes in the Other?* (technical report). London: EPPI-Centre, Social Science Research Unit, Institute of Education, University of London.

Lawrence, D. (2006) *Enhancing Self Esteem in the Classroom* (3rd edition). London: Paul Chapman.

Lester, S. (2007) *Evidence-Based Practice.* Available online from www.sld.demon.co.uk/ebp.pdf (accessed 9 December 2013).

Lindsley, O. (1991) 'From technical jargon to plain English for application'. *Journal of Applied Behavior Analysis*, 24(34), 449–458.

Littlejohn, A. (2001) 'Motivation: Where does it come from? Where does it go?' *English Teaching Professional*, 19.

Long, R. (1999) *Challenging Confrontation: Information and Techniques for School Staff.* Tamworth: NASEN.

Long, R. and Fogell, J. (1999) *Supporting Pupils with Emotional Difficulties.* London: David Fulton.

Lord, P. and O'Donnell S. (2005) *Learner Motivation 3–19: An International Perspective.* Slough: NFER/QCA.

Lunenberg, F. (2012) 'Power and leadership: An influence process'. *International Journal of Management, Business and Administration*, 15(1), 1–9.

McGrath, H. and Noble T. (2010) 'Supporting positive pupil relationships: Research to practice'. *Educational and Child Psychology*, 27(1), 79–90.

McGuiness, J. (1993) *Teachers, Pupils and Behaviour: A Managerial Approach.* London: Cassell.

McLean, A. (2009) *Motivating Every Learner.* London: Sage.

McNally, J., L'Anson, J., Whewall, C. and Wilson, G. (2005) '"They think swearing is ok": First lessons in behaviour management'. *Journal of Education for Teaching*, 31(3), 169–85.

McPhillimy, B. (1996) *Controlling Your Class.* Chichester: Wiley.

Maloney, J. (2007) 'Children's roles and use of evidence in science: An analysis of decision making in small groups'. *British Educational Research Journal*, 33(3), 371–402.

Martin, A. and Dowson, M. (2009) 'Interpersonal relationships, motivation, engagement, and achievement: Yields for theory, current issues and educational practice'. *Review of Educational Research*, 79(1), 327–65.

Maslow, A. (1962) *Towards a Psychology of Being.* Princeton, NJ: D. van Nostrand.

Meyerhoff, M. (1996) 'Natural and logical consequences'. *Pediatrics for Parents*, 16(9), 8–10.

Miles, M., Huberman, A. and Saldana, J. (2013) *Qualitative Data Analysis: A Methods Sourcebook* (3rd edition). London: Sage.

Miller, A. (1996) *Pupil Behaviour and Teacher Culture.* London: Cassell.

Miller, W. (1989) 'Increasing motivation for change', in Hestor, R. and Miller, W. (eds) *Handbook of Alcoholism Treatment Approaches.* New York: Pergamon.

Miller, D. and Moran, T. (2005) 'One in three? Teachers' attempts to identify low self-esteem children'. *Pastoral Care in Education*, 23(4), 25–30.

Moore, A. (2004) *'The Good Teacher': Dominant Discourses in Teaching and Teacher Education.* London: RoutledgeFalmer.

Mosley, J. and Sonnet, H. (2005) *Better Behaviour Through Golden Time.* Wisbech: LDA.

NASUWT (National Association of Schoolmasters Union of Women Teachers) (2012) *The Big Question.* Birmingham: NASUWT.

Neill, S. and Caswell, C. (1993) *Body Language for Competent Teachers.* London: Routledge.

Nelsen, J., Lott, L. and Glenn, S. (2000) *Positive Discipline in the Classroom* (3rd edition). Rocklin, CA: Prima Publishing.

Neuman, W.L. (1997) *Social Research Methods: Qualitative and Quantitative Approaches.* Boston. MA: Allyn and Bacon.

Nevo, I. and Slonim-Nevo, V. (2011) 'The myth of evidence-based practice: Towards evidence-informed practice'. *British Journal of Social Work*, 41(6), 1176–97.

NFER (National Foundation for Educational Research) (2012) *Teacher Voice Omnibus February 2012 Survey: Pupil Behaviour.* Nottingham: DfE.

O'Brien, T. and Guiney, D. (2001) *Differentiation in Teaching and Learning*. London: Continuum.

O'Connor, J. and Seymour, J. (2003) *Introducing NLP Neuro-Linguistic Programming*. London: Thorsons.

O'Flynn, S. and Kennedy, H. (2003) *Get Their Attention!* London: David Fulton.

O'Leary, K. and O'Leary, S. (eds) (1977) *Classroom Management: The Successful Use of Behavior Modification* (2nd edition). New York: Pergamon.

Ofsted (2004) *Special Educational Needs and Disability Review: Towards Inclusive Schools*. London: Ofsted.

Ofsted (2005) *Managing Challenging Behaviour*. London: Ofsted.

Ofsted (2010) *The Special Educational Needs and Disability Review: A Statement is Not Enough*. London: Ofsted.

Ofsted (2011) *The Annual Report of Her Majesty's Chief Inspector of Education, Children's Services and Skills 2010/11*. London: Ofsted.

Ofsted (2014) *The framework for school inspection* January 2014 No. 120100 London: Ofsted.

Olsen, J. and Cooper, P. (2001) *Dealing with Disruptive Students in the Classroom*. London: Kogan Page.

Pease, A. and Pease, B. (2004) *The Definitive Book of Body Language*. London: Orion Books.

PEEL (2009) *PEEL in Practice: Principles of Teaching*, Project for Enhancing Effective Learning, available online from www.peelweb.org (accessed 19 January 2013).

Porter, L. (2007) *Behaviour in Schools* (2nd edition). Maidenhead: Open University Press.

Poulou, M. and Norwich, B. (2000) 'Teachers' causal attributions, cognitive, emotional and behavioural responses to students with emotional and behavioural difficulties'. *British Journal of Educational Psychology*, 70(4), 559–81.

Powell, S. and Tod, J. (2004) *A Systematic Review of how Theories Explain Learning Behaviour in School Contexts*. London: EPPI-Centre, Social Science Research Unit, Institute of Education, University of London.

Robertson, J. (1996) *Effective Classroom Control* (3rd edition). London: Hodder and Stoughton.

Roffey, S. (2010) 'Content and context for learning relationships: a cohesive framework for whole school development'. *Educational and Child Psychology*, 27(1), 156–67.

Rogers, B. (1990) *You Know the Fair Rule* (1st edition). London: Pitman Publishing.

Rogers, B. (1997) *The Language of Discipline* (2nd edition). Plymouth: Northcote House.

Rogers, B. (2007) *Behaviour Management: A Whole-School Approach* (2nd edition). London: Paul Chapman.

Rogers, B. (2011) *Classroom Behaviour* (3rd edition). London: Sage.

Rogers, B. (2012) *You Know The Fair Rule* (3rd edition). Harlow: Pearson.

Rogers, C. (1951) *Client-centred Therapy*. London: Constable.

Rogers, C. and Freiberg, H. (1994) *Freedom to Learn* (3rd edition). New York: Merrill.

Roseth, C., Johnson, D. and Johnson, T. (2008) 'Promoting early adolescents' achievement and peer relationships: The effect of co-operative, competitive and individualistic goal structures'. *Psychological Bulletin*, 134(2), 223–46.

Rotter, J. (1954) *Social Learning and Clinical Psychology*. Englewood Cliffs, NJ: Prentice Hall.

Sackett, D., Rosenberg, W., Grey, J., Haynes, R. and Richardson, W. (1996) 'Evidence based medicine: What it is and what it isn't'. *British Medical Journal*, 312(7023), 71–2.

Sackett, D.L., Straus, S.E., Richardson, W.S., Rosenberg, W. and Haynes, R.B. (2000) *Evidence-Based Medicine: How to Practice and Teach EBM* (2nd edition). New York: Churchill Livingstone.

Schön, D. (1983) *The Reflective Practitioner: How Professionals Think in Action*. New York: Basic Books.

Seligman, M. (1975) *Helplessness: On Depression, Development and Death*. New York: W.H. Freeman.

Sharp, C., Eames, A., Sanders, D. and Tomlinson, K. (2006) *Leading a Research-engaged School*. Nottingham: National College for School Leadership.

Silverman, D. (2011) *Interpreting Qualitative Data* (4th edition). London: Sage.

Slavin, R. (2004) 'When and why does cooperative learning increase achievement?', in Edwards, A. and Daniels, H. (eds) *Reader in Psychology of Education*. London: RoutledgeFalmer.

Smith, C., Dakers, J., Dow, W., Head, G., Sutherland, M. and Irwin, R. (2005) *A Systematic Review of what Pupils, aged 11–16, Believe Impacts on their Motivation to Learn in the Classroom*. London: EPPI-Centre, Social Science Research Unit, Institute of Education, University of London.

Stobbs, P. (2012) 'Addressing inequality'. *Special*, January 18–20.

TA (Teaching Agency) (2012) *Improving Teacher Training for Behaviour*. Available online from www.gov.uk/government/uploads/system/uploads/attachment_data/file/200406/TA-00079-2012.pdf (accessed 17 December 2013).

TDA (Training and Development Agency for Schools) (2007) *Professional Standards for Teachers: Qualified Teacher Status*. London: TDA.

Thomas, G. (2005) 'What do we mean by "EBD"?', in Clough, P., Garner, G., Pardeck, J. and Yuen, F. (eds) *Handbook of Emotional and Behavioural Difficulties*. London: Sage.

Thomas, G. (2009) *How to do your Research Project: A Guide for Students in Education and Applied Social Sciences*. London: Sage.

Tobe, E. (2009) 'An exploration into teachers' and educational psychologists' causal attributions of secondary pupil misbehaviour'. *Debate*, 131, June 7–15.

TTA/DfES (Teacher Training Agency/Department for Education and Skills) (2002) *Qualifying to Teach: Professional Standards for Qualified Teacher Status and Requirements for Initial Teacher Training*. London: TTA.

United States Department of Health and Human Services (1999) *Enhancing Motivation for Change in Substance Abuse (Treatment Improvement Protocol [TIP] Series, No. 35)*. Rockville, MD: Department of Health and Human Services. Available online from www.adp.ca.gov/SBI/pdfs/TIP_35.pdf (accessed 23 August 2010).

Upton, G. (1983) *Educating Children with Behaviour Problems*. Cardiff: Faculty of Education, Cardiff University.

Visser, L. (2006) *The Teacher's Voice*. Melbourne: Thomson Social Science Press.

Watkins, C. (2011) *Managing Classroom Behaviour*. London: Association of Teachers and Lecturers. Available online from www.atl.org.uk/publications-and-resources/classroom-practice-publications/managing-classroom-behaviour.asp (accessed 7 July 2014).

Watkins, C. and Wagner, P. (2000) *Improving School Behaviour*. London: Paul Chapman.

Webb, S. (2001) 'Some considerations on the validity of evidence-based practice in social work'. *British Journal of Social Work*, 31(1), 57–79.

Weiner, B. (1985) 'An attributional theory of achievement motivation and emotion', *Psychological Review*, 92, 548–73.

Weiner, B. (2000) 'Interpersonal and Intrapersonal theories of motivation from an attributional perspective.' *Educational Psychology Review*, 22(1), 1–14.

Wheldall, K. and Glynn, T. (1989) *Effective Classroom Learning*. Oxford: Blackwell.

Wheldall, K. and Merrett, F. (1989) *Positive Teaching in the Secondary School*. London: Paul Chapman.

Wiliam D. (2008) 'Taking assessment for learning to scale'. Paper presented to OECD CERI 40th anniversary conference. Available online at www.oecd.org/dataoecd/26/43/40756772.pdf (accessed 21 July 2014).

Wubbels, T., Brekelmans, M., Brok, P. and Tartwijk, J. (2006) 'An interpersonal perspective on classroom management in secondary classrooms in the Netherlands', in Evertson, C. and Weinstein, C. S. (eds) *Handbook of Classroom Management: Research, Practice and Contemporary Issues*. New York: Lawrence Erlbaum Associates.

Zwozdiak-Myers, P. and Capel, S. (2005) 'Communicating with pupils', in Capel, S., Leask, M. and Turner, T. (eds) (2005) *Learning to Teach in the Secondary School* (4th edition). Abingdon: Routledge.

Index